PRENTICE HALL STUDIES
IN INTERNATIONAL RELATIONS
ENDURING QUESTIONS IN CHANGING TIMES

CHARLES W. KEGLEY, JR., *SERIES EDITOR*

In the era of globalization in the twenty-first century, people cannot afford to ignore the impact of international relations on their future. From the value of one's investments to the quality of the air one breathes, international relations matter. The instantaneous spread of communications throughout the world is making for the internationalization of all phenomena, while the distinction between the domestic and the foreign, the public and the private, and the national and the international is vanishing. Globalization is an accelerating trend that is transforming how virtually every field of study in the social sciences is being investigated and taught.

Contemporary scholarship has made bold advances in understanding the many facets of international relations. It has also laid a firm foundation for interpreting the major forces and factors that are shaping the global future.

To introduce the latest research findings and theoretical commentary, a new publication series has been launched. *Prentice Hall Studies in International Relations: Enduring Questions in Changing Times* presents books that focus on the issues, controversies, and trends that are defining the central topics dominating discussion about international relations.

ATLANTICISM FOR A NEW CENTURY
THE RISE, TRIUMPH, AND DECLINE OF NATO

CARL CAVANAGH HODGE
Okanagan University College

PEARSON
Prentice
Hall

UPPER SADDLE RIVER, NEW JERSEY 07458

Library of Congress Cataloging-in-Publication Data

Hodge, Carl Cavanagh.
  Atlanticism for a new century: the rise, triumph, and decline of NATO/Carl Cavanagh Hodge.
      p. cm.—(Prentice Hall studies in international relations)
  Includes bibliographical references and index.
  ISBN 0-13-048129-7
  1. North Atlantic Treaty Organization.   2. Security, International.   I. Title.   II. Series.
JZ5930.H63   2004
355'.031'091821—dc22

                                                                    2004002794

Editorial Director: Charlyce Jones Owen
Acquisitions Editor: Glenn Johnston
Assistant Editor: John Ragozzine
Editorial Assistant: Suzanne Remore
Marketing Manager: Kara Kindstrom
Marketing Assistant: Jennifer Bryant
Prepress and Manufacturing Buyer: Sherry Lewis
Interior Design: John P. Mazzola
Cover Design: Bruce Kenselaar
Composition/Full-Service Project Management: Kari Callaghan Mazzola and John P.
   Mazzola
Printer/Binder: RR Donnelley & Sons Company
Cover Printer: Phoenix Color Corp.

This book was set in 10/12 Electra.

Pearson Education LTD.
Pearson Education Singapore, Pte. Ltd
Pearson Education, Canada, Ltd
Pearson Education–Japan
Pearson Education Australia PTY, Limited

Pearson Education North Asia Ltd
Pearson Educación de Mexico, S.A. de C.V.
Pearson Education Malaysia, Pte. Ltd
Pearson Education, Upper Saddle River, NJ

PEARSON
Prentice
Hall

10 9 8 7 6 5 4 3 2 1
ISBN 0-13-048129-7

To Senator and Patty Everett,
with gratitude and affection

CONTENTS

PREFACE

Alliances are formed as often to avoid wars as to win them. Because the Atlantic Alliance can be said to have won its war unconditionally without actually fighting it, its claim to be the most successful alliance of modern history is unassailable. Its survival as a military coalition is not. In fact, the NATO of 2004 scarcely resembles that of 1989. In the spring of 1999 it went to war for the first time in its fifty-year history, not to defend Western Europe against the massed might of Soviet and Warsaw Pact forces but rather against Serbia, a single republic of the former Federal Republic of Yugoslavia. What's more, NATO did not fight in defense of sovereign territory in accordance with Article V of its founding document. It in fact abridged the principle of sovereignty, officially for the higher goal of arresting a campaign of ethnic cleansing against the Albanian population in the Serb province of Kosovo. The Alliance's commitment to peace-support and political trusteeship in the Balkans constitutes an expansion every bit as meaningful as the offer of membership NATO extended to the Czech Republic, Hungary, and Poland in 1997, in the first round of post–Cold War enlargement, and the offer to seven additional East European states made official at the 2002 Prague summit. The Alliance has "gone East" to an extent few would have imagined at the conclusion of the Cold War, and it has changed fundamentally in the process.

The great contradiction of NATO's presence in the former Yugoslavia is that it is primarily the result of American determination, yet no member of the Alliance is more concerned with extracting itself from the region than is the United States. Armed intervention in Kosovo in particular can be viewed as the redemption of a warning registered by the first Bush administration and reiterated by the Clinton administration, that repressive actions by Belgrade in the province would result in a military response from Washington. It was the United States that led the way to the Dayton Accords and to the Rambouillet ultimatum, yet almost weekly American foreign policy commentary maintained during the 1990s that a Europe whose unity is worth anything ought to be able to handle a neighborhood problem alone. In Kosovo, *Operation Allied Force* demonstrated that Europe's collective military resources pale in comparison with those of the United States and that Europeans are collectively far from equal to the challenges posed by a region that has been a vector for war since the nineteenth century.

The Alliance's future as a political community is related to, though not wholly determined by, its radically altered military mission—in particular where its commitment to the safety and international vitality of democratic government is concerned. This book makes no claim to be a history of NATO, nor is it a comprehensive study of the Alliance's post–Cold War transformation.[1] What follows, rather, is an extended essay on the American commitment to European peace and security through NATO, an organization that has always had an overtly political as well as a military mandate, and the change in the definition of that commitment since the end of the Cold War. It argues that NATO is the agent of Atlanticism, the notion that the democracies of the North Atlantic realm have a common political heritage and a joint responsibility to it—a responsibility that now reaches beyond Europe to the hills of Afghanistan. More specifically, the Alliance has successfully adopted and adapted principles developed by President Woodrow Wilson as a prescription for international peace at the end of World War I to the extent that key aspects of the Wilsonian legacy are dominant features of the Alliance's political and diplomatic culture. Disagreements between the United States and its European allies over which principles have been vindicated by the experience of the twentieth century provide a good deal of the grist for present acrimony within NATO. Indeed, they are in many instances disagreements about the very nature of contemporary international affairs.

But they are not the whole story. Of equal importance is the strategic and political drift that has occurred between the United States and Western Europe over the past fifteen years. This drift has been accelerated by, yet did not begin with, the national trauma experienced by the people and government of the United States on the morning of September 11, 2001. Its roots go deeper and are found both in the enormous differential in military power between the United States and its allies as well as in an American strategic culture that is increasingly global rather than Eurocentric in perspective. Especially since the diplomatic fracture of the Alliance occasioned by the UN debate on Iraq, some of the most prominent scholars of Atlanticism view this drift as little short of tragic.[2] This book is less pessimistic. It does not hold that NATO's internal conflicts were inevitable—nothing in politics is inevitable—but attempts to show that they were probable and need not be terminal to the political vitality of Atlanticism.

---

[1]See Lawrence Kaplan, *The Long Entanglement: NATO's First Fifty Years* (Westport, CT: Praeger, 1999) and David S. Yost, *NATO Transformed: The Alliance's New Roles in International Security* (Washington, D.C.: USIP, 1998).

[2]David P. Calleo, "Power, Wealth, and Wisdom: The United States and Europe after Iraq," *The National Interest*, no. 72 (2003): 5–15.

ACKNOWLEDGMENTS

In writing this book, I have been helped by many friends and colleagues. Adrian U-jin Ang, Martin Cook, Grant Hammond, Robert J. Jackson, Tom Nichols, Ralf Schumacher, and Philip Towle helped in a variety of ways in the research effort and the manuscript development. Special thanks go to Chuck Kegley and Greg Raymond for including *Atlanticism for a New Century* in their series, *Enduring Questions in Changing Times,* and to Joel Rosenthal at the Carnegie Council on Ethics and International Affairs for alerting them to the manuscript's potential. I would like to acknowledge the gracious cooperation of the editors of *Ethics & International Affairs* and of the *Journal of Military Ethics* for permitting me to use material originally published by them for Chapters 5 and 6 of this book. I hope I have vindicated their faith in me. John Ragozzine at Prentice Hall/Pearson Education and Kari Callaghan Mazzola at Big Sky Composition demonstrated a constant and patient professionalism in steering the book through production. My dear friend Cathal Nolan has been a constant source of professional inspiration and useful criticism in this as in other projects. My wife, Jane Everett, has commented on and corrected successive drafts of every chapter and has been an invaluable intellectual influence throughout. Lastly, I am deeply indebted to the NATO Euro-Atlantic Partnership Council and to the International Security Research Outreach Program of the Department of Foreign Affairs and International Trade of Canada for their generous financial assistance.

Carl Cavanagh Hodge

Our magistrates and commanders were eager to win the greatest praise solely by endeavoring to defend our provinces and allies with justice and fidelity. As a result "protectorate of the world" rather than "empire" would have been a truer title.

—Marcus Tullius Cicero, *On Obligations*, Book Two

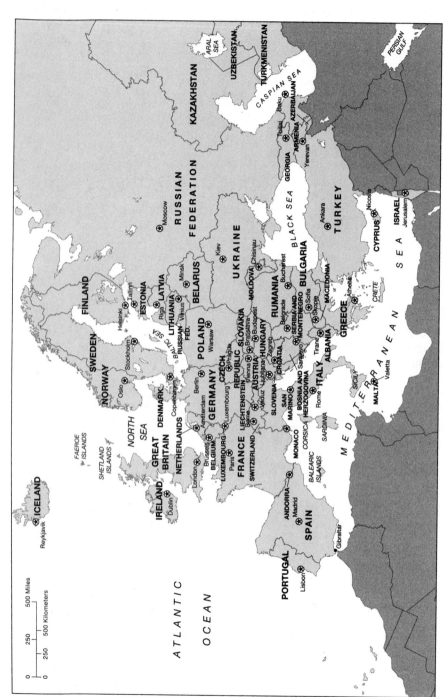

POST–COLD WAR EUROPE

ATLANTIC OCEAN

500 Miles
250
0

500 Kilometers
250
0

ICELAND
Reykjavik

FAEROE ISLANDS

SHETLAND ISLANDS

NORTH SEA

IRELAND
Dublin

GREAT BRITAIN

London

PORTUGAL
Lisbon

SPAIN
Madrid

ANDORRA

Gibraltar

BALEARIC ISLANDS

FRANCE
Paris

NETHERLANDS
Amsterdam

BELGIUM
Brussels

LUXEMBOURG

MONACO

CORSICA

SARDINIA

SWITZERLAND
Berne

LIECHTENSTEIN
Vaduz

NORWAY
Oslo

DENMARK
Copenhagen

GERMANY
Berlin

SWEDEN
Stockholm

FINLAND
Helsinki

ESTONIA
Tallinn

LATVIA
Riga

LITHUANIA
Vilnius

RUSSIAN FED.

BALTIC SEA

POLAND
Warsaw

CZECH REPUBLIC
Prague

SLOVAKIA
Bratislava

AUSTRIA
Vienna

HUNGARY
Budapest

SLOVENIA
Ljubljana

CROATIA
Zagreb

ITALY
Rome

SAN MARINO

BOSNIA AND HERZEGOVINA
Sarajevo

SERBIA AND MONTENEGRO
Belgrade

MALTA
Valetta

SICILY

MEDITERRANEAN SEA

BELARUS
Minsk

RUSSIAN FEDERATION
Moscow

UKRAINE
Kiev

MOLDOVA
Chisinau

RUMANIA
Bucharest

BULGARIA
Sofia

MACEDONIA
Skopje

ALBANIA
Tirane

GREECE
Athens

CRETE

BLACK SEA

KAZAKHSTAN

ARAL SEA

UZBEKISTAN

TURKMENISTAN

CASPIAN SEA

Baku

AZERBAIJAN

ARMENIA
Yerevan

GEORGIA
Tbilisi

TURKEY
Ankara

CYPRUS
Nicosia

ISRAEL
Jerusalem

SEA

PERSIAN GULF

THE AMERICAN MISSION IN EUROPE

Confronted with the political disintegration of the Yugoslav federation in the early 1990s, the historian John Lukacs observed that Woodrow Wilson was in retrospect beginning to make Lenin look like small fry. "The ideas of this pale Presbyterian professor-president," he wrote, "were more revolutionary than those of the Bolshevik radical from the middle Volga region."[1]

Indeed, any appreciation of the American mission in Europe in the twentieth century logically begins with Wilson. The twenty-eighth president of the United States articulated an alternative to the abstention from European affairs that had been a cornerstone of American diplomacy since Washington's *Farewell Address* initiated an essentially Europhobic tradition labeled ever since as *isolationism*. He provided both the justification for American entry into WWI and the principles for the postwar settlement at the Paris Peace conference of 1919. His most durable contribution has been the conviction that "a steadfast concert for peace can never be maintained except by a partnership of democratic nations. No autocratic government could be trusted to keep faith within it or observe its covenants."[2] Wilson's larger legacy is rooted as much in his fourteen-point prescription for lasting peace as in the settlement of 1919 itself. The first six points covered general principles such as an end to secret diplomacy, free navigation of the seas, free trade, arms control and disarmament, and impartial settlements of colonial claims. The remaining points were specific, calling upon Germany to evacuate all territory occupied by its armies in Russia, Belgium, and elsewhere, and calling for the liberation of France and the return of Alsace-Lorraine to France; self-determination for the peoples of the Austro-Hungarian Empire; the evacuation by Austria of Rumania, Serbia, and Montenegro; independence for the non-Turkish peoples from the Ottoman Empire and the internationalization of the Dardanelles; an independent Poland with access to the sea through the port of Danzig; the creation of a League of Nations to guarantee the independence of all states through a system of collective security. But the "ideas that conquered the world" achieved their victory through Atlanticism, a partnership of the democracies of the North Atlantic based on the notion that they had a common heritage and a shared destiny.

A popular half-truth about Wilson is that his judgment was clouded by idealism that led him to expect commitments from the victorious powers that were unrealistic. Yet the American delegation in Paris was by far the best informed at the conference, and a British representative later wrote that had the treaty been drafted by the Americans, "it would have been one of the wisest as well as the most scientific ever devised."[3] In February 1919 the Europeans understood that Wilson did not represent majority opinion in the United States; since a Republican majority had captured Congress the preceding November and rejected American membership in the League, democracy itself hobbled his diplomacy. Democracy was also a big part of British and French inflexibility. Had David Lloyd George disavowed his election pledges of 1918 to make Germany pay for the cost of the war, he would have faced a hostile House of Commons; had Georges Clemenceau not sought to obtain territory and reparations from Germany, "he would have been 'hurled from power' and replaced by a leader in 'closer accord with the prevailing temper of France.'"[4] In Germany progressive opinion agreed that autocracy and militarism had led the country to war, and the hope of a just peace nurtured support for democracy across social classes and religious confessions before and after the armistice.

When these hopes were disappointed, many Germans who had embraced Wilson's vision joined the nationalist extremism that tormented the Weimar Republic until its collapse. Others who had never been friends of democracy used the compromise of Wilson's principles as an excuse for a relentless assault on the republic and the Versailles settlement.[5] In the 1920s and 1930s British Conservative and Labour leaders, disgusted by French revanchism against Germany, sought to avoid security commitments to France but, in the effort, routinely dressed up Francophobia in a high-minded internationalism that assumed a moral equilibrium between France and Germany long after Hitler had come to power and made his intentions all too obvious. In 1936 "League procedure" permitted Paris to save face during German reoccupation of the Rhineland when British support for a military response was not forthcoming.[6] When a second catastrophic war again led to American intervention, revived and revised Wilsonian ideas helped to create the League's successor in the United Nations, but the end of isolationism was signified by the continuation after 1945 of the Anglo-American wartime coalition against the wartime Soviet ally.

President Franklin Roosevelt was as much the spiritual father of the United Nations as Wilson had been of its predecessor. His approach was nonetheless that of a conservative reformer for whom national sovereignty was not "a millstone fatally attached to the neck of humanity" to be thrown off in the cause of global peace.[7] Above the level of the UN's array of specialized agencies, whose work channelled the enthusiasm of believers in world government,[8] the UN Security Council made war and peace the business of great power cooperation. Because the United

States, Britain, and the Soviet Union "Big Three" had together borne the brunt of the 1939–1945 military struggle, they represented an oligarchic elite of the Security Council's five permanent members, while France and China occupied a second rank.[9] The fracturing of that oligarchy's unity signified the onset of the Cold War and gave the Anglo-American partnership a role in Europe that utterly eclipsed the United Nations. In a sense, Britain and the United States had declared war on the Soviet Union years earlier by drafting the Atlantic Charter.

THE ATLANTIC CHARTER

Like Wilson, Roosevelt believed that the New World was morally superior to the Old and that the future belonged to a dynamic civilization led by the United States.[10] Unlike Wilson, Roosevelt personally shunned neutral disinterestedness and had moved incrementally but relentlessly to align the United States on the side of the Western democracies after war broke out in Europe in 1939.[11] In signing the *Atlantic Charter*, a statement of principles agreed on by Roosevelt and Prime Minister Winston Churchill aboard the cruiser *Augusta* off the coast of Newfoundland in August 1941, Roosevelt was concerned to assuage the anxiety of Americans that a war fought in alliance not only with Britain but also with Soviet Russia might contaminate democratic ideals. The *Charter* pledged its signatories to seek a postwar peace upholding the principles of self-determination, free trade, nonaggression, and freedom of the seas. The 1948 Treaty of Brussels created an alliance among Britain, France, and the Benelux states, based on enduring fear of Germany as much as on the emerging threat of the Soviet power in Central Europe. Its members then asked Washington for security assistance and were joined by Canada, Denmark, Iceland, Italy, Norway, Portugal, and the United States in signing the North Atlantic Treaty in Washington in April 1949. The impulse behind the Brussels Pact was thereby combined with the vision of the *Charter* for the purpose of keeping, in the oft-quoted words of the Alliance's first Secretary-General, Lord Hastings Ismay, "the Americans in, the Russians out, and the Germans down."

The North Atlantic Treaty Organization (NATO), established officially to "safeguard the freedom, common heritage and civilization" of the peoples of the North Atlantic area, was from the start more than a military alliance. Whereas the *Atlantic Charter* harkened back to nineteenth-century notions of a federal union of English-speaking peoples, the effect of the wars of the twentieth century was to broaden the concept to a union to include France, Benelux, and Scandinavia "based on the universal democratic enlightenment culture of the Atlantic rather than the particular culture of Englishmen"; war had deprived populations of their sense of sovereign safety, but the comradeship-of-arms had given many of them a sense of common citizenship for the duration of the fighting.[12] The greater Atlantic Alliance of 1949 was a tribute to that kinship and a manifesto for future security.

To say that all this had been a work of British foreign policy is only a modest overstatement. Troubled by Washington's reluctance to share nuclear materials and information, the postwar Labour government of Clement Attlee decided in 1946 to embark secretly on its own nuclear weapons program. But a British nuclear capacity could not of itself compensate for the lack of collective conventional strength that after 1919 had left the European democracies ever more vulnerable. A permanent American presence in Europe was thus indispensable to Britain's strategic relationship with the continent, and it was at the urging of Attlee's foreign minister, Ernest Bevin, that talks with Washington about a broad Atlantic alliance got underway.[13] In a noteworthy nod to collective security, Article V of the North Atlantic Treaty stated that an armed attack against any member-state "shall be considered an armed attack against them all," thus establishing an institutional entanglement of the United States in European affairs, the durability of which nobody guessed at the time.

The Alliance became the cornerstone of American Cold War policy in Europe, the security dimension of what George Kennan prescribed as the "patient but firm and vigilant *containment* of Russian expansionist tendencies" in his legendary article of 1947—a response to Western European concerns about long-term American intentions and simultaneously a call for the American people to answer, "with a certain gratitude to providence," the role of leadership "that history plainly intended them to bear."[14] Kennan was subsequently critical of much of the implementation of containment, but his recommendation that the United States "confront the Russians with *unalterable counterforce at every point* where they show signs of encroaching upon the interests of a peaceful and stable world"[15] inevitably required massive military resources.

The recent experience of WWII made containment prudent. The logistics of a conflict fought in distant theaters of war was for defense planners a lesson in the importance of power projection and the forward deployment of forces. When President Truman advised Congress that it was "far wiser to act than to hesitate,"[16] he meant that practical military considerations, combined with uncertainty about Soviet designs, favored an unambiguous commitment to Western Europe's defense; containment redeemed some of the wartime sacrifice of blood and treasury in the form of a strategic posture that anticipated future conflict. It could be regarded as anti-Wilsonian in its acceptance of power realities. Kennan cautioned that, "if we insist at this moment in our history in wandering about with our heads in the clouds of Wilsonian idealism and universalistic conception of world collaboration," then "we run the risk of losing even that bare minimum of security which would be assured to us by the maintenance of humane, stable and cooperative forms of human society on the immediate shores of the Atlantic."[17]

Still, the Truman administration was nurturing and articulating a national willingness to be "at the forefront of the struggle to control the ideological direction of the world,"[18] and it does not follow that strategic prudence was a choice against Wilsonian liberal principles. A primary concern was Soviet *political* influence beyond the sphere occupied by the Red Army and Western Europe's economic, moral, and political recovery. The *Truman Doctrine*, promulgated in March 1947 in the face of communist insurgency in Greece, promised American aid to "all free peoples" similarly threatened. Secretary of State Dean Acheson denied to the Senate Foreign Relations Committee that the United States had embarked on an anticommunist crusade yet conceded that "where a free people is coerced to give up its free institutions, we are interested."[19] The Alliance was enlarged to admit Greece and Turkey, despite the fragile condition of democracy in both, due to their utility as a bulwark against Soviet encroachment in the Eastern Mediterranean. Containment became the *leitmotif* of an array of initiatives, in which the European Recovery Program (ERP), better known as Marshall Aid, was as important as military alliance.[20]

Bringing in Germany

The inclusion of Turkey in particular was an important step in broadening the Atlantic ambit yet pales in significance compared to Germany. When Moscow responded to the unification of Western Allied zones of occupation in Germany with a blockade of West Berlin in June 1948, the massive 324-day-long U.S. airlift of supplies to West Berliners symbolized the central role their city and country was to play in the East-West struggle. That there was also a military mission in and for Germany became obvious when American global commitments stretched dramatically with the outbreak of the Korean War in June 1950. The rearmament of the fledgling West German state promised to reduce the direct American military burden in Europe, especially as the idea of an integrated European Defense Community (EDC) had been under discussion since its proposal by French Premier René Pleven the same year.[21] For Truman's successor in the White House, former Supreme Allied Commander Dwight Eisenhower, a major priority became the institutionalization of containment for the long siege its logic implied. With a German contribution to Western Europe's defense, the continuing American presence there could be justified to public opinion; once the collective European contribution reached a threshold of credibility, American troops could be reduced or withdrawn altogether.

For Konrad Adenauer, first chancellor of the Federal Republic of Germany constituted on the terrain of the Western zones of occupation in May 1949, the opposite obtained: West Germans would deem containment credible only if the American presence in Europe were made permanent. Adenauer's first term in office was devoted to *Westpolitik*, a policy of reconciliation with France, German participation in West European economic integration, and the establishment of strong ties to the United States. The Korean War only intensified his concern that American energies might be directed away from Europe.[22] In response to these conflicting pressures, Eisenhower tied the theme of security to that of European economic integration by throwing his support behind the EDC, and he never tired of making public statements to the effect that heaven and earth depended on the

EDC's success in the court of European parliaments. In reality, the utility of integrated European forces was limited while the need for German rearmament, regardless of its format, was self-evident; the Belgian, Danish, Dutch, and Norwegian governments maintained that West Germany's participation was vital both to its political rehabilitation and to the forward defense of their own countries.[23] The Eisenhower administration therefore attempted to buttress Adenauer's domestic political position. In the months leading up to the chancellor's reelection bid in the fall of 1953, American interventions on his behalf strained the limits of discretion. When the electorate handed Adenauer a second term, Eisenhower confessed that he had become the pivot of "our whole political program in Europe" and expected that the EDC would now proceed to fruition — an expectation dashed by the failure of the ratification effort in the French parliament by 319 to 264 votes.[24]

The significance of this event cannot be overemphasized, because it shunted Western Europe's security from a continental to an Atlantic track and established the conditions in which an ever-more prosperous continent was to remain militarily a modest adjunct to American power.

British Foreign Secretary Anthony Eden is rightly given credit for providing the procedural formula for bringing West Germany into NATO by way of the Brussels Pact and the Western European Union (WEU). Given British skepticism concerning the EDC from the very outset, Eden could congratulate himself that he had at last persuaded the United States to adopt the concept of a German army in a NATO rather than a European framework.[25] In order to placate French concerns over the resurrection of a national German army, Chancellor Adenauer declared that West Germany would forswear the production of nuclear, biological, or chemical weapons; because the French government could make no such commitment, Adenauer was agreeing in principle to accept French military superiority. When West Germany joined NATO on May 9, 1955, the Atlantic alliance initially formed in 1941 to defeat Nazi German arms admitted a German democracy to the anti-Soviet coalition. German national aspirations were themselves to be restrained by a Western military alliance, even as the Bonn Republic contributed territory and troops to balancing the Soviet threat. Whereas Germany after 1919 had maneuvered between East and West to loosen the shackles of Versailles, it was now locked institutionally into a Western security system. This was an equally historic change for both Germany and the United States. Eisenhower had been determined to "get out of Europe," but with the NATO solution to German rearmament the United States was to remain entangled in Europe indefinitely; meanwhile, the extension of an American security guarantee to the Bonn republic facilitated West Germany's domestication as a reliable member of the Atlantic community of democratic states by removing certain issues from the immediate political agenda.[26] That Germany was to remain divided was apparent when Moscow created the Warsaw Pact immediately after and in response to West Germany's admission to NATO. Any doubt that the pact was in reality the vehicle of enforced East European alliance with the Soviet Union dissolved when in 1956 Hungary announced its intention to withdraw and was promptly invaded by the Red Army. After three days of street fighting in which 20,000 Hungarians and 3,000 Soviets were killed, the Hungarian rebels surrendered.

The hardening of the Cold War's fault line was underscored by the erection of the Berlin Wall in August 1961. For Moscow, stopping the flow of refugees from East Germany was necessary to maintain the East German regime and possibly the entire Warsaw Pact. The newly inaugurated President Kennedy was aware that the United States was in no military position to threaten action against the Soviet Union over Berlin, save that of nuclear war. The American nuclear advantage was enormous, but as long as the access of the Western powers to West Berlin was respected, the closing of the border with the East was not a shooting issue. Kennedy is remembered for his emotional identification with West Berliners during a trip to Germany in 1963, but in 1961 he held himself to symbolic gestures—above all in the dispatch of General Lucius Clay, commander of the 1948 airlift, to assure Berliners of American support.[27] For the time being, he sought the stabilization rather than the overthrow of the status-quo in Europe; if the principle of self-determination and the *idea* of a united Germany were kept alive by the *fact* of the protected freedom of West Berlin, the United States would be surrendering neither advantage nor principle to Moscow.[28] Kennedy's adaptation of Wilson—if Washington and Moscow could not bury their differences, they could at least make the world safe for diversity—held that the interest of American policy "was not to remake the world, but to balance power within it."[29]

ANGLO-FRENCH POLARITIES

As the Eisenhower and Kennedy administrations stabilized American relations with West Germany, those with Britain and France entered a stage of flux. In October 1956, a combined Anglo-French-Israeli action to overturn Egypt's nationalization of the Suez Canal triggered international outrage and condemnation in the United Nations by both of the superpowers. The Suez crisis distracted international attention from Moscow's repression of the Hungarian revolt and also prompted Soviet threats of action against London and Paris, to which the United States would be obliged to respond. President Eisenhower condemned his European allies for the attack and had the U.S. delegation to the UN propose a resolution demanding immediate withdrawal of their forces. Additionally, Washington brought extraordinary economic pressure to bear on Britain through the IMF, the World Bank, and a U.S. Treasury sell-off of American sterling reserves.[30] This public humiliation for a late-imperial misadventure was a trauma for London and Paris equally, but their long-term reactions were different. Anthony Eden resigned from the British premiership and was replaced by Harold Macmillan, while the French National Assembly expressed continuing confidence in Prime Minister Guy Mollet. Britain in effect accepted a subordinate status in NATO and looked to repair its relationship with Washington; France resolved to recover a capacity for independent action and made ostentatious independence of American leadership within the Western camp the cornerstone of its foreign policy.

The "terminal calamity of Empire," Suez struck Britain's confidence a blow at a point where the question of its future role in Europe was approaching a cross-roads.[31] Macmillan acknowledged that Britain could no longer stand alone as a great power but rejected outright that the logical alternative was to join the project of European integration. Whereas the Eisenhower administration retained its interest in building Europe, through an independent European nuclear force and NATO forces that might eventually be commanded by a European, Macmillan saw Britain's future role as "Greece to America's Rome," the counsel of the wise to the powerful in global affairs for which the country needed a nationally controlled nuclear deterrent.[32] Both the Eisenhower and Kennedy administrations found the policy at odds with Britain's ability to pay its way, a problem highlighted by a fiscal crisis in the summer of 1957. The crisis, coming in the same year in which six continental states[33] signed the Treaty of Rome officially establishing EURATOM and the European Economic Community (EEC), was from the American perspective a symbol both of British decline and the role of foreign policy choices in it.

In the early 1960s, Britain suffered two further setbacks to its prestige. The first was Washington's decision to abandon production of the Skybolt air-to-ground missile it had promised to share with Britain. The Macmillan government frothed up the Skybolt affair into something of an Anglo-American crisis, which had the unintended effect of damaging the optics of the special relationship by making British national interest appear less rather than more secure due to dependence on the United States.[34] The second was more serious. The fiscal crisis of 1957 was followed by balance-of-payments crises in 1961 and 1964, just as the economies of Germany and France were visibly prospering. Macmillan therefore decided in 1961 to cut the nation's losses by applying for British membership in the EEC—a move he regarded as complementary to the special relationship, especially as the Kennedy administration was eager that British participation make the European project less parochial and more open and Atlanticist in nature. For the opposite reason, namely that British membership would represent a "trojan horse" for American influence in Europe and endanger French leadership of the EEC, French President Charles de Gaulle announced in January 1963 a French veto to London's application, a colossal blow both to Macmillan's plan for new directions in foreign policy and to Kennedy's vision of European partnership with the United States.[35] Britain did not manage to join the EEC until 1973, at the end of a decade of prosperity on the continent but just in time for economic recession and the worst of its crisis years.

For all the hardness of his veto, de Gaulle was correct in assuming that French leadership of the EEC would have been undermined by British membership. Notwithstanding a rhetoric of national *grandeur* long on symbolism, as first president of the Fifth Republic de Gaulle reconstituted France's domestic politics to give the country the most effective executive leadership of its democratic history and recovered a measure of great power status sufficient to make France a force to be reckoned with. At the core of his foreign policy was a view that the American and Soviet superpowers had in effect divided Europe into two spheres of influence and that Europe, led by France, had to assert itself as a third force. De Gaulle welcomed the American nuclear umbrella for NATO but rejected the idea of an Atlantic Multilateral Force, and developed instead an independent nuclear *force de frappe* of sufficient strength to induce circumspection from any potential adversary.[36] The supranational aspect of the EEC had no place in de Gaulle's worldview, but he welcomed the advantages of economic integration for the French economy and saw the EEC both as an instrument for controlling a revived Germany and a vehicle for leveraging greater independence from the United States. In de Gaulle's view, such independence was not to be bought at the price of surrendering sovereignty to Europe in proportion; supranational or federal Europe was a soulless concept that could never replace the shared historical experience of the nation-state. David Calleo once labelled de Gaulle's attitude toward Europe as "commonsensical," in that it sought to create a revived France "unfettered in her revisionist initiatives by the need for achieving consensus among a half dozen or more heterogeneous partners."[37]

This did not prevent France from capitalizing on the integrationist enthusiasm of other states, the Franco-German Friendship Treaty of 1963 being a case in point. The treaty's spirit of reconciliation was in harmony with Bonn's effort to rehabilitate Germany through both Atlantic and European arrangements. To de Gaulle, Franco-German entente presented other possibilities. Between the drafting of the treaty in the fall of 1962 and the ceremony scheduled for its signing in January 1963, he held the press conference vetoing EEC British membership—at which point the Friendship Treaty took on a different complexion. The Kennedy administration saw Adenauer falling in with a Gaullist plan to create a continental bloc as an alternative rather than a supplement to the Atlantic community and possibly to arm it with a collective nuclear capacity. Kennedy told Bonn through a variety of channels that it could not have it both ways and that France's small nuclear umbrella could never replace the deterrent nuclear firepower of the United States.[38] After the crisis over the erection of the Berlin Wall in 1961 and the Cuban Missile Crisis of 1962, Kennedy was additionally concerned to put superpower relations on a less volatile footing. This included Anglo-American talks with Moscow over a treaty banning nuclear tests—a treaty negotiated over Bonn's head, on which Washington nonetheless expected a German signature—thereby locking in West Germany's non-nuclear status and underscoring its fundamental dependence on the United States. Because de Gaulle would have no part of a test ban agreement, the episode did three things. It signalled the end of the Adenauer era in West Germany after the chancellor's less-than-adroit Euro-Atlantic balancing act, exposed the barrenness of de Gaulle's overture to West Germany, and committed the United States to maintain sizeable conventional forces in Germany, more or less permanently, to compensate the frontline ally for its non-nuclear status.[39] The German Bundestag approved the Franco-German Treaty but with a preamble stipulating that the document would not affect Bonn's commitments to NATO.

De Gaulle's efforts to revise and then to scupper the Fouchet Plan for a common European defense and foreign policy, followed by his withdrawal of France from NATO's command in 1966, testify to his abiding suspicion that Washington would use either the Atlantic Alliance or the EEC to dominate Western Europe, and Kennedy's enthusiasm for the EEC as a "partner" in establishing stronger trans-Atlantic ties deepened this suspicion. An aggravating factor was disagreement over Kennedy's embrace of the nuclear doctrine of "flexible response" and insistence on centralized control of nuclear decisions. Yet even allowing for genuine strategic disputes, it is difficult to avoid the conclusion that de Gaulle was simply bent on maximum French autonomy, given that nuclear independence was integral to France's domestic Gaullist reconstitution. "By eliminating discussions about what one would fight for and how France's defense was to be achieved," Beatrice Heuser observes, nuclear weapons permitted the country to "overcome internal disagreements which had arguably contributed to France's defeats in 1870–1871 and 1940."[40] When de Gaulle then adopted a *stratégie tous azimuts* for his nuclear forces, France adopted the strategic doctrine of a neutral country. He continued to hope that the Soviet Union would eventually recognize France as its interlocutor in the West, that the Americans would go home, and that he would be free to orchestrate a new security system for Europe based on a Franco-Russian condominium to contain Germany.[41]

THE EMERGENCE OF HELSINKI EUROPE

The ambiguities of French independence did not, in the long run, influence the outcome of the Cold War. With its rearmament and induction into NATO, West Germany became the Alliance's frontier state; due to its gathering economic strength in the 1970s and 1980s it evolved into the motor of European integration as well as a loyal and diplomatically active member of NATO. If any state earned the title of "interlocutor," it was West Germany, not least of all because the German nation straddled the Cold War divide while German *Ostpolitik* supplemented the superpower détente of the 1970s.

As the Kennedy administration took containment to Vietnam and the Johnson administration increased the American military burden there past the point at which disaster might have been averted, critical European press and public opinion claimed that the United States had sacrificed its moral authority as the champion of self-determination.[42] This was a cruel twist, considering that Kennedy judged support for South Vietnam a symbol of American credibility, and Johnson described the conflict as "a struggle for freedom on every front of human activity."[43] Most governments in Western Europe were not openly critical but were disturbed by the political radicalism of the European New Left, partly influenced by opposition to the Vietnam war but also fueled by demands for domestic reform. The leftward gravitation of moderate public opinion occasioned the establishment of left-of-center governments in many European countries, the Social

Democratic/Liberal coalition led by Willi Brandt in Bonn being the most important. An appetite for superpower détente was evident in the efforts of the Kennedy
and Johnson administrations to stabilize relations with Moscow, notwithstanding
the Warsaw Pact invasion of Czechoslovakia in 1968 to overthrow the reformist
government of Alexander Dubček, but it was the need for a consolidation of American overseas commitments in light of the Vietnam failure that made détente the
centerpiece of U.S. foreign policy under Richard Nixon.

Détente involved a determination to stress the diplomatic over the military tools
of statecraft in an era of negotiations with the Soviet Union, rapprochement with the
People's Republic of China, and devolution of greater responsibility for containment to regional powers.[44] At the nuclear level it initiated the Strategic Arms Limitation Talks (SALT I), 1969–1972, and produced the 1972 Anti-ballistic Missile
Treaty (ABM). In the atmosphere of demilitarization the Brandt government saw
an opportunity to become an regional power by improving relations with the Soviet Union, the Warsaw Pact, and East Germany.[45] Nixon and his national security advisor, Henry Kissinger, were initially worried that Brandt might move West
Germany in the direction of a nationalist neutrality that would divide Bonn from
its allies. But they chose to "give the inevitable a constructive direction," and
Brandt's *Ostpolitik* fit into the logic of détente by permitting Bonn to assume more
diplomatic responsibility for East-West relations without undermining its loyalty to
NATO.[46] Brandt's efforts led to the Treaty of Moscow in August 1970, the Treaty
of Warsaw the following December, and in 1972 a capstone treaty with East Germany, recognizing its sovereignty and renouncing West Germany's claim as the
sole rightful representative of the German people. A parallel agreement on Berlin
among the four occupying powers acknowledged that West Berlin was not a constituent part of the Federal Republic in exchange for a Soviet concession that neither did it belong to East Germany. The Berlin agreement reduced the city's potential
as a flashpoint while improving access to West Berlin. Collectively the treaties renounced the use of force and recognized the inviolability of borders, most significantly the Oder-Neisse line between East Germany and Poland. They additionally
declared a mutual commitment to peace and the relaxation of tension—platitudes
that in time took on greater significance—increased human traffic between the
German states, and extended West German economic assistance and financial
credit to the East. *Ostpolitik* confirmed the status quo diplomatically while seeking to undermine it politically. The German states were admitted to the United
Nations as equals in 1972, but Moscow became progressively accustomed to talking over the head of its East German ally to the prospering German democracy
governed from Bonn.[47]

In the circumstance of the early 1970s the Soviets saw an opportunity to insert
a wedge between Washington and its West European allies by way of a European
security conference. They were initially opposed to American participation, but
their highest priority was to gain general acceptance of the territorial and political
status quo in Central and Eastern Europe in accordance with the *Brezhnev Doctrine*.[48] Entered into reluctantly by a skeptical Nixon administration and continued

by the Ford administration, the Conference on Security and Cooperation in Europe (CSCE) led to interlinking agreements on the military, economic, and human aspects of security. The 1975 CSCE Helsinki Final Act was not considered a diplomatic triumph for the West; indeed, it was widely deemed a defeat by virtue of its acceptance of the division of Europe. But the human rights dimension of the "Helsinki process" ultimately had greater popular resonance inside the Soviet bloc than anyone expected. Despite the repression of the dissident groups that emerged, the growth of organized opposition inside the Warsaw Pact contributed to the unraveling of the Soviet sphere in the 1980s. The irony is that Nixon, recoiling from Vietnam with a self-consciously hard-headed pursuit of national interests, supplemented efforts to stabilize relations with Moscow by initiating a human rights diplomacy with implications for national self-determination more sweeping than at any time since 1919.[49]

ATLANTIC ACRIMONY

A primary motive behind West German *Ostpolitik*, the need to show progress on the national issue, was clearly domestic in origin. As long as Germany remained divided and Moscow retained a veto over unification, the Bonn republic was primarily an object rather than a subject of East-West relations, a mature industrial economy but a semisovereign state. Economic maturity meant that West Germany could nonetheless practice a measure of leadership both within and beyond Europe in international trade and monetary policy. A vehicle for so doing, the Group of Seven (G-7),[50] began as a response both to Nixon's termination of the postwar Bretton Woods system of monetary governance and the OPEC oil embargo of 1973. The group's purpose was to coordinate national efforts for monetary stability, energy conservation, and preservation of the global financial system against the transfer of wealth generated by a dramatic rise in oil prices.[51] The sense among West European governments was that the United States was applying the strategic retrenchment brought about by Vietnam to the realm of economics and trade. As the G-7 established regular summits, West Germany's Helmut Schmidt and France's Valéry Giscard D'Estaing made a major contribution to Western Europe's collective diplomatic heft. As successor to Brandt, Schmidt invested in G-7 summitry in part to improve on the diplomatic room for maneuver Brandt had won. West Germany's strategic options were still extremely limited, but in international commerce Bonn could exercise a measure of European leadership. When the United States abandoned Bretton Woods it also surrendered its global monetary leadership and, Schmidt later wrote, "a portion of its de facto leadership of the West."[52].

This sentiment deepened with the election to the White House in 1976 of James Earl Carter, Jr., a man for whom Schmidt had slight regard and an uncommon willingness to express it.[53] Schmidt understood that calculated abandonment of the etiquette of diplomacy was an attention-grabber, and over Carter's four-year tenure the chancellor contrived to build his European leadership partly at the expense of Carter's

Atlantic leadership. In substantive terms he sought to make the EEC a zone of relative monetary stability. Once Schmidt had drafted Giscard to this cause, the creation of the first European Monetary System (EMS) in 1978 facilitated the "transition of West Germany's economic might into a more assertive political stance," in which the Franco-German partnership set the pace and agenda of European integration and Germany enjoyed an ever-stronger position.[54] Positioning himself as the champion of European interests, Schmidt made Carter the scapegoat of his public defiance and skepticism of American economic policy while leaving the president with the odium for difficult security policy decisions, such as the production and then cancellation of the "neutron bomb." And yet Schmidt tried to control the damage. He routinely lit into colleagues who indulged the German public in petty anti-Americanism and focused his own criticisms on the person of Jimmy Carter.[55]

There were limitations on how far this could go. The first three years of the Carter administration found the United States in a phase of uncertain retrenchment that strengthened the position of the Europeans and made G-7 summits an approximation of discussions among equals. With the second OPEC oil shock, the Iranian revolution of 1979, and the Soviet invasion of Afghanistan in December of the same year, Washington was forced to assume again the mantle of the assertive superpower. Carter punished Moscow for Afghanistan with an embargo on grain sales and high-technology transfers and looked to European allies for similar measures. Schmidt and Giscard stopped short of anything beyond public condemnation of the Soviet invasion. But Schmidt's ability to stand by the logic of NATO's "double-track" decision of December 1979, a policy of deployment/negotiation for theater nuclear weapons in Europe initially championed by the chancellor himself, became a test of his government and of Bonn's fidelity to NATO. The double-track policy was a response to competing pressures. The Soviet Union was deploying SS-20 medium-range mobile missiles targeted on West European cities at a time when NATO states had been reducing their own defenses. Schmidt wanted to go the extra mile for détente without appearing weak and neutralist to Moscow. He therefore committed West Germany to accept the deployment of a new generation of intermediate-range nuclear forces (INF) consisting of Cruise and Pershing II missiles, provided that parallel arms negotiations with Moscow were initiated for the purpose of reducing the number of all medium-range weapons.[56] The last year of Carter's term in office presaged in many ways the first of Reagan's, in that the end of superpower détente put arms reduction negotiations under a cloud and exposed the dependence of the Western Europe states on American security guarantees as thoroughly as the G-7's focus on trade issues had temporarily eclipsed it.

Reagan's presence alone changed the chemistry of Western leadership, but the election of Margaret Thatcher to Downing Street in 1979 brought in a politician as ideologically committed to free markets and the anti-Soviet cohesion of the Alliance as Reagan, as intelligent, impatient, fearless, and inexhaustible as Schmidt. The personal political affinity between Reagan and Thatcher was durable enough to make the Anglo-American relationship more special than at any time since the formation of NATO.[57] Within the G-7 it was sufficient to position a London-Washington Atlantic axis somewhat athwart the Bonn-Paris European axis, the latter missing Giscard after his defeat by the Socialist François Mitterrand in the French *présidentielle* of 1981.

Schmidt's coalition government faltered in a parliamentary nonconfidence vote in which Foreign Minister Hans-Dietrich Genscher's Free Democrats, troubled by pacifism among Schmidt's Social Democrats, abandoned Schmidt to form a center-right coalition with the Christian Democratic Union headed by Helmut Kohl. The subtext to this shift was the rising popularity of the Green Party and its pacifist platform—not to mention the diffuse anti-American sentiment of its social milieu—which made many Social Democrats nervous over their electoral base. Domestic economic issues also contributed to the chancellor's downfall, but insofar as he stood by the double-track deployments even as his party deserted him, Schmidt staked his fate on NATO unity and took a political bullet for the Alliance.[58] In his first speech to the Bonn parliament as chancellor, Kohl signaled acceptance of the new urgency of the European security agenda when he stated that membership in NATO constituted the core element of the Federal Republic's very political identity.[59]

The political turnovers that brought Kohl and Thatcher to power strengthened the Reagan administration's effort to use G-7 summits as symbols of Western unity in a more confrontational stance with Moscow. President Mitterrand was meanwhile concerned that the peace movement in Germany might endanger the durability of Kohl's coalition and push Bonn in a neutralist direction. With Kohl seeking a popular mandate for his government in general elections in March 1983, Mitterrand turned away from Giscard's détente policy and put his energies into pushing through the INF deployments. In January 1983 he used the twentieth anniversary of the Franco-German Treaty to plead Kohl's case in a guest address to the Bundestag. Mitterrand condemned any attempt to "decouple" Western Europe from North America over the primacy of nuclear deterrence in preserving peace. Yet while the French president spoke as the senior partner of the Franco-German relationship in defense, by 1983 Mitterrand's government was reversing the course of Socialist economic policy in acknowledgement that the exchange rate mechanism of the EMS would punish any French divergence from German monetary discipline.[60]

THE COLD WAR ENDGAME

It is doubtful that the Helsinki norms would have yielded the political dividend of the 1990s without Reagan's re-militarization of the Cold War in the 1980s. Carter had found it increasingly difficult to defend détente in light of intensified Soviet strategic competition in Europe, but the invasion of Afghanistan—interpreted by Carter partly as an attempt by Moscow to exploit American expulsion from Iran and improve Soviet access to the oil-rich Persian Gulf—demolished any chance of salvaging a decade's work in superpower cooperation. Prior to Afghanistan, Democrats and Republicans in Congress had used human rights issues to question the legitimacy of détente in very public ways.[61] These initiatives had in turn prefigured Carter's use of the theme of human rights in his own 1976 presidential campaign and in his administration's effort to revive moral purpose in American foreign policy.[62] To the human rights theme Reagan added a massive increase in defense expenditure and fastened upon the Soviet regime as the principal enemy of human dignity. His speech to the National Association of Evangelicals, denouncing the Soviet state as an "Evil Empire," and his televised address to the nation announcing the Strategic Defense Initiative (SDI), both delivered in March 1983, combined intensified ideological attack with the spectre of a whole new dimension of armed confrontation. Because Reagan believed both that foreign policy must necessarily have a moral core and that the tides of history favored democracy, he has since been judged an unmatched political descendant of Wilson.[63]

Still, his was a Wilsonianism cool to the notion that arms control was inherently wholesome. Reagan proceeded with development of the MX missile, the B-1 bomber, the B-2 stealth bomber and stealth fighter, the Trident missile, as well as the European deployments of the Pershing II and cruise missiles. After only two weeks in office he had approved an increase on defense spending of $32.6B, over and above the $200.3B requested by Carter. Most troubling to Moscow was SDI, the research and development of a space-based antimissile system in violation of the 1972 ABM Treaty and the reigning strategic doctrine of nuclear deterrence.[64] This was a return to Kennan. From the outset, the father of containment had denied that it was an inherently defensive policy, because the United States had in its power "to increase enormously the strains under which Soviet policy must operate."[65]

The administration also formulated human rights diplomacy to argue that right-wing dictatorships, many of whom enjoyed U.S. support by virtue of their anti-communism, were incidentally abusive of the rights of their populations, while Soviet-style socialist states were *inherently* hostile to individual liberty. Senior Democratic Senator Daniel Patrick Moynihan put it best when he noted that authoritarian regimes committed abominations in practice while communist systems committed them "on principle."[66] When the Polish government of General Wojciech Jaruzelski proclaimed martial law and banned the dissident Solidarity trade union movement, Reagan blamed Moscow for the repression and called for economic sanctions against the Soviets and their allies. This endangered the commitments of British, French, German, and Italian firms to build a pipeline across the Soviet territory to deliver natural gas to West European markets. Reagan eventually backed off the call for a pipeline embargo, but the episode illustrated the potential for division within NATO due to the economic investment West European governments, Germany above all, had made in détente.[67]

The Reagan administration's willingness both to contemplate abandoning nuclear deterrence in favor of SDI and to upgrade its missile capability in Europe posed a novel challenge to the Soviet leadership. In the 1972 ABM Treaty the superpowers had made a virtue of necessity due to the limitations of available technologies, but the "ripening plums" of American defense research in the 1980s meant that Washington would not be bound to the assumptions of that virtue indefinitely. The argument that SDI might one day facilitate the defense of the United States against a nuclear attack, moreover, put Western critics of the idea on the problematic terrain of arguing that continuing reliance on mutual deterrence was a superior moral position.[68] To the extent that governments and publics of Western Europe in the early 1980s became almost as apprehensive as the Kremlin at both SDI and the INF deployments, the double-track policy adopted to assuage West European security concerns in the late 1970s became for Reagan a test of alliance loyalty.

Thatcher and Kohl were confronted with well-organized protest movements against the INF deployments, but the disposition of their respective governments to the deployments, popular protest, and the Reagan administration were qualitatively different. From her first day in office Thatcher was unequivocal in her support not only for modernizing NATO theater missile forces in response to the Soviet SS-20 threat but additionally in her determination to upgrade Britain's nuclear capacity through the purchase of American Trident missiles. Clear parliamentary majorities in the elections of 1979 and 1983 spared her the perils of coalition politics. So unflinching was Thatcher's determination to buttress American resolve and NATO unity—in spite of periodic embarrassments such as the surprise U.S. invasion of Grenada in October 1983—that domestic enemies called her "Reagan's poodle." There is no evidence that she was troubled by the epithet or that she listened to opponents of the deployments, all of whom she considered either deluded or mendacious.[69] By contrast, Kohl's center-right coalition itself was the result of a government collapse brought about by the Green Party's appeal to pacifist, neutralist, and nationalist sentiment. The German dispute over the INF deployments was one of the greatest tests of the resilience of the *Westpolitik* established by Adenauer, of Bonn's ability to deliver on the double-track commitment made by Schmidt, and of West German democracy's capacity to resist Soviet attempts to use the fear of war to draw the Bonn republic away from its NATO allies.[70] This test was passed. Despite Moscow's efforts to exploit the alliance-breaking potential of the peace movement, Soviet foreign policy analysts during this period were themselves surprised by the size of the protest movement but otherwise convinced not only that NATO remained strong but additionally that German-American relations were "especially solid."[71]

By the mid-1980s such perceptions enabled Reagan to steer peace-through-strength diplomacy toward the ambitious arms control and reduction proposals that led from the Geneva talks to the Reykjavik Summit of 1986 and the Washington Summit of 1987—breakthroughs to which SDI may have been as critical as any other factor.[72] At the same time, the administration's covert support for the democratic goals of the Solidarity movement in Poland helped to further undermine Warsaw's communist government; support for guerrilla opposition in national circumstances as different as Nicaragua and Afghanistan was articulated in the tradition of national self-determination.[73] After Reagan's 1985 State of the Union address these initiatives fell under the *Reagan Doctrine*, a pledge of aid to all anticommunist insurgent movements — in Europe a recapitulation of the *Truman Doctrine* and a direct challenge to the *Brezhnev Doctrine*. As Reagan promised aid to the hostage populations of the Soviet system in Eastern Europe, Spain brought new vitality to Western Europe by joining NATO in 1982 and applying for EEC membership in the same year. Spain's unquestioned geostrategic value made it attractive militarily, but a Francoist regime dating to the 1930s had made its membership unsavory until its democratic transformation after 1975. Like West Germany in 1955, Spain was recasting itself as a modern West European democratic state.[74]

The motives for Soviet reaction to Reagan's words and actions are difficult to sort out.[75] A sober verdict, however, is that the U.S. defense buildup, Reagan's rhetorical assault on the barbarism of the Soviet system, support for dissident communities inside the Warsaw Pact, and NATO discipline in the INF deployments collectively exerted significant influence on the Kremlin leadership after the death of Leonid Brezhnev in 1982. A process of leadership succession and transition in Moscow led subsequently to Mikhail Gorbachev's abandonment of the tenets of Soviet foreign policy maintained since 1945. Gorbachev's effort to jolt the Soviet system out of the stagnation of the Brezhnev years was a domestic project, but the mounting burden of a military budget conditioned by intensified strategic competition with the United States and a war in Afghanistan were inherited features of a political economy incompatible with reform. To be rid of them Gorbachev was prepared to sacrifice Soviet hegemony in Eastern Europe, make disproportionate arms reductions, withdraw troops from Afghanistan, and withhold support for Cuban adventures in the Third World.[76]

Reagan wanted more. The discussions that led to the INF Treaty of December 1987, eliminating all American and Soviet intermediate-range ballistic and cruise missiles in Europe, were accompanied by repeated challenges to Gorbachev to demonstrate a genuine desire for peace, the most famous Reagan's June 1987 speech at the Brandenburg Gate in which he called upon the Soviet leader to tear down the Berlin Wall. Among the most symbolic testimonies to Gorbachev's intentions, therefore, was his 1989 speech in East Berlin on the occasion of the regime's fortieth anniversary. In the face of mass street demonstrations against the Honecker government, Gorbachev quoted Reagan's appeal to tear down the Berlin Wall and pledged that "all walls of enmity, estrangement, distrust between Europeans will fall."[77] If military retrenchment and the language of popular sovereignty were principal features of Gorbachev's new relationship with the West, the Soviet leader was taking many of his cues from Reagan — on occasion, unabashedly so. East-West relations had returned to détente, with the difference that NATO enjoyed a stronger military and moral posture than at any time since the 1950s.[78]

Gorbachev's speech, given after Reagan had retired from office, represents one of the first steps in the process of German reunification. That process was managed by Reagan's successor, George Bush, Gorbachev, and West German Chancellor Helmut Kohl. Of pivotal importance was Bush's role in providing the kind of face-saving assurances to Gorbachev that permitted the Soviet leader to eventually accept German reunification while cautioning Chancellor Kohl against words or actions that might imperil that goal. At his discussions with Gorbachev at Malta in December 1989—a month after the East German regime had begun to demolish the Berlin Wall in an attempt to salvage a morsel of legitimacy—Bush and Secretary of State James Baker listened to Gorbachev's characterization of divided Germany as "the decision of history," yet urged him to accept changes already underway according to the Helsinki principles of respect for "universal" democratic values and self-determination, which in Germany were reversing that decision.[79] Among the Warsaw Pact states, Hungary authorized the formation of opposition parties in January 1989. The threat of nationwide strikes in Czechoslovakia the following autumn brought about non-Communist participation in a coalition government and forced the Communist Gustav Husak from the presidency in favor of the dissident playwright Vaclav Havel. When the Romanian hardliner Nicolae Ceauçescu attempted to flee the country in the face of mass street demonstrations in December 1989, he was caught and summarily executed. The tide of democratic and nationalist rebellion spilled over into the constituent republics of the Soviet Union itself, in Armenia, Azerbaijan, the Central Asian republics, Ukraine, Georgia, and Moldavia. An anti-Soviet government came to power in Lithuania in March 1990 and promptly declared its secession from the Soviet Union.

In response to secessionism in the geopolitically sensitive Baltic republics, Soviet military units intervened early in 1991 in an action that prefigured, in its failure to arrest change, the coup attempt by conservative forces against Gorbachev in August of the same year. In the political flux hastened by the intensified strategic competition of the 1980s, in other words, ethnic nationalism and the Helsinki principles dismembered the Soviet system within months.[80] Atlantic arms and Wilson's principles had won the twentieth-century struggle for Europe.

NOTES

1. John Lukacs, "The End of the Twentieth Century," *Harper's*, January 1993, p. 41.
2. Quoted in Robert W. Tucker, "A Benediction on the Past: Woodrow Wilson's War Address," *World Policy Journal* (Summer 2000): 84; Michael Mandelbaum, *The Ideas That Conquered the World: Peace, Democracy, and Free Markets in the Twenty-First Century* (New York: Public Affairs, 2002), 17–44.
3. Harold Nicolson, *Peacemaking 1919* (New York: Grosset & Dunlap, 1965), 28.
4. Ibid., 89–94; Charles Loch Mowat, *Britain Between the Wars, 1918–1940* (London: Methuen, 1955), 46–52; Denis Brogan, *The Development of Modern France, 1870–1939* (London: Hamish Hamilton, 1967), 544–545.
5. Heinrich August Winkler, *Der lange Weg nach Westen: Deutsche Geschichte vom Ende des Alten Reiches bis zum Untergang der Weimarer Republik*, 2 vols. (Munich: C. H. Beck, 2001), I, 376–398.
6. Patrick Salmon, "Reluctant Engagement: Britain and Continental Europe, 1890–1939," *Diplomacy & Statecraft* 8, no. 3 (1997), 146–147; Nicole Jordan, *The Popular Front & Central Europe: The Dilemmas of French Impotence* (New York: Cambridge University Press, 1992), 72–76; Frank Ninkovich, *The Wilsonian Century: U.S. Foreign Policy since 1900* (Chicago, IL: University of Chicago Press, 1999), 77.

7. Inis L. Claude, Jr., *Swords into Plowshares: The Problems and Progress of International Organization* (New York: Random House, 1964), 54–56, 62–63.

8. Ibid., 346.

9. Ibid., 56.

10. John Lamberton Harper, *American Visions of Europe: Franklin D. Roosevelt, George F. Kennan, and Dean G. Acheson* (New York: Cambridge University Press, 1994), 34.

11. Priscilla Roberts, "The Anglo-American Theme: American Versions of an Atlantic Alliance, 1914–1933," *Diplomatic History* 21, no. 3 (1997): 363; Robert Dallek, *Franklin Roosevelt and American Foreign Policy, 1932–1945* (New York: Oxford University Press, 1979), 199–313.

12. Ira Straus, "Atlantic Federalism and the Expanding Atlantic Nucleus," *Peace & Change* 24, no. 3 (1999): 284.

13. Kenneth O. Morgan, *The People's Peace, 1945–1989* (New York: Oxford University Press, 1990), 53–58.

14. "The Sources of Soviet Conduct," *Foreign Affairs* 25, no. 4 (July 1947): 582–575; David Mayers, *George Kennan and the Dilemmas of U.S. Foreign Policy* (New York: Oxford University Press, 1988), 29–47, 89–131; Wilson D. Miscamble, *George F. Kennan and the Making of American Foreign Policy* (Princeton, NJ: Princeton University Press, 1992), 20–33; Ninkovich, *Wilsonian Century*, 164–185.

15. Ibid.; Mayers, *Kennan*, 105–160; Harper, *Visions of Europe*, 183–232; also Joel H. Rosenthal, *Righteous Realists: Political Realism, Responsible Power, and American Culture in the Nuclear Age* (Baton Rouge, LA: Louisiana State University Press, 1991), 23–24.

16. Quoted in David McCullough, *Truman* (New York: Simon & Schuster, 1992), 608; Melvyn Leffler, *A Preponderance of Power* (Stanford, CA: Stanford University Press, 1992), 11.

17. Quoted in Mayers, *Kennan*, 96.

18. Ninkovich, *Wilsonian Century*, 155; Melvyn Leffler, "The American Conception of National Security and the Beginnings of the Cold War, 1945–1948," *American Historical Review* 89, no. 2 (1984): 346–400.

19. Quoted in John Lewis Gaddis, *Strategies of Containment: A Critical Appraisal of Postwar American National Security Policy* (New York: Oxford University Press, 1982), 66.

20. Mark Smith, *NATO Enlargement during the Cold War: Strategy and System in the Western Alliance* (London: Palgrave, 2000), 67–68; Michael Hogan, *The Marshall Plan: America, Britain, and the Reconstruction of Europe* (New York: Cambridge University Press, 1987).

21. F. Roy Willis, *France, Germany, and the New Europe, 1945–1963* (Stanford, CA: Stanford University Press, 1965), 130–156; Irwin M. Wall, *The United States and the Making of Postwar France, 1945–1954* (New York: Cambridge University Press, 1991), 263–275.

22. Hans-Jürgen Schröder, "Kanzler der Alliierten? Die Bedeutung der USA für die Aussenpolitik Adenauers," in Joseph Foschepoth, ed., *Adenauer und die deutsche Frage* (Göttingen: Vandenhoeck und Ruprecht, 1988), 118–145; Wilfred Loth, "The Korean War and the Reorganization of West European Security, 1948–1955," in R. Ahmann, A. M. Birke, and M. Howard, eds., *The Quest for Stability: Problems of West European Security, 1918–1955* (London: Oxford University Press, 1993), 481–484.

23. Smith, *Nato Enlargement*, 104–105.

24. *The Papers of Dwight David Eisenhower*, 17 vols., Louis Galambos and Duan Van Ee, eds. (Baltimore, MD: Johns Hopkins University Press, 1996), 14, 569; Wall, *The United States and the Making of Postwar France, 1945–1954*, 284–286; Kevin Ruane, *The Rise and Fall of the European Defence Community: Anglo-American Relations and the Crisis in European Defence, 1950–1955* (London: Macmillan, 2000).

25. Marc Trachtenberg, *A Constructed Peace: The Making of the European Settlement, 1945–1963* (Princeton, NJ: Princeton University Press, 1999), 121–122; Saki Dockrill,

Britain's Policy for West German Rearmament, 1950–1955 (New York: Cambridge University Press, 1988); Ruane, *The Rise and Fall of the European Defence Community*, 197–199.

26. Ibid., 143–145; Thomas Alan Schwartz, *America's Germany: John J. McCloy and the Federal Republic of Germany* (Cambridge, MA: Harvard University Press, 1991).

27. Ibid., 323–324; Lawrence Kaplan, *The Long Entanglement: NATO's First Fifty Years* (Westport, CT: Praeger, 1999), 85–86; Thomas Alan Schwartz, "Victories and Defeats in the Long Twilight Struggle: The United States and Western Europe in the 1960s," in Diane B. Kunz, ed., *The Diplomacy of the Crucial Decade: American Foreign Relations in the 1960s* (New York: Columbia, 1994), 120–123.

28. Ibid., 327. The italicization is Trachtenberg's.

29. Gaddis, *Strategies of Containment*, 201.

30. Diane B. Kunz, *The Economic Diplomacy of the Suez Crisis* (Chapel Hill, NC: University of North Carolina Press, 1991).

31. Hugo Young, *This Blessed Plot: Britain and Europe from Churchill to Blair* (Woodstock, CT: Overlook Press, 1998), 99.

32. Trachtenberg, *A Constructed Peace*, 215–216; Beatrice Heuser, *Nuclear Mentalities? Strategies and Beliefs in Britain, France, and the FRG* (New York: St. Martin's, 1998), 3–74.

33. Belgium, France, Italy, Luxembourg, the Netherlands and West Germany.

34. Compare Morgan, 215–219 with Trachtenberg, 359–363.

35. Ibid., 219–221; Trachtenberg, *A Constructed Peace*, 369–370.

36. Jean Lacouture, *De Gaulle, The Ruler: 1945–1970*, trans. Alan Sheridan (New York: W. W. Norton, 1991); Philip H. Gordon, *A Certain Idea of France: French Security Policy and the Gaullist Legacy* (Princeton, NJ: Princeton University Press, 1993), 3–22; Maurice Larkin, *France Since the Popular Front: Government and People, 1936–1986* (Oxford: Clarendon Press, 1988), 309–316.

37. David Calleo, *The Atlantic Fantasy: The U.S., NATO, and Europe* (Baltimore, MD: Johns Hopkins University Press, 1970), 67.

38. Trachtenberg, *A Constructed Peace*, 371–377; Wolfram F. Hanrieder, *Germany, America, Europe: Forty Years of German Foreign Policy* (New Haven, CT: Yale University Press, 1989), 260–262.

39. Ibid., 392–398; Hanrieder, *Germany, America, Europe*, 261–262.

40. Heuser, *Nuclear Mentalities?* 143.

41. Ibid., 129; John Newhouse, *De Gaulle and the Anglo-Saxons* (New York: Viking Press, 1970), 248–249.

42. See André Fontaine in *Le Monde* quoted by Raymond Aron, *The Imperial Republic: The United States and the World, 1945–1973* (Cambridge, MA: Winthrop, 1974), 93. Larry Berman, *Planning a Tragedy: The Americanization of the War in Vietnam* (New York: W. W. Norton, 1982). Lawrence J. Basset and Stephen E. Pelz, "The Failed Search for Victory: Vietnam and the Politics of War," in Thomas G. Paterson, ed., *Kennedy's Quest for Victory: American Foreign Policy, 1961–1963* (New York: Oxford University Press, 1989), 223–252; David Kaiser, "Men and Policies, 1961–1969," in Kunz, *The Diplomacy of the Crucial Decade*, 19.

43. Stephen Ambrose, *Rise to Globalism: American Foreign Policy since 1938* (New York: Penguin, 1991), 201–235. Johnson is quoted by Ninkovich, 218.

44. Raymond L. Garthoff, *Détente and Confrontation: American-Soviet Relations from Nixon to Reagan* (Washington, D.C.: Brookings, 1985), 248–261; Robert S. Litwak, *Détente and the Nixon Doctrine: American Foreign Policy and the Pursuit of Stability, 1969–1976* (New York: Cambridge University Press, 1984), 192–193.

45. Dennis L. Bark and David R. Gress, *A History of West Germany*, 2 vols. (Oxford: Blackwell, 1993), II, 159–160.

46. Henry Kissinger, *White House Years* (Boston: Little, Brown & Company, 1979), 530, 408–412, 423–424, 529–534; Angela Stent, *From Embargo to Ostpolitik: The Political Economy of West German-Soviet Relations, 1955–1980*, (New York: Cambridge University Press, 1981), 156–157, 249–250.
47. Winkler, *Der lange Weg nach Westen*, 283–296.
48. Ibid., 195–196; Garthoff, *Détente and Confrontation*, 473–475. Promulgated a month after the Warsaw Pact invasion of Czechoslovakia in August 1968, which toppled the reform government of Alexander Dubček in Prague, the Brezhnev Doctrine declared the right of the Soviet Union to intervene in any state within the Soviet sphere of influence where Moscow deemed socialism and the leading role of the Communist Party to be threatened by "counter-revolutionary" forces.
49. Daniel C. Thomas, *The Helsinki Effect: International Norms, Human Rights, and the Demise of Communism* (Princeton, NJ: Princeton University Press, 2001); Henry Kissinger, *Years of Renewal* (New York: Simon & Schuster, 1999), 648.
50. The G-7 consisted of the United States, Canada, Britain, France, Germany, Italy, and Japan.
51. Kissinger, *Years of Renewal*, 606.
52. Helmut Schmidt, *Menschen und Mächte* (Berlin: Goldmann, 1987), 196. Haig Simonian, *The Privileged Partnership: Franco-German Relations in the European Community* (Oxford: Clarendon, 1985), 139.
53. Zbigniew Brzezinski, *Power and Principle: Memoirs of the National Security Advisor, 1977–1981* (New York: Farrar, Strauss, Giroux, 1983), 291.
54. Simonian, *The Privileged Partnership*, 253–254, 274–306; Keith Middlemas, *Orchestrating Europe: The Informal Politics of European Union, 1973–1995* (London: Fontana, 1995), 87–88.
55. Jonathan Story, "The Launching of the EMS: Analysis of Change in Foreign Economic Policy," *Political Studies* 36, no. 3 (1988): 397–412; Jimmy Carter, *Keeping Faith: Memoirs of a President* (Fayetteville, AR: University of Arkansas Press, 1995), 546–547.
56. Garthoff, *Détente and Confrontation*, 859–863.
57. Geoffrey Smith, *Reagan and Thatcher* (London: The Bodley Head, 1990).
58. Hanrieder, *Germany, America, Europe*, 359–360.
59. Winkler, *Der lange Weg nach Westen*, II, 404; Bark and Gress, *A History of West Germany*, II, 376–385.
60. Simonian, *The Privileged Partnership*, 321–327; Sten Rynning, *Changing Military Doctrine: Presidents and Military Power in Fifth Republic France, 1958–2000* (Westport, CT: Praeger, 2002), 126–128.
61. In 1973 Congress passed the Jackson-Vanik Amendment, which denied most-favored trade status to the Soviet Union unless Moscow relaxed restrictions on Jewish emigration. The amendment "let members of Congress curry constituent favor; use the power of the purse to participate in key decisions about foreign policy; and hold the executive branch increasingly accountable to the sense of Congress." Sandy Vogelgesang, *American Dream, Global Nightmare: The Dilemma of U.S. Rights Policy* (New York: W. W. Norton, 1980), 120–124.
62. Brzezinski, *Power and Principle*, 148–149; Cyrus Vance, *Hard Choices: Critical Years in America's Foreign Policy* (New York: Simon & Schuster, 1983), 46.
63. Tony Smith, *America's Mission: The United States and the Worldwide Struggle for Democracy in the Twentieth Century* (Princeton, NJ: Princeton University Press, 1994), 269. On Reagan's inspirational leadership, see William Ker Muir, Jr., *The Bully Pulpit: The Presidential Leadership of Ronald Reagan* (San Francisco, CA: Institute for Contemporary Studies, 1992), 78.
64. Raymond Garthoff, *The Great Transition: American-Soviet Relations and the End of the Cold War* (Washington, D.C.: Brookings, 1994), 33–35.

65. Quoted by Harper, *Visions of Europe*, 195.
66. Quoted in Joshua Muravchik, *The Uncertain Crusade: Jimmy Carter and the Dilemmas of Human Rights Policy* (Lanham, MD: Hamilton Press, 1986), 62; Jeane Kirkpatrick, "Dictatorships and Double Standards," *Commentary* 68, no. 5 (November 1979): 34–45.
67. Michael J. Sodaro, *Moscow, Germany, and the West from Khrushchev to Gorbachev* (Ithaca, NY: Cornell University Press, 1990), 276–277.
68. See Colin Gray's commentary in Ashton B. Carter and David N. Schwartz, eds., *Ballistic Missile Defense* (Washington, D.C.: Brookings, 1984), 400–407; also Richard Perle, "Military Power and the Passing Cold War," in Charles W. Kegley, Jr. and Kenneth L. Schwab, eds., *After the Cold War: Questioning the Morality of Nuclear Deterrence* (Boulder, CO: Westview, 1991), 33–38.
69. John Baylis, *Anglo-American Defense Relations, 1939–1984: The Special Relationship* (London: Macmillan, 1984), 181–194.
70. Paul Sharp, *Thatcher's Diplomacy: The Revival of British Foreign Policy* (New York: St. Martin's, 1997), 107–111; Margaret Thatcher, *The Downing Street Years* (New York: HarperCollins, 1993), 156–160; Jeffrey Herf, *War by Other Means: Soviet Power, West German Resistance, and the Battle of the Euromissiles* (New York: Free Press, 1991), 196–233.
71. Sodaro, *Moscow, Germany and the West*, 266–316; Harry Gelman, *The Brezhnev Politburo and the Decline of Détente* (Ithaca, NY: Cornell University Press, 1984), 206–209.
72. John Lewis Gaddis's interpretation in *The United States and the Cold War: Implications, Reconsiderations, Provocations* (New York: Oxford University Press, 1992), 43–46.
73. Tony Smith, *America's Mission*, 298–300.
74. Mark Smith, *NATO Enlargement during the Cold War: Strategy and System in the Western Alliance* (London: Palgrave, 2000), 127–161.
75. Compare Walter McDougall's balanced verdict in *Promised Land, Crusader State: The American Encounter with the World since 1776* (Boston, MA: Houghton Mifflin, 1997), 171, with Thomas's *The Helsinki Effect*, 285–286.
76. Michael McFaul, *Russia's Unfinished Revolution: Political Change from Gorbachev to Putin* (Ithaca, NY: Cornell University Press, 2001), 33–60; Peter Reddaway and Dmitri Glinski, *The Tragedy of Russia's Reforms: Market Bolshevism Against Democracy* (Washington, D.C.: USIP, 2001), 30, 259–260; Garthoff, *The Great Transition*, 762–770.
77. Quoted in Sodaro, *Moscow, Germany, and the West*, 377.
78. Gaddis, *The United States and the Cold War*, 120–123.
79. Philip Zelikow and Condoleezza Rice, *Germany Unified and Europe Transformed: A Study in Statecraft* (Cambridge, MA: Harvard University Press, 1995), 127–131; Sodaro, *Moscow, Germany, and the West*, 380–383; Garthoff, *The Great Transition*, 407–408.
80. McFaul, *Russia's Unfinished Revolution*, 86–95; Thomas, *The Helsinki Effect*, 244–256.

ATLANTIC *OSTPOLITIK* NORTH AND SOUTH

Beginning in the summer of 1989 the Cold War ended where it began, in the city of Berlin. That it ended in Soviet capitulation on Western terms was a product of the political miscalculations inherent in the Gorbachev reforms of the Soviet state and of the agility of Western governments, particularly of George Bush and Helmut Kohl, in capitalizing on the opportunities for change. In August 1989 free elections were held for the Polish parliament in which Solidarity candidates won most of the contested seats and subsequently formed Poland's first non-Communist government since 1946. A reformist government in Hungary meanwhile abandoned the state ideology of Marxism-Leninism, opened its border with Austria, and refused to return East German citizens attempting to transit Hungary for West Germany. The point of no return was passed when Gorbachev declined to back the Honecker regime in East Berlin in its desire to meet street demonstrations with firmness and possibly force. In response to Chancellor Kohl's request for a public tribute to Western unity in encouraging democratic change in Soviet Europe, President Bush told the *New York Times* that "I don't share the concern that some European countries have about a reunified Germany," and thereby erased any notion that the United States had misgivings about the full legitimacy of West German democracy or the ability of a reunified Germany to live in peace with its neighbors.

Neither Prime Minister Thatcher nor President Mitterrand was as prepared as Bush to welcome change so unequivocally. Mitterrand was ambivalent and his statements were oblique; Thatcher revealed a lack of appreciation of the society democratic Germany had become and an overconfidence that Moscow could determine the pace of East European change. Bush's statement came on October 24, 1989, a full sixteen days before the fall of the Berlin Wall. After four decades of platitudes about the grail of German unity Chancellor Kohl and his people could see that, possibly alone among the NATO allies, the United States had meant what it had said. Just as in the inauguration of Brandt's *Ostpolitik* in the late 1960s Washington demonstrated that it had conquered its fear of German nationalism, Bush now expressed confidence in the success of the policy begun in 1949 of westernizing German civic culture, a policy in which NATO membership had been so vital.[1]

In 1989 Germany was poised to benefit from a NATO and EU *Ostpolitik* for the democratization of Eastern Europe. That such an approach would be needed had been evidenced by the 1989 elections to the USSR's Congress of People's Deputies in which popular front organizations fielded nationalist and anti-Soviet candidates within constituent units of the Soviet Union itself, the Baltic Soviet republics, Georgia, and Armenia.[2] As early as February 1991, leaders of former Warsaw Pact states such as President Lech Walesa of Poland, President Václav Havel of Czechoslovakia, and Prime Minister József Antall of Hungary met in the Hungarian town of Visegrad to discuss a joint strategy for pursuing closer ties with NATO and the EU. Thereafter their countries were commonly referred to as the "Visegrad Three," or "Visegrad Quartet," after the division of Czechoslovakia into two sovereign states. The post–Cold War decade thus witnessed the elimination of the political East-West divide in Europe. But it also saw the emergence of a North-South divide in NATO's policies toward the future of former communist states. This in turn involved a paradox. Although the Alliance did not expand officially into the Yugoslav successor states, it became more substantively present there than in any of three former Warsaw Pact states to whom it offered NATO membership in 1997—the Czech Republic, Hungary, and Poland—and was itself transformed by the Yugoslav experience. Alliance expansion in Northeastern Europe was the product of comparatively coherent diplomacy, incorporating a guarantee of military security into a process of economic transformation and political reform that extended the frontier of Western Europe to the borders of Belarus and Ukraine. The NATO presence in the former Yugoslavia was the result of hesitant and ad hoc security crisis-management. In effect, NATO's cumulative actions put military force behind the self-determination claims of Croats, Slovenes, Bosnians, and Kosovars against the Yugoslav Rump State of Serbia. The serial wars of the Yugoslav succession changed the definition of European security more radically than a decade's worth of official declarations and visionary documents on new strategic concepts.

THE DEMILITARIZATION OF SECURITY

Germany's reunification was the first act of post–Cold War NATO expansion. While the United States did not share Anglo-French apprehension at the reappearance of a single German state, President Bush *was* adamant that Germany remain in NATO.

Gorbachev instinctively opposed such a shift in the strategic balance on principle. After the breach of the Berlin Wall in November 1989 and the victory of the non-Communist parties in East Germany's first free elections in March 1990 demonstrated that he could not prevent reunification, however, the restraint continuing

Scale

```
0        250        500 Miles
0    250    500 Kilometers
```

Kola

Arkhangel'sk
(Archangel)

Oulu

FINLAND

Umeå

Lake
Onega

Konosha

Trondheim

NORWAY **SWEDEN**

Tampere

Lake
Ladoga

Vologda

Bergen

Turku
(Abo)

Helsinki

St. Petersburg

Oslo

Stockholm

Tallinn

Yaroslavl

Novgorod

RUSSIAN

Nizhniy
Novgorod

Göteborg

ESTONIA

Lake
Peipus

Tartu

Tver

Jonköping

Riga

Pskov

Moscow

FEDERATION

Ryazin

Alborg

Liepaja

LATVIA

Daugavpils

Arhus

DENMARK

Copenhagen

LITHUANIA

Vitebsk

Smolensk

Tula

Malmo

**RUSSIAN
FEDERATION**

Kaunas

Vilnius

Minsk

Mahilyow

Klaipeda

Kaliningrad

Orel

Rostock

Gdansk

BELARUS

Bryansk

Hamburg

Szczecin

Bialystok

Voronezh

Bremen

Berlin

Hormel

Kursk

Hanover

Posnan

Warsaw

Brest

Pinsk

GERMANY

Leipzig

POLAND

Lodz

Dresden

Wroclaw

Lublin

Luts'k

Kharkov

Frankfurt

Krakow

Zhytomyr

Kyiv

Poltava

Prague

Opole

Lviv

UKRAINE

Lugansk

Nürmberg

Plzen

**CZECH
REPUBLIC**

Brno

Vinnytsia

Dnepropetrovsk

Munich

Zilina

SLOVAKIA

Kosice

Cherniytsi

Kryvyi Rih

Mariupol

Rostov

Linz

Vienna

Bratislava

Miskolc

Balti

**REP. OF
MOLDOVA**

Mykolayiv

Sea
of
Azov

Innsbruck

Budapest

Debrecen

Cluj-
Napoca

Chisinau

Krasnodar

SWITZ.

AUSTRIA

HUNGARY

Bacau

Odessa

Novorossiysk

Milan

SLOVENIA

Ljubljana

Pecs

Szeged

ROMANIA

Verona

Trieste

Zagreb

Novy
Sad

Sevastopol.

Venice

CROATIA

Timisoara

Ploiesti

BLACK SEA

Genoa

Bologna

Banja
Luka

Belgrade

Bucharest

Constanta

**BOSNIA
AND
HERZEGOVINA**

Sarajevo

**SERBIA
AND**

Florence

Split

Mostar

Pleven

Varna

ITALY

MONTENEGRO

BULGARIA

Rome

Podgorica

Sofia

Plovdiv

Burgas

Tirana

Skopje

Istanbul

Naples

MACEDONIA

Bari

ALBANIA

Thessalonika

Ankara

TURKEY

SICLIY

Palermo

GREECE

Smyrna

Athens

CRETE

RHODES

CYPRUS

M E D I T E R R A N E A N   S E A

BALTIC SEA

CENTRAL AND EASTERN EUROPE

German membership in the Atlantic Alliance would impose on nationalist revisionism offered significant compensation. So long as the Americans were in, by Lord Ismay's logic, the Germans would be down. For his part, Chancellor Kohl based the German claim to unity on the right of self-determination to which all CSCE states were bound by the Helsinki Final Act of 1975.[3] It was thus to discuss the terms of reunification that the Two-Plus-Four talks (the two German states plus Britain, France, the United States, and the U.S.S.R) convened and in an eight-month flurry of innovative negotiations on bilateral and multilateral levels led to agreement that a united Germany was to consist of the two existing German states and the city of Berlin; was free to join the alliance of its choice but would reduce the size of its armed forced to 370,000 men; was bound by existing arms limitations honored by West Germany (the renunciation of nuclear, chemical, and biological weapons); and acknowledged the Oder-Neisse line as its border with Poland. Moscow agreed to withdraw its 300,000 troops from former East German territory by the end of 1994, after which no foreign troops or nuclear weapons were to be stationed there. On these terms the Federal Republic of Germany remained a member of NATO and absorbed its East German nemesis on October 3, 1990. Its capital was henceforth to be Berlin. Germany's center-of-gravity shifted eastward and with it the frontier of democratic Europe.

These momentous events took place against the backdrop of negotiations for the Treaty on Conventional Armed Forces in Europe (CFE), signed at the CSCE summit in Paris on November 19, 1990. Talks on Mutual and Balanced Force Reductions (MBFR), inaugurated under the auspices of superpower détente during the mid-1970s, had the source of their failure written on their very name. Because the Soviet Union enjoyed a significant quantitative advantage in conventional arms in Europe, only *asymmetrical* reductions could improve the West's strategic position. By the mid-1980s the Gorbachev reforms in the Soviet Union made radical arms reductions plausible. As these very reforms led to revolutionary political change within the Soviet Union, the dismantling of the Soviet state, and the dissolution of the Warsaw Pact, the much greater Soviet troop reductions in the CFE Treaty reflected the evolution of Moscow's position toward "what appeared to be a one-sided pell-mell Soviet retreat."[4] Together with the INF Treaty of 1987, the CFE Treaty represents a major substantive triumph for arms-control and the demilitarization of the European continent. By the time the treaty was signed, official diplomacy had been overtaken by events in Warsaw Pact capitals that eventually led to the reunification of Europe. The Charter of Paris, signed at the 1990 summit, formally ended the Cold War and declared that security in Eurasia was to be governed by the liberal-democratic principles of the 1975 Helsinki Accords.

The CFE Treaty eliminated the Soviet Union's edge in conventional weapons by setting equal ceilings on the number of tanks, armored combat vehicles (ACVs), heavy artillery, combat aircraft, and attack helicopters that NATO and the Warsaw Pact were permitted to deploy between the Atlantic Ocean and the Ural Mountains. Under the CFE provisions for Treaty Limited Equipment (TLE) each alliance was permitted 20,000 tanks, 30,000 ACVs, 20,000 heavy artillery pieces, 6,800 combat aircraft, and 2,000 attack helicopters for the treaty's area of application. The member states of each alliance then divided their alliance limits among themselves, thereby establishing "national" ceilings. After the Soviet Union's dissolution its national total was distributed among eight of its successor states. The Soviet Socialist Republics of Estonia, Latvia, and Lithuania were removed from the CFE area of application on October 18, 1991, after they had received independence. As part of the dissolution of Czechoslovakia in January 1993 the successor Czech and Slovak Republics agreed on respective national limitations.

Because the CFE's territorial application ended at the Ural Mountains, Russia's vast interior space afforded it an advantage unavailable to NATO forces in Europe. A large amount of equipment could be withdrawn from Europe to storage east of the Urals and yet remain at Moscow's disposal. Still, the advantage was mostly theoretical. The reintroduction of the equipment to the European theater would take several weeks and could easily be monitored. Additionally, storage conditions east of the Urals were less than ideal, so that the condition of the equipment could deteriorate rapidly absent the investment to maintain it. This was a problem even before the post-Soviet economy of Russia went into steep decline in the mid-1990s. Lastly, the balance between the two alliances became fictive when the Warsaw Pact was dissolved in March 1991, because it could not be assumed that former members would again combine their forces with a recidivist Russia against NATO.[5] By May 1996, when the treaty's first review conference was held, more than 58,000 pieces of TLE had been destroyed and 2,700 inspections conducted to ensure compliance.[6] Beyond these reductions the CFE's inspection regime itself did much to reduce tensions and build confidence during a phase of critical change. The treaty soothed concern over the headlong rush to German reunification and facilitated the withdrawal of Soviet forces from Eastern Europe. Its significance was enormous. By the mid-1990s Europe had greater assurance against the risk of large-scale conventional warfare than at any time since the Franco-Prussian War of 1870.

The issue of NATO's possible enlargement to include former members of the Warsaw Pact prompted occasionally threatening comments from recidivist political forces in Moscow. The Partnership for Peace (PfP) established at the NATO summit of 1994 was in part intended to avoid a hasty decision on NATO enlargement, but when the Russian foreign minister Andrej Kzoyrev signed an agreement giving Moscow less than full equality with Washington in the PfP, communists and nationalists in the Duma denounced it as "American imperialism" and compared it to *Operation Barbarossa*, Germany's invasion of the Soviet Union in 1941.[7] The resolution of the "flank dispute" is an example of how the CFE forum eased these anxieties. In order to avoid having to declare Russia "noncompliant" with treaty standards, the CFE signatories permitted Moscow higher force levels than initially stipulated for the Leningrad Military District in Russia's north and the North Caucasus Military District in the south. The concessions were an acknowledgement of Russia's vast geography and of the fact that the force limits on the southern flank in particular were irksome to Moscow in light of the revolt in Chechnya.[8] Among the arguments against NATO expansion in the mid-1990s, meanwhile, was the claim that the CFE Treaty had already solved the problem expansion would answer: the emergence of a power vacuum between Germany and Russia in Central and Eastern Europe. In this argument the CFE was regarded as a principal feature of a "new, different, and supremely valuable security order," extending from the Atlantic to the Urals and based on the mutual confidence-building aspects of the CFE and other arms control agreements negotiated in the last years of the Cold War and early post–Cold War years.[9] But the argument was unsustainable against the array of national and Alliance rationales for extending NATO eastward. In its 1995 *Study on NATO Enlargement* the Alliance cited seven goals to be pursued in adding to its membership:

- Supporting democratic reform, including civilian control of the military
- Fostering among new members the habits of cooperation that characterize relations among the current members
- Promoting neighborly relations among all states of the Euro-Atlantic area, both members and non-members of NATO
- Emphasizing and extending the benefits of common defense while increasing transparency in defense planning and military budgets
- Reinforcing the trend in Europe toward integration based on shared democratic values, thereby curbing the danger of political disintegration on ethnic and territorial lines
- Enhancing NATO's capacity to contribute to European and international security and peacekeeping operations through vehicles such as the OSCE and the United Nations
- Strengthening and broadening the trans-Atlantic partnership

Between 1990 and 1994 discussion on both sides of the Atlantic dealt with the merits and risks of expansion. Critics cited the danger of aggravating Moscow's anxieties over Western encroachment into the Russian "near abroad," recommending alternatives ranging from a cautious approach to expansion to a plan for making Russia itself a member of NATO. Some warned that NATO enlargement might become "the catalyst that would enable extreme chauvinist elements in Russia to exploit frustrations, resentments, and wounded national pride in ways that would have unpleasant consequences both internally and internationally."[10] Enlargement enthusiasts countered that instability in post-Soviet Eastern Europe could revive old rivalries between Germany and Russia; consolidating Germany's security substantively merited higher priority than stroking Russian sensibilities symbolically. This argument paid tribute to the historic reason for admitting West Germany to NATO in 1955, namely to lock Germany permanently in a Western community of democratic states. A new and expansive *Ostpolitik* underwritten by NATO promised to reward that diplomatic investment by broadening democratic Europe's horizons on a scale nobody had dared to hope for only a few years previous.[11]

While the United States is rightly regarded as the initiator of an enlargement agenda that called for the Visegrad states of the Czech Republic, Poland, and

Hungary to begin talks leading to the signing of accession protocols in December 1997, Germany too was a key supporter of eastern enlargement. Geography dictated that its government had a sharp sense of exposure to crises and threats from the East. The commitment to enlargement was additionally influenced by economic and cultural ties as well as a sense of moral obligation to Eastern Europe in light of Germany's historic transgressions there.[12] Equally, enlargement created a new set of problems and opportunities between Berlin and Moscow, the most important bilateral relationship in Europe.[13] By virtue of the Franco-German partnership in European integration, Germany occupied a pivotal position both within NATO and the EU. The conduct of *Ostpolitik* during the Cold War was designed to open up human contact and commerce with East Germany, Poland, and the Soviet Union in particular. After national reunification, democratic Germany was free to pursue through Atlantic and European multilateral vehicles the sphere of influence it sought through intimidation and conquest in the first half of the twentieth century.[14]

As early as November 1989, the Kohl government offered Poland an unprecedented debt reduction plan along with financial aid to encourage investment by the German private sector. Additionally, Germany was in a position to orchestrate EU financial commitments in support of postcommunist economic reform. Though initially ambivalent about the French initiative to create the European Bank for Reconstruction and Development (EBRD), the Kohl government came to appreciate that a multilateral approach to economic aid could do in the East what the European Community had done in Western Europe over the previous four decades. Investment and credit under EU auspices fostered the development of new markets on Germany's doorstep, yet eased the fears of Germany's Eastern and Western neighbors that Bonn's goal was to create a German-dominated zone in the East.[15] In a number of ways these developments were truly revolutionary. In the 1920s and 1930s French diplomacy in Eastern Europe sought above all to thwart German aspirations in the region. Now German and French firms were involved in joint ventures there, and their governments acquired EU subsidies to mitigate costs. Large firms such as Siemens AG found it a form of enlightened self-interest to plow Deutschmarks into the upgrading of East European nuclear power plants, if only to prevent another Chernobyl disaster and a public relations nightmare for the nuclear power industry.[16]

The Kohl government articulated an important differentiation between relations with Eastern Europe and Russia. Defense Minister Volker Rühe worked to integrate a strong security dimension into Germany's eastern diplomacy, in which Poland in particular played a central role. In the wake of the 1994 NATO summit in Brussels, Rühe claimed in a Bundestag debate that it was in Germany's "vital interest" to open the Alliance to eastern neighbors. Drawing the connection between soft and hard security particularly close, he went on to say that it required no strategic genius to see that Germany's eastern border must not be permitted to become the eastern frontier of either NATO or the EU. "Either we export stability," Rühe argued, "or we will import instability."[17] In the same debate Foreign Minister Klaus Kinkel observed that the government saw itself as an "advocate for the interests of our eastern neighbors" and that former members of the Warsaw Pact had justifiably high expectations of Germany.[18] The fact that enlargement spoke to specific regional concerns and brought to Germany a particularly cost-effective improvement of its security enhanced domestic support across the political spectrum. Karsten Voigt, opposition foreign policy spokesman, observed that without alliance expansion Germany's ties with its eastern neighbors would become bilateral; it was "much better to embed *Ostpolitik* within NATO structures."[19]

The very anticipation of these changes in itself helped to promote political reform and a redefinition of security in post-Soviet Europe. In 1991, well in advance of any formal agreement on EU enlargement, Polish President Lech Walesa observed that "having a Frenchman or an Englishman here with his factory is like having a division of troops."[20] Corporate *Ostpolitik* represented the less-visible yet equally important private-sector dimension of the economic transformation required of governments of post-Soviet Europe in reforming their practices in accordance with the *acquis communautaire* required for EU membership. Although membership in NATO could not of itself "spread democracy," early NATO expansion into the Visegrad states nurtured a popular sense of enhanced security, thereby permitting national governments to concentrate their efforts on the economic requirements of membership in the European Union.[21] The goal of NATO membership prompted the same governments to undertake military reforms to enhance their eligibility. The reforms required by the CFE and those required by NATO ran parallel. Military reform for NATO enlargement in Central and Eastern Europe began to replace the CFE norms, while Alliance expansion drastically reduced the importance of arms control as such. For major states such as Germany and Russia, CFE norms were still highly valued after 1991 because of the transparency and assurance they provided,[22] but NATO enlargement too encouraged reforms with a similar outcome in terms of building confidence in potential conflict zones.

In a demilitarized environment the prospect of EU enlargement meanwhile alters the nature of security between former adversaries, while pushing the frontier of the Euro-Atlantic community eastward. The establishment of border-free "Schengen" standards among the core EU states of Western Europe and the demilitarization of the German-Polish border means that one of Germany's immigration borders is for all functional purposes now in Eastern Poland.[23] Although the size and deployment of conventional forces in Poland and Belarus remains important, security relations between Poland and Germany are in large part governed by cooperation in "microsecurity," regulating the flow and quality of civilian traffic into the European Union.

Not all relationships have been so dramatically changed. The Western aspirations of the former Soviet Baltic republics of Estonia, Latvia, and Lithuania complicate regional security in Northeast Europe. Because they were constituent republics of the Soviet Union rather than members of the Warsaw Pact, their early assertion of secessionism during the period of the Gorbachev reforms signaled that Moscow had lost control of the pace of domestic change. The governments of the Baltic states did not join the CFE, because in the early 1990s they were primarily

concerned with getting Soviet troops to leave their soil, and the treaty was regarded as a vehicle by which that very presence could be legitimated. Prior to 1997,
Russian policy toward the "near abroad"—initially the "diaspora linkage" aspect
of the withdrawal of Russian troops[24]—testified to an inability to accept the Western aspirations of the Baltic peoples. Even after the 1997 Helsinki Summit with
President Clinton, at which President Yeltsin and Foreign Minister Yevgeny Pri-
makov announced a new approach to the region, Moscow asserted more than once
its right to intervention based on the continuing presence of ethnic Russians. An
unwillingness to provide the reassurance the Baltic republics needed from their
former master produced the result Moscow wished above all to avoid. It foreclosed
Baltic neutrality by heightening the concern of Sweden, Finland, Denmark, Germany, Poland, and the United States for the security of the republics and thereby
made their admission to NATO more rather than less likely.[25]

The Russian *oblast* of Kaliningrad on the Baltic coast nestled between Lithuania and Poland adds a geopolitical wrinkle. The *oblast* has a population of about
900,000. It is home to the Russian Baltic Sea Fleet and the Yanter shipyard. It offers the only ice-free port on the Baltic, without which the Russian navy would be
unable to operate effectively in the area. It also has the Baltic's largest fishing fleet
and possesses undeveloped oil reserves, a reputation as a haven for organized crime,
decaying industry, and the worst pollution problem in northeastern Europe.[26] Although the Putin government obviously feels the need to maintain a military presence in the enclave in order to deter potential secessionism, it appears to have
decided against a "fortress Kaliningrad" policy and is scaling back its commitment.
The contrast between Moscow's often petulant reaction to the first round of NATO
enlargement and its relaxed reception of the much more ambitious second round
agreed upon by Alliance members at the Prague Summit of 2002 is remarkable, especially as the Prague meeting included a NATO offer of accession talks to the
Baltic republics.[27]

Given its economic dimension, it is encouraging that Moscow and the EU
have reached a compromise on visa controls for Russian citizens in Kaliningrad
who, once the Baltic states join the EU, will have to travel through Lithuania and
then Belarus or Latvia in order to reach any other part of Russia by land.[28] The
work of the EU in "societal security" will be possibly more important than innovative military arrangements over the long term. The promotion of economic renewal and the fight against crime resulting from social decay in Kaliningrad are
goals of the joint multilateral efforts of the EU and the Council of Baltic Sea States
(CBSS).[29]

The *Founding Act on Mutual Relations, Cooperation and Security* with Moscow
and the *Charter on a Distinctive Partnership* with Kiev each acknowledge NATO as
a positive force for peace and stability in Europe.[30] The extension of Atlantic institutions eastward—through the PfP, Russian inclusion in meetings of the G-7, and evolution of the NACC into the Euro-Atlantic Partnership Council (EAPC) in
1997—provide a layer of multilateral consultation overarching these regional arrangements. Most inclusive of all is the child of Helsinki, the OSCE, in light both of its

BALTIC STATES

broad definition of Europe and the breadth of its nonmilitary security functions, ranging from observer and monitoring missions to conflict-mediation services.

What is striking, then, about post–Cold War change in Northeast Europe is the extensive demilitarization of security and the multilayered presence of regional, European, and Atlantic institutions in a concerted, and fairly coherent, effort in economic and political stabilization. The impact on NATO has been profound but pales by comparison with the Alliance's travail in Europe's Southeast. For if it is true that "the most significant development of NATO's post–Cold War adaptation is not its enlargement but its transformation, which entails acceptance of a power projection role and the unilateral assumption of responsibility for European security broadly defined,"[31] it is equally true that the territorial disintegration of Yugoslavia has done more to redefine the Alliance's strategic perspective and to introduce new tensions to the relationship of the United States with its principal European allies.

THE BALKAN CATALYST

The process began on December 23, 1991, when the Kohl government in Germany announced its intent to extend diplomatic recognition to the secessionist Yugoslav states of Croatia and Slovenia. In so doing, Germany in effect renounced the legitimacy of the existing Yugoslav state and pressured other European governments to do the same. Nobody at the time guessed that Germany's initiative was the first step of a diplomacy that led ultimately to NATO trusteeship for the political future of the Yugoslav republic of Bosnia-Herzogovina and the Serb province of Kosovo.

Germany's declaration represented a sudden break with forty years of foreign policy embedded in multilateral solutions to European problems, but there was also a degree of hard-headed pragmatism in acting preemptively. In 1991, after all, Germany had only just realized the goal of national reunification and sought no responsibilities beyond the integration of seventeen million East Germans into West German society. But in 1991 Gorbachev's fragile political position in the Kremlin—underscored by the abortive coup in August and the specter of Soviet territorial disintegration—threatened the implementation of the unification agreements. With so much at stake in its bilateral relationship with Moscow, Yugoslavia was an issue that Bonn was anxious not to handle. It has been argued additionally that popular German support for Croat independence, combined with the ambition of German foreign minister Hans-Dietrich Genscher to chalk up a policy success with a bold initiative, pushed Bonn toward basing a case for recognition on the principle of self-determination, which had, after all, just brought national fulfillment to Germany itself. In the fall and winter of 1991, meanwhile, the member states of the European Community found themselves in the final negotiations for the Maastricht *Treaty on European Union* (TEU), which represented the culmination of the effort underway since the Single European Act of 1986 to create a fully integrated European market free of restrictions on the movement of capital and labor. The TEU included a commitment to develop a Common Foreign and Security Policy (CFSP) and a European Security and Defense Identity (ESDI), both promoted by Germany; the Kohl government considered a unified European voice in international affairs a logical and wholesome aspect of integration as well as a way to strengthen the European contribution to NATO.[32] None of these considerations, singly or in combination, speak against the proposition that what appeared at first glance to be a German initiative in European leadership was at root an attempt to get Yugoslavia as quickly as possible into the diplomatic out-basket and to minimize direct German and European responsibility for the Yugoslav crisis. With its diplomacy on the cusp of national and European achievements of this magnitude, what were the odds that Bonn would have permitted the calm negotiation of the New Europe to be interrupted by the distant chatter of small arms fire in the Balkans?

Washington considered the crisis an inherently European problem. Unlike the Iraqi invasion of Kuwait, which the United States had reversed between August 1990 and February 1991 with a series of resolutions from the United Nations and help from some of its European allies, civil war in Yugoslavia touched upon no American vital interests, nor did it pose a threat to vulnerable global oil markets. In Europe the Bush administration focused its attention on the great unravelling in Moscow, with its sweeping implications for the global balance of power. Its policy on Yugoslavia was to convince Belgrade and the republics to consider seriously the possibilities of reforming and renewing the existing federation. The administration sought, in the words of Secretary of State James Baker III, "to work with the Europeans to maintain a collective nonrecognition policy against any republic that unilaterally declared independence, as a lever to moderate behavior."[33] Baker later confessed that there existed a measure of resentment in Washington over European ambitions to develop a defense and security identity over American protests that Europe was not yet equal to the task. But there was also, he concedes, "an undercurrent in Washington, often felt but seldom spoken, that it was time to make the Europeans step up to the plate and show that they could act as a unified power. Yugoslavia was as good a first test as any."[34]

As it turned out, Germany's recognition initiative represented the first installment on European failure. An alternative approach to recognition, admittedly, would not necessarily have produced a more peaceful transformation of Yugoslavia.[35] But withholding recognition pending guarantees for minority rights might have established a respectable principle for recognition over the tawdry claims of ethnic self-determination that ultimately set the agenda for Yugoslavia's further disintegration. Additionally, withholding recognition might also have flushed out the Serbian government in Belgrade on what it wanted all along, a Greater Serbia patched together by uniting through force those regions of the federation where ethnic Serbs represented a preponderance of the population. As the situation deteriorated to progressively more brazen violence from all parties to the dispute, Genscher insisted that only an international response through the United Nations stood any chance of bringing the fighting to an end.[36] When Secretary General Javier Peres de Cuellar warned that a premature Western recognition of Slovenian and Croatian sovereignty could further inflame the military conflict, Dutch Foreign Minister Hans van der Broek chimed in that, on the contrary, Bonn was on the right track with its recognition initiative. Genscher then took his diplomacy into de Cuellar's arena with an address to the UN General Assembly in September 1991, in which he defended external intervention in domestic situations involving offenses to human rights and democratic order. Other European governments lined up behind Bonn as Genscher sought UN Security Council involvement in the Yugoslav crisis.

Thus began a particularly difficult phase of the Atlantic Community's post–Cold War experience, resulting in part from the relative disinterest that the United States and Germany shared with regard to the future of Yugoslavia. Germany's recognition forced the hand of other European states and thereby lent legitimacy to the breakaway Yugoslav republics. A crisis that in American eyes had been Europe's to solve in principle, because it was a crisis in Europe, was now doubly Europe's to solve in deed, because European governments had stampeded events inside Yugoslavia.[37] The great mischief in German policy, of course, was that "Germany herself could not really contribute to an implementation of the policies that logically flowed from her attitude."[38] At the time, Germany had not so much as scratched the surface of the reforms necessary to convert the *Bundeswehr* from an army of territorial defense to a mobile force capable of rapid deployment for regional crisis management.[39] Because the Kohl government was still engrossed in a domestic constitutional debate over the use of the German troops in NATO "out of area" operations, moreover, the German contribution at this juncture was to support in principle actions by an international community that did not necessarily include Germany in any military capacity.

Indeed, the manner in which Yugoslavia eventually became a crisis of legitimacy for the United Nations itself, in turn, complicated even NATO's ability to succeed where the broader international community could not. When the Republic of Bosnia-Herzogovina declared its own independence and the term "ethnic cleansing" entered the vocabulary of international media, the perceived moral stakes of ending the violence were ratcheted upward. Televised scenes of brutality provoked *Resolution 781* from the UN Security Council, banning all flights over Bosnia not approved by the UN. "Where is Europe?," wondered Senator John McCain to the U.S. Congress, "We have seen Germany recognize the sovereignty of some Yugoslav nations, but what evidence of leadership have they demonstrated beyond that action?"[40] While NATO's European member states vetoed an American motion that all violators of the no-fly zone be shot down, European governments consented to provide peacekeepers under UN auspices. Guessing that NATO might eventually have to assume a burden in Yugoslavia, France filed a note of dissent to the effect that a humanitarian or peacekeeping mission could easily turn into a Western confrontation with one of the parties to the dispute, namely the Serb Republic. The government in Paris had no answer to Senator McCain's question but was, in its own way, worried where any collective crisis-management effort might lead, especially when France's traditional partner in Europe, Germany, was apparently not to be part of it.[41]

This was understandable. It did not require a self-consciously realist interpretation of events to conclude that Germany had a diplomatic strategy for Yugoslavia that possibly went beyond the immediate issues of the crisis itself.[42] When in doubt about which multilateral institution best suited a given situation during the Cold War years, Germany typically resorted to all of them. Though at times this habit made German policy seem self-contradictory, it reflected a determination to maintain a low profile in international security affairs. It was natural and advantageous for Bonn to approach the Yugoslav crisis with the habits acquired over forty years; keeping the United States involved in Europe had been a priority of German foreign policy since the foundation of the Federal Republic. Only in its *haste* to extend recognition to Croatia and Slovenia did Bonn's diplomacy seem unusually assertive. By virtue of its address, the United Nations, recognition diplomacy remained consistent with the German multilateralist tradition. When the Bush administration assumed a comparatively arms-length posture on the crisis, the United Nations offered both Germany and the European Union far and away the best diplomatic vehicle for eventual American involvement. No government understood better than Germany's that international crisis management consists of a complex of diplomatic rivers, all of which flow into the Potomac.[43]

In the case of Yugoslavia there was a certain historical appropriateness to this attitude. The principle of self-determination was made respectable by its central place in President Wilson's blueprint for European peace after 1919, though prior to the armistice it had been an article of war-fighting diplomacy employed to weaken the Habsburg Empire through the cultivation of ethno-nationalist zeal within its borders. This turned a legitimate article of anti-imperialist foreign policy into the child of nationalism and strategic expedience, but did not in principle rob it altogether of the capacity to contribute to civilized politics between nations. Hence its inclusion alongside the commitments to respect for sovereignty and the inviolability of frontiers governing security in Europe of the 1975 Helsinki Final Act. Wilson also envisaged the opening of Europe's subjugated peoples to the penetration of American commerce; their acceptance of the liberal values; and their ultimate attainment of self-government. But national self-determination was always open to a variety of interpretations. It is hard to disagree with Wilson's Secretary of State Robert Lansing that the idea was "loaded with dynamite"; certainly, it became one of the great lessons of the twentieth century that "minorities not infrequently seek self-determination for themselves in order to deny it to others."[44] Wilson's inclination as a progressive had been to assume that in the 1920s a wave of democracy would follow upon a disastrous war for which European autocracies were responsible. Yet only as the twentieth century drew to a close was it reasonable to speculate that democracy was on its way to becoming a global entitlement,[45] while its relationship to the century's experience of nationalist movements remained as problematic as ever. The message received in the Balkans from Western recognition diplomacy was essentially that the principle of self-determination could legitimately break up multinational states. Nationalists were encouraged to believe that the surest way to succeed with a project of secession was to "instigate a defensive war and win international sympathy and then recognition."[46] In the 1990s the Yugoslav example moved a body of opinion to conclude that Lansing's caution was closer to the mark than Wilson's optimism. Much of the democracy available in the Balkans was illiberal in intent and deed.[47]

This verdict, as it turns out, was unduly harsh in light of the genuine progress made by democratic governments internationally. The more legitimate criticism was that reserved for the United Nations, for that body's response to the Yugoslav crisis was only one of a number for which it earned failing grades. In the 1930s the League's dream of preventing great power wars with the organized weight of "world opinion" proved illusory; in the 1990s even the modest goal of quelling regional conflicts "was cast into doubt as the growing American reluctance to lead was more than matched by a reluctance of its partners to follow."[48]

THE AMBIT OF ATLANTICISM

Even as NATO contemplated official enlargement into the Visegrad states, therefore, it was simultaneously drawn into the vacuum created in Yugoslavia by the EU's impotence and the UN's failure. Its member states began to discuss simultaneously the need to change the form and purpose of the Alliance from that of prosecuting a war of territorial defense of Western Europe. Attention was given to the possibility of security crises in the Mediterranean and the Middle East, but the social, economic, and political difficulties now faced by Central and Eastern Europe were deemed most likely to produce the conditions leading to armed conflict.[49] The continued disintegration of Yugoslavia—moving over the decade from the Slovenian and Croatian secessions to the Bosnian crisis and the humanitarian outrages in the Serb province of Kosovo—exerted a constant influence on NATO reform and enlargement.

Voted from office in November 1992, the Bush administration had no opportunity to consider NATO expansion systematically, and in the Clinton administration a decision to back expansion was reached only incrementally. Clinton faced conflicting arguments between those who sought above all to avoid alarming Russia and those who worried that the momentum of political reform in Eastern Europe would stall without the carrot of NATO membership. He came to accord higher priority to the political transformation of the former Warsaw Pact states for a number of reasons, among them personal discussions with Lech Walesa and Václav Havel; the need to demonstrate American Alliance leadership; an emerging domestic political consensus on the issue, and his own vague commitment to spreading liberal values through the globalization of commerce and communications.[50] At the NATO summit of January 1994, at which Clinton unveiled the Partnership for Peace initiative that included Russia, it was evident that some partners had nonetheless become more important than others.[51]

Clinton's White House made an astute tactical choice to fast-track Senate approval and thus separate the NATO expansion issue from congressional debates on strategic arms reduction and the Comprehensive Test Ban Treaty (CTBT), both of which faced vigorous opposition from congressional Republicans.[52]

In response to mounting public outrage at televised vignettes of the carnage in Srebrenica in March 1993, Clinton meanwhile pondered another kind of expansion. He ordered a review of U.S. policy on the Balkans and gravitated toward a "lift and strike" approach to Bosnia, despite protests from the Europeans against an end to the arms embargo on Bosnia. But a lack of consensus within the administration—combined with the awareness that an American diplomatic lead would mean that Bosnia would become, above all, Washington's problem—kept Clinton from more decisive action until the open differences within NATO looked like they could fracture the Alliance itself. After the use of air strikes to lift the Serb siege of Sarajevo in the summer of 1995, the Europeans secured at last the quid pro quo of American ground deployments as part and parcel of the implementation of the Dayton Accords brokered by Clinton the following autumn.

Thus, the period of European and UN-led crisis management in Yugoslavia came to an end and NATO's career in peacemaking began. The Clinton administration's slowly emerging geo-strategic vision of post–Cold War European security required that it tie the various strands of its policy together. Bosnia could not be permitted to question the very unity and credibility of the Alliance at the moment its spokesmen publicly pondered the "projection of stability" into Poland, the Czech Republic, and Hungary.[53] As early as the July 1990 summit, NATO's heads of government had agreed upon a *New Strategic Concept*, identifying a broadened concept of security in which "management of crisis" and "conflict prevention" assumed special prominence, but few of them guessed the press of necessity in Bosnia would eventually make the price of unity a redefinition of the Alliance's very purpose.[54] The document noted additionally that "integrated and multinational European structures, as they are further developed in the context of an emerging European Defence Identity would enhance Alliance cohesion; reinforce the transatlantic partnership, and strengthen the European pillar."[55] This, in retrospect, was by contrast both an overstatement of impending change and a tribute to the optimism of the early post–Cold War years. The Maastricht Treaty came into effect in November 1993, transforming the European Community into the European Union (EU). In January 1994 the Alliance acknowledged this development; gave its formal blessing to ESDI; and recorded its intention to strengthen the European pillar by making NATO assets available, through the vehicle of combined joint task forces (CJTF), for operations undertaken solely by European member states in the name of a common foreign and security policy.

Among the European Allies, France was drawn to the CJTF concept by virtue of what it seemed to hold out in terms of greater European self-reliance. Yet President Chirac was also annoyed that the attempt to innovate a European autonomy within NATO by way of CJTFs was to be subject to approval of the North Atlantic Council and thus of the United States.[56] This attitude reflected a French willingness to reassess the traditional Gaullist policy toward NATO in light of both the challenges and the opportunities the end of the Cold War possibly portended. Relative to Germany, post–Cold War France also demonstrated both a greater concern with Southern European and Mediterranean affairs and a greater willingness to pursue both defense reforms and structural change within the Alliance. French units of the multinational Eurocorps, agreed to in principle by Bonn and Paris in 1987, were integrated into the defense planning of the Alliance. A willingness to make available to the Supreme Allied Commander in Europe (SACEUR) additional troops with a high degree of readiness also broadened France's former cooperation agreements with NATO.

But none of this meant that Paris had abandoned its goal of creating a more independent Europe. It signaled rather the beginning of an attempt to change NATO from within.[57] France's failed demand that in the future a European should be given responsibility for NATO's Southern Command (AFSOUTH), for example, reflected two things. The first was the recurrent Gaullist appetite for seeking major and immediate diplomatic capital for France in return for marginal and even hypothetical concessions to allies. The second was a more legitimate attempt to focus NATO's attention more forthrightly to Southeastern Europe, where the security scenario was too frequently anarchic relative to the political transformations on Germany's doorstep.

A constant French concern between 1991 and 1995, moreover, was that eastern enlargement of the Alliance would divert energies from the creation of a ESDI as the basis of reduced European dependence on American military capacity. Germany regarded ESDI as "primarily a political concept developed by the West European member states in their search for greater convergence or identity of interests while not changing the basic political and military structure of the Alliance."[58] It is fair to say that since 1989 Europe's largest economy, Germany, had become a predominantly conservative force on the issue of collective European military capabilities. The result was that Franco-German partnership in the early 1990s proceeded on two levels, more or less independent of each other. The creation of Maastricht Europe represented for both governments the capstone of three decades of economic integration in which the overlap of hard interests was considerable; the repeated invocation of CFSP and ESDI reflected a common fear of perceived failure rather than a reflection of genuine common security priorities.[59]

The Kohl government found it easy to agree in principle with Paris that a more genuinely European defense capacity was necessary and that Europe *ought* to have the ability to launch a military operation in which the United States would not be involved. It also devoted a good deal of diplomatic energy to revamping the institutional "architecture" of continental security by co-authoring the proclamation of a CFSP and helping to revive the long-dormant Western European Union (WEU) as a possible cornice for the European pillar of the Alliance. Additionally, it endorsed a French proposal that the WEU should become an integral part of the EU, an institution to which it historically had no formal link. But German enthusiasm for such initiatives was integral to what has been dubbed the European "masque of institutions," an incessant multilateral deliberation of security issues at summits and subministerial meetings that is too often a diversion "from direct discussion of the vital interests, regional policies and needed military readiness."[60] While governments tinkered with institutional relationships at the European level, national defense industries spent the 1990s in a struggle to survive.

Both center-right and and center-left coalitions pursued post–Cold War cuts in defense spending as a symbol of the national commitment to fiscal rigor and the commitment to meeting Maastricht monetary criteria while covering the cost of absorbing East Germany. In the spring of 1994 the management of Rheinmetall, a long-time German defense contractor, noted that between 1990 and 1993 the number of jobs in the defense sector had declined from 280,000 to 140,000. Rheinmetall claimed further that the country was approaching a critical threshold beyond which further contraction of the defense industry would make it difficult both to equip the *Bundeswehr* with German weapons and to sustain Germany's technological competence in arms development.[61] Among the major Western European states no armed forces were as thoroughly organized as Germany's for the mission of territorial defense implied by the Cold War balance of forces in Europe. No thought was given to deploying the *Bundeswehr* outside the NATO area — indeed, the mid-1990s occasioned a national legal pantomime as to whether such a deployment was even constitutional — quite apart from the rapid reaction and expeditionary warfare contingencies with which NATO's *New Strategic Concept* began to grapple in 1990. Germany represented the extreme example of rationalization in defense expenditure, coterminous with a need for radical restructuring and the acquisition of entirely new capabilities. As *primas inter pares* of the EU member states, Germany was also a symbol of the lopsided nature of the New Europe, an economic superpower lacking the military capacity to deal with security emergencies on its frontiers.

Britain and France were much less comfortable with the want of European clout, especially in light of their experience on the Bosnian crisis. The new Bosnian state, with its three-cornered struggle between ethnic Croats, Serbs, and Muslim Bosnians, experienced the bloodiest episodes in ethnic cleansing. Washington's initial position that the fighting constituted a civil war in which all three ethnic communities were equally culpable became progressively more difficult to defend. Warren Zimmerman, the Bush administration's ambassador to Belgrade, charged that the government of Slobodan Milošević in the Serb Republic was in fact waging a war of aggression in Bosnia on behalf of Serbian irredenta.[62] Because Britain and France became the first principal European contributors to the UN peacekeeping effort, it was over the issue of punitive air strikes against Serb forces that Washington found itself in open conflict with London and Paris. Dual-key provisions written into the creation of the UN force — according to which the UN Secretary General was to approve NATO air strikes — meant that Britain and France could use their positions on the UN Security Council and the UN Bosnian command to veto any American move to bomb Serb forces. Their reason for doing so was that they had troops on the ground in Bosnia vulnerable to Serb reprisals, while the United States did not. It was evident that European initiatives to ensure the integrity of UN "safe areas," such as that of French President Jacques Chirac after the fall of Srebrenica in July 1995, were crafted to draw the United States more deeply into the conflict—which ultimately they did.[63] But these Anglo-French maneuvers at no point represented a common European strategy. In fact, the first and second installments of the Balkan crisis (Slovene-Croatian secession, then Bosnian) turned out to be "a boon for all those who argue that in the absence of American leadership, Europe, now habituated to dependence, cannot act."[64] For this conclusion there was plenty of support from other member states involved in the UN effort. "Unless America is engaged," observed the Canadian Chargé d'Affaires in Croatia, "it simply doesn't work."[65]

NOTES

1. Philip Zelikow and Condoleezza Rice, *Germany Unified and Europe Transformed: A Study in Statecraft* (Cambridge, MA: Harvard University Press, 1995), 93–98; Paul Sharp, *Thatcher's Diplomacy: The Revival of British Foreign Policy* (New York: St. Martin's, 1997), 202–224; Frank Ninkovich, *The Wilsonian Century: U.S. Foreign Policy since 1900* (Chicago, IL: University of Chicago Press, 1999), 239, 276.
2. Michael McFaul, *Russia's Unfinished Revolution: Political Change from Gorbachev to Putin* (Ithaca, NY: Cornell University Press, 2001), 69–73.
3. Zelikow and Rice, *Germany Unified and Europe Transformed*, 102–188.
4. Raymond L. Garthoff, *The Great Transition: American-Soviet Relations and the End of the Cold War* (Washington, D.C.: Brookings, 1994), 411–413, 434; Richard A. Falkenrath, *Shaping Europe's Military Order: The Origins and Consequences of the CFE Treaty* (Cambridge, MA: MIT Press, 1995), 1–31.
5. *The Conventional Armed Forces In Europe (CFE) Treaty at a Glance*, Arms Control Association, <http://www.armscontrol.org/subject/caec/cfeback2.asp>; Pál Dunay, "The CFE Treaty: History, Achievements and Shortcomings," *PRIF Report No. 24*, Peace Research Institute Frankfurt, October 1991, 26.
6. Implementation was delayed by the disintegration of the Soviet bloc. It did not get underway until November 1992, after the signing and ratification of protocols for the Soviet successor states of Belarus and Kazakhstan.
7. John Borwaski, "Partnership for Peace and Beyond," *International Affairs* 71, no. 2 (1995): 233–246; and *Neue Zürcher Zeitung*, June 24, 1994, 2.
8. Richard A. Falkenrath, "The CFE Flank Dispute: Waiting in the Wings," *International Security* 19, no. 4 (1995): 118–144; Sherman Garnett, *The CFE Flank Agreement* (Washington, D.C.: Carnegie Endowment for International Peace, 1997).
9. Michael Mandelbaum, *The Dawn of Peace in Europe* (New York: Twentieth Century Fund), 62–65, 90–109; Idem., *NATO Expansion, A Bridge to the Nineteenth Century* (Chevy Chase, MO: Center for Political and Strategic Studies, 1997).
10. Coral Bell, "Why an Expanded NATO Must Include Russia," *Journal of Strategic Studies* 17, no. 4 (1994): 27–41; Owen Harries, "The Collapse of The West," *Foreign Affairs* 72, no. 4 (1993): 43.
11. Ronald D. Asmus, Richard L. Kugler, F. Stephen Larrabee, "Building a New NATO," *Foreign Affairs* 72, no. 4 (1993): 32–34; Wolfram F. Hanrieder, *Germany, America, Europe: Forty Years of German Foreign Policy* (New Haven, CT: Yale University Press, 1989), 37–62.

12. David S. Yost, NATO *Transformed: The Alliance's New Roles in International Security* (Washington, D.C.: USIP, 1998), 103–112.

13. Ibid., 178–179; Lawrence S. Kaplan, *The Long Entanglement: NATO's First Fifty Years* (Westport, CT: Praeger, 1999), 194–199; Frederick P. A. Hammersen, "The Disquieting Voice of Russian Resentment," *Parameters* 28, no. 2 (1998): 39–55.

14. Angela Stent, *From Embargo to Ostpolitik: The Political Economy of West German-Soviet Relations, 1955–1980* (New York: Cambridge University Press, 1981); Idem., *Russia and Germany Reborn: Unification, The Soviet Collapse, and the New Europe* (Princeton, NJ: Princeton University Press, 1999), 233–245; Jean-Pierre Froehly, "Frankreich-Deutschland-Russland im neuen Dialog: eine Troika für Europa," *Politische Studien* 52, no. 376 (March/April 2001): 24–30.

15. George Kolankiewicz, "Consensus and Competition in the Eastern Enlargement of the European Union," *International Affairs* 70, no. 3 (1994): 477–495; Steven Webber, "Origins of the European Bank for Reconstruction and Development," *International Organization* 48, no. 1 (1994): 8–9, 27–28.

16. *Wirtschaftswoche* (March 13, 1992): 202–204.

17. *Das Parlament* (January 21, 1994): 5.

18. *Das Parlament* (January 21, 1994): 4.

19. Quoted in Stent, *From Embargo to Ostpolitik*, 223.

20. Quoted in Zbigniew Dobosiewicz, *Foreign Investment in Eastern Europe* (London: Routledge, 1992), 25.

21. Mark Smith, *NATO Enlargement During the Cold War: Strategy and System in the Western Alliance* (Basingstoke: Palgrave, 2000); Dan Reiter, "Why NATO Enlargement Does Not Spread Democracy," *International Security* 25, no. 4 (2001): 41–67; Jiri Sedivy, Pál Dunay, and Jacek Saryusz-Wolski, "Enlargement and European Defence after 11 September," *Chaillot Paper No. 53*, European Union Institute for Security Studies (June 2002): 58.

22. Celeste A. Wallander, *Mortal Friends, Best Enemies: German-Russian Cooperation after the Cold War* (Ithaca, NY: Cornell University Press, 1999), 127.

23. The first Schengen agreement involved the lifting of border controls among France, Germany, and the Benelux states and was signed in 1985 in the Luxembourg town of Schengen. Twelve states currently participate in the Schengen system. Heather Grabbe, "The Sharpe Edges of Europe: Extending Schengen Eastwards," *International Affairs* 76, no. 3 (2000): 519–536.

24. Sven Gunnar Simonsen, "Compatriot Games: Explaining the 'Diaspora Linkage' in Russia's Military Withdrawal from the Baltic States," *Europe-Asia Studies* 53, no. 5 (2001): 771–791.

25. Stephen Blank, "Russia, NATO Enlargement, and the Baltic States," *World Affairs* 160, no. 3 (1998): 115–125.

26. Garthoff, *The Great Transition*, 394–399, 419–420; Stephen J. Blank, "Russia and the Baltics in the Age of NATO Enlargement," *Parameters* 28, no. 3 (1998): 50–68; John Burbank, "What to Do about Kaliningrad?" *Europe*, Issue 421 (November 2002).

27. Dmitri Trenin, "Silence of the Bear," *NATO Review* (Spring 2002) <http://www.nato.int/docu/review/2002/issue1/art3.html>. In all, seven states were invited to accession talks: Bulgaria, Estonia, Latvia, Lithuania, Rumania, Slovakia, and Slovenia.

28. "EU Seen Approving Compromise on Kaliningrad," *Russia Journal Daily*, October 23, 2002, <http://www.russiajournal.com/print/russia_news_28050.html>. See the *Joint Statement on Transit between the Kaliningrad Region and the Rest of the Russian Federation* issued by the Tenth EU-Russia Summit, of November 11, 2002, at <http://europa.eu.int/comm/external_relations/russia/summit_11_02/js_kalin.htm>.

29. Graeme P. Herd and Joan Löfgren, "Societal Security, the Baltic States, and EU Integration," *Cooperation and Conflict* 3, no. 3 (2001): 273–296; Peer Lange, "Das Baltikum als eine Aufgabe für die integrative Gestaltung Europas," *Aus Politik und Zeitgeschichte*,

B37/1998, 3–13. The CBSS membership includes Denmark, Estonia, Finland, Germany, Iceland, Latvia, Lithuania, Norway, Poland, Russia, and Sweden. On the EU approach to Kaliningrad, see Commission of the European Communities, *Communication from the Commission to the Council: The EU and Kaliningrad*, Brussels, January 17, 2001.

30. *The Founding Act on Mutual Relations, Cooperation and Security between the Russian Federation and the North Atlantic Treaty Organization*, <http://www.usia.gov/products/washfile/eu.shtml>; *Charter on a Distinctive Partnership Between the North Atlantic Treaty Organization and Ukraine*, <http://www.nato.int/docu/basictxt/ukrchrt.htm>.

31. Thomas S. Szayna, *NATO Enlargement, 2000–2015: Determinants and Implications for Defense Planning and Shaping* (Santa Monica, CA: RAND, 2001), 132.

32. Angela E. Stent, *Russia and Germany Reborn: Unification, the Soviet Collapse, and the New Europe* (Princeton, NJ: Princeton University Press, 1999), 21, 153–154; Susan L. Woodward, *Balkan Tragedy: Chaos and Dissolution after the Cold War* (Washington, D.C.: Brookings, 1995), 177–185; Beverly Crawford, "Explaining Defection from International Cooperation," *World Politics* 48, no. 4 (1996): 482–521; John S. Duffield, *World Power Forsaken: Political Culture, International Institutions, and German Security Policy after Unification* (Stanford, CA: Stanford University Press, 1998), 126–129.

33. James Baker III, *The Politics of Diplomacy: Revolution, War and Peace, 1989–1992* (New York: G. P. Putnam's), 482–483.

34. Ibid., 637.

35. A key argument in Michael Libal, *Limits of Persuasion: Germany and the Yugoslav Crisis, 1991–1992* (Westport, CT: Praeger, 1997), 144. German Foreign Minister Hans-Dietrich Genscher argued the contrary, namely that withholding recognition of Croatia and Slovenia would be regarded in Belgrade as Western complicity toward Serbian military aggression. Hans-Dietrich Genscher, *Erinnerungen* (Berlin: Siedler, 1995), 959.

36. Ibid., 161.

37. Kaplan, *The Long Entanglement*, 204–205.

38. Libal, *Limits of Persuasion*, 163.

39. Bernhard Fleckenstein, "Bedingt einsatzfähig: Der lange Weg zur Neugestaltung der Bundeswehr," *Aus Politik und Zeitgeschichte* 43 (October 2000): 13–23.

40. Kaplan, *The Long Entanglement*, 205; *Foreign Policy Bulletin*, no. 3 (September/October 1992): 8.

41. Michael Meimeth, "France and the Organization of Security in Post–Cold War Europe," in Carl C. Hodge, ed., *Redefining European Security* (New York: Garland, 1999), 152.

42. Hanns W. Maull, "Germany and the Use of Force: Still a Civilian Power?" *Trierer Arbeitspapiere zur internationalen Politik*, no. 2 (November 1999): 9.

43. John S. Duffield, *Power Rules: The Evolution of NATO's Conventional Force Posture* (Stanford, CA: Stanford University Press), 83–143.

44. N. Gordon Levin, Jr., *Woodrow Wilson and World Politics: America's Response to War and Revolution* (New York: Oxford University Press, 1968), 247–249; Daniel Patrick Moynihan, *Pandemonium: Ethnicity in International Politics* (New York: Oxford University Press, 1993), 63–106.

45. Thomas M. Franck, "The Emerging Right to Democratic Governance," *American Journal of International Law* 86, no. 46 (1992): 46–91.

46. Woodward, *Balkan Tragedy*, 189.

47. Frank Ninkovich, *The Wilsonian Century: U.S. Foreign Policy since 1900* (Chicago, IL: University of Chicago Press, 1999); and Fareed Zakaria, "The Rise of Illiberal Democracy," *Foreign Affairs* 76, no. 6 (1997): 22–43.

48. Ibid., 286–287.

49. Duffield, *Power Rules*, 270.

50. James M. Goldgeier, "NATO Expansion: The Anatomy of a Decision," *Washington Quarterly* 21, no. 1 (1998): 85–102.
51. Kaplan, *The Long Entanglement*, 194–195.
52. *Congressional Quarterly Weekly Report* (October 4, 1997): 2415.
53. Ivo H. Daalder, *Getting to Dayton: The Making of America's Bosnia Policy* (Washington, D.C.: Brookings, 2000), 8–36; Kaplan, *The Long Entanglement*, 205–206; Yost, *NATO Transformed*, 192–199.
54. NATO, *The Alliance's New Strategic Concept*, available at <http://www.nato.int/docu/comm/49-95/c911107a.htm>.
55. Ibid., Pt. IV, paras. 51–53.
56. Yost, *NATO Transformed*, 204–205.
57. Peter Schmidt, "Frankreichs neues Verhältnis zur NATO. Preisgabe oder Verwirklichung gaullistischer Prinzipien?" SWP-AP 2957, May 1996.
58. Peter Schmidt, "ESDI: A German Analysis," in Charles Barry, ed., *Reforging the Trans-Atlantic Relationship* (Washington, D.C.: National Defense University Press, 1996), 37.
59. Michael Meimeth, "France and the Organization of Security in Post–Cold War Europe," in Hodge, *Redefining European Security*, 159; Kori Schake, "NATO after the Cold War, 1991–1996: Institutional Competition and the Failure of the French Alternative," *Contemporary European History* 7, no. 3 (1998): 379–407.
60. Philip Zelikow, "The Masque of Institutions," in Philip H. Gordon, ed., *NATO's Transformation: The Changing Shape of the Atlantic Alliance* (Lanham, MD: Rowman and Littlefield, 1997), 77–89.
61. *Handelsblatt*, May 25, 1994, 5; Trevor Taylor, "European Security and Defense Cooperation," *International Affairs* 70, no. 1 (1994): 12–15; Karl-Heinz Kamp, "Die Zukunft der Bundeswehr: Die Diskussion in der CDU/CSU," *Aus Politik und Zeitgeschichte* 34 (October 2000): 29–33.
62. Woodward, *Balkan Tragedy*, 200–201, 221–222; Sanya Popovic, "Debating Operation Quagmire Storm: U.S. Crisis Management in Bosnia," in Raju G. C. Thomas and H. Richard Friman, eds., *The South Slav Conflict: History, Religion, Ethnicity and Nationalism* (New York: Garland Publishing, 1996), 291–292.
63. Daalder, *Getting to Dayton*, 22–23, 68–69.
64. Stanley Hoffmann, "Yugoslavia: Implications for Europe and for European Institutions," in Richard H. Ullman, ed., *The World and Yugoslavia's Wars* (New York: Council on Foreign Relations Press, 1996), 116.
65. Quoted in Lenard J. Cohen and Alexander Moens, "Learning the Lessons of UNPRO-FOR: Canadian Peacekeeping in the Former Yugoslavia," *Canadian Foreign Policy* 6, no. 2 (1999): 85–101.

Expeditionary NATO

This dependence on uniquely American capabilities became more evident as the Alliance reoriented its strategy toward other peace-support operations in Europe or expeditionary warfare beyond. A redefinition of peacekeeping proceeded against the backdrop of revolutionary changes in the conduct of war, demonstrated in the UN-mandated campaign to reverse the Iraqi invasion of the Persian Gulf state of Kuwait in August 1990, to which select NATO members made contributions. Both required capable, mobile, flexible, self-reliant, and tailored-to-need forward-deployed forces, usually on short notice, for rapid deployment in joint and often multinational operations. Although the mounting of multinational expeditionary operations overseas was a common practice of imperial powers in the nineteenth century, the limited wars and humanitarian interventions of the late twentieth century were governed by a different moral universe, in which the success or failure of military actions were judged according to exacting ethical and operational criteria.[1] New standards were themselves made conceivable by the emerging technologies and accompanying operational concepts commonly if somewhat sloppily referred to as the Revolution in Military Affairs (RMA). These standards simultaneously ratcheted up accepted measurements of military success, highlighted the widening "capabilities gap" within NATO, and provoked debates on the appropriate application of force.

Peace-support and political trusteeship missions in Yugoslavia made the most immediate contributions to NATO's transformation. The Alliance's intervention in Bosnia had the effect of eclipsing its traditional role of collective defense in favor of a version of collective security. In contrast to the disinterested and altruistic Wilsonian approach, NATO's presence in Bosnia was the result of "multilateral intervention, undertaken with the implicit or explicit consensus of the major powers, directed against international aggression or internal conflict or disorder."[2]

The revision of collective security found in the United Nations Charter does not assume selfless motives on the part of the intervening powers. It provides that action can take place in cases that are not a matter of dispute among them. The Alliance intervened in Bosnia not to thwart the UN goals there but rather to pursue them more robustly. When the Clinton administration took the steps that lead to the Dayton Accords, altruism was not entirely absent. The United States had little of substance to gain by ending the fighting and little to lose by allowing it to continue.[3] The 1991 Persian Gulf War, by contrast, had the hard interest of the free flow of Middle Eastern oil as a primary motive for collective action. Yet its prosecution was as purely Wilsonian as a war is ever likely to be. It involved a collective response to a naked act of territorial aggression in violation of international law and was mandated by a succession of UN Security Council Resolutions. The defeat of Iraqi forces, lastly, was followed by a return to the international *status quo ante.*

What the Bosnian and Persian Gulf operations had in common was a significant qualification of coalitional warfare. Both were so dependent on American military capabilities and leadership that they would have been impossible in the absence of the requisite determination in Washington. Both operations were undertaken in the unusual international atmosphere of the immediate post–Cold War years, yet neither delivered a fundamental improvement in security—the 1991 Persian Gulf War was refought in 2003, while the jury remains out on the viability of a self-governing Bosnia. What is important for our purposes here is their profound impact on NATO as a military alliance and political community.

DESERT STORM

In organizing an international diplomatic response to the Iraqi invasion of Kuwait, the United States benefited from the liquidation of the Cold War order in Europe, above all in the form of Moscow's new policy of cooperation with the West. As a result of that cooperation the UN Security Council was able to meet its mandate in a fashion that had been impossible since the Korean War. By August 9, 1990, it had approved trade sanctions against Baghdad; when the combination of sanctions and diplomatic pressure failed to prompt an Iraqi withdrawal, the Security Council passed UNSC Resolution 678 authorizing "all necessary means" by member states to "restore international peace and security in the area" and set January 15, 1991, as the deadline for Iraqi compliance.

The international coalition fashioned by the Bush administration to put a credible threat of force behind the UN demands on behalf of the international community was extraordinary, as was the success of *Operation Desert Storm* in evicting the Iraqi army from Kuwait. Altogether, 540,000 personnel from 31 countries contributed in some capacity. Although *Desert Storm* was not a NATO operation, a sufficient number of member states were involved to make the Alliance a vehicle for the coordination within the coalition during the campaign and to raise the issue afterward as to whether NATO should remain regional or aspire to global reach.[4]

The radical implications of the latter for an organization shaped by fifty years of territorial defense of Western Europe are obvious. Among the states composing the multinational force for *Desert Storm,* only a minority offered wholehearted support of the war. Many governments wanted to demonstrate fidelity to the UN resolutions but were simultaneously troubled by ambivalent public opinion concerning the use of force. Besides the United States, a grouping of "Anglo-Saxon" countries — NATO members Britain and Canada, joined by Australia and New Zealand — demonstrated a readiness for war unmatched by other groups.[5]

Britain was far and away the most significant in the robustness of its diplomatic position and the size of its military contribution. The Thatcher government, backed by public opinion in favor not only of liberating Kuwait but also of toppling the regime of Saddam Hussein, saw part of its role as a buttress to American resolve and contributed to the military effort an armored division amounting to almost a quarter of the entire British army. British forces were also fully integrated with U.S. forces and demonstrated from the outset a determination to be in the thick of the action.[6]

The French role in *Desert Storm* was in many respects a mirror image of the British. The notion that France needed to buy political influence within the coalition by making a serious military contribution was controversial within the Mitterrand cabinet. Defense Minister Jean-Pierre Chevènement consistently sought to limit the French role and to distance it as far as possible from Anglo-American actions. The posture was adopted possibly to give France standing in the event of a last minute search for a settlement, yet succeeded mostly in annoying the coalition allies and the French army itself. On the eve of the January 15 deadline for Iraqi compliance with Resolution 678, France made new proposals to the UN Security Council, calling for Iraqi withdrawal and suggesting a Middle East peace conference for some undetermined date in the future — a gambit of which France's European partners were not notified at a meeting the EC Foreign Ministers held that very morning. President Mitterrand ultimately put French forces under U.S. command, but the impression of half-heartedness created prior to the campaign was then reinforced by the modest contribution French aircraft were able to make due to technical shortcomings and interoperability problems once it was underway.[7]

Preoccupied with reunification, Germany was singularly slow to wake up to the growing probability of war in the Middle East. The Kohl government was further hampered by the largest antiwar demonstrations in Europe and a national intellectual community ostentatious in its concern for a nation cleansed of its militarist past. As a consequence, Germany's contribution was primarily financial, accounting for ten percent of the total cost of the war. But the revelation that German companies had been involved in supplying Iraq's chemical and nuclear weapons program — a guilt aggravated by Iraqi Scud missile attacks on Israel — had as much to do with the size of Germany's subsidy as the merits of the international case against Iraq as an aggressor. In fact, Germany's hesitation regarding its obligation to defend Turkey, a NATO ally, in the event of Iraqi attacks suggested that the post–Cold War Alliance might encounter "cohesion problems" even in subregional collective defense contingencies. The opposition Social Democrats were joined by some members of the governing coalition in arguing that by permitting U.S. aircraft to operate against Iraq from Turkish bases, Turkey had provoked Iraq to possible retaliation and thereby nullified German obligations under Article V of the North Atlantic Treaty. Those who took this position under conditions of a UN-mandated war "appeared to run away from any German political or moral obligation whatsoever, let alone political debt" when Germany was being asked "only to grant a small fraction of the support which it had received over four decades."[8]

The contributions of smaller European states to the coalition effort in the Gulf varied considerably. The Netherlands backed military action due to the importance of the territorial integrity of the Middle Eastern states to Europe; its government put two frigates under U.S. command and sent Patriot missiles and support personnel to Turkey. At the other extreme, Belgium delayed sending naval vessels to the Gulf and sought a WEU blessing for doing so. Late in 1990 Belgium actually refused to sell ammunition to Britain. Prime Minister Thatcher characterized the European contribution to *Desert Storm* as "patchy and disappointing" and did not miss the chance to argue that it gave the lie to the many statements about a common foreign and security policy.[9]

At the time this verdict was somewhat premature, as was the expectation that NATO would be able to project power into the Persian Gulf with anything other than overwhelmingly American military capabilities. Euro-Atlantic perceptions and institutions had only just begun to adjust to post–Cold War reality. For that reason NATO's experience in the former Yugoslav republic of Bosnia-Herzegovina is more telling in terms of the implications of the expeditionary era for the gap in military capabilities between the United States and its European allies. Whereas the first Persian Gulf War was an international crisis of the first order, the conflict in Bosnia was a regional European contingency that became a crisis in alliance management.

PEACE AND DEMOCRACY IN BOSNIA

Between 1992 and 1995 Bosnia divided NATO to an extent that imperiled the Clinton administration's slowly emerging vision for Europe. Inconsistency and genuine differences over policy, even among the Europeans, were partly to blame for this. In the first phase of Yugoslavia's disintegration, German support for Slovenian and Croatian secession ran up against open French sympathy for Serbia. When the Slovenian and Croatian episodes led to the secession of Bosnia-Herzegovina, Britain and France dispatched troops under UN auspices to provide humanitarian aid in the republic while the United Nations embargoed all military aid to the Serb, Croat, and Bosnian Muslim parties to the conflict. The Vance-Owen Peace Plan for Bosnia painfully constructed by the United Nations and the European Community then proposed to partition Bosnia into ten ethnically based cantons.

The Clinton administration rejected the Vance-Owen Plan on the grounds that it essentially rewarded Serbian military successes and was unfair to Bosnia's Muslims both in its ethnic definition of nationhood and the unequal impact of the arms embargo.[10] Its preference for a "lift-and-strike" approach in defending the Muslim population, lifting the embargo on arms supplies to them while subjecting the Serbs to such punitive air strikes as would motivate them to negotiate—failed to secure European participation due to the vulnerability of lightly armed British and French troops in Bosnia to retaliation by Serb forces.

Clinton also sought to separate events on the ground in Bosnia, along with transatlantic differences about how to respond, from the issue of NATO enlargement as he moved toward a decision in 1994. At a meeting of the North Atlantic Council in December of that year, Secretary of State Warren Christopher insisted that the continuing chaos in Bosnia "does not diminish our responsibility to build a comprehensive European security architecture that consolidates stability."[11] The fact that Bosnia could render such an architectural enterprise irrelevant, however, brought Clinton to realize that, even if Bosnia itself was not so vital as to justify the deployment of American ground troops, the unity of NATO was. He therefore pushed the United Nations aside to end the Bosnian bloodshed but also to end NATO disunity. *Operation Deliberate Force,* NATO's precision bombing of Serb military positions, broke the siege of Sarajevo and paved the way for the peace accord brokered by Clinton at Dayton, Ohio, in November 1995, among the three parties to the Bosnian conflict for a multiethnic and federal Bosnian republic. Its guarantee was the deployment of 60,000 NATO troops, 20,000 of them American. The Dayton Accords had the effect of ensuring NATO's transformation in two critical ways. First, it stressed the new priority of extending the stability of Western Europe eastward and did so with a military presence involving American boots on the ground. Second, it underscored the commitment to NATO enlargement and drew together its two strands, formal admission and regional crisis management, when discussions convened with the Visegrad states about the terms of Alliance membership even as the implementation of Dayton made Bosnia a NATO protectorate.[12]

The Bosnian episode was, additionally, "the means by which the Europeans trapped the United States into taking a role of leadership toward the conflict,"[13] a goal dating to Germany's recognition of Croatia and Slovenia, and a measure of European military impotence. It was less NATO than American airpower that brought Serbia to heel. Of a total of 3,515 sorties flown, the United States accounted for 2,318 or 65.9 percent; of the 1,026 bombs and missiles used, the fact that 708 were precision-guided munitions (PGMs) permitted the air campaign to achieve the fastest possible results while minimizing collateral damage and casualties. *Deliberate Force* expended in total about the equivalent of a busy day's munitions for *Desert Storm* and required nowhere near an equivalent expeditionary capacity from the participating forces.[14] Yet the precision needed for the application of force in what was in large part a humanitarian effort "highlighted the mismatch between the EU's declared foreign policy objectives and the means available to achieve those objectives"[15] in a fashion that *Desert Storm* never could have.

The Combined Joint Task Force (CJTF) concept approved by the Brussels summit of 1994 was an integral part of the effort to adapt the Alliance's political and military structures to non–Article V missions and to reflect the aspirations of the European states for a European Security and Defense Identity (ESDI) within NATO through the European institution of the Western European Union (WEU). The fact that a good deal of fudge was applied in order to win consensus on the change — such as the statement that WEU and NATO functions were to be "separate but not separable" — testifies to the urgency given to institutional innovation for building the European pillar without appearing to qualify Atlantic unity. If an ESDI worthy of the name was nowhere in evidence prior to the Dayton Accords, the history of failure before 1995 could be compensated somewhat by genuinely joint efforts in enforcing Bosnia's peace. A de facto CJTF emerged in the form of the Implementation Force (IFOR) for the enforcement of the military aspects of the accords. Both IFOR and the Stabilization Force (SFOR), which replaced it in December 1996, were NATO-dominated multinational forces that included non-NATO members of the North Atlantic Cooperation Council (NACC) and the Partnership for Peace (PfP).[16] If the purpose of CJTFs during a transitional phase in NATO's life was to raise the European while lowering the American profile, however, the contribution of IFOR and SFOR was limited. When the schedule was initially set for SFOR to operate from December 1996 to June 1998, the European Allies, including France, insisted that the force would have to include American ground forces. In early 1998 the Clinton administration acknowledged that a deadline for the withdrawal of American troops would be unrealistic and effectively "relinquished the vain hope that Europeans would carry the military burden while Americans provided only communications and logistical services."[17]

THE CAPABILITIES GAP

In the defense and security community the discussion of the Revolution in Military Affairs (RMA) and its possible impact on NATO's effectiveness and cohesion meanwhile became the *basso continuo* of the Alliance's missions in the 1990s. Among the more serviceable definitions of an RMA is that it occurs "when the application of new technologies into a significant number of military systems combines with innovative operational concepts and organizational adaptations in a way that fundamentally alters the character and conduct of conflict."[18] For a wide swath of opinion among defense intellectuals in the United States there was a consensus that "such an RMA is now occurring and those who understand it and take advantage of it will enjoy a decisive advantage on future battlefields."[19] While other analysts considered this judgment "eminently contestable," the revolutionary potential of advanced technologies — in particular "the use of information technology to gain strategic advantage by networking one's forces, gaining complete knowledge of the battle, and striking from any range with near-perfect precision"[20] — assumed a position of privilege in Washington's vision of the military future. In that vision, the use of dispersed yet integrated forces enables one to attack all enemy targets from all ranges while it remains comparatively more difficult for the enemy to engage effectively in response. As important as the possession of technologies is, it is the development of innovative doctrine, tactics, training, and organization for their use that produces transformative results.

The evolution of modern war suggests that decisive advantage can turn out to be a strangely elusive goal when too much is expected from technology alone. To expect that technological or conceptual innovation will eliminate either the "friction" or "fog" of war could turn out to be the gravest of follies.[21] During the 1990s Americans and Europeans differed significantly over the meaning of airpower, precision munitions, and information technology for the future of war. The disagreement was to some extent explained by the wide differential in technological capabilities alone. But it was also influenced by a difference in strategic culture and the stress that the American way of war has historically placed on exploiting technological advantage to the fullest. "In and of itself, a quest for technical improvement is strategically innocent," notes a prominent critic of American strategic tradition, but if "the benefit of better military tools becomes an article of faith in the power of machines, great harm can be done."[22] Moreover, although progress in electronics and computer systems is genuinely revolutionary, it is much slower in other areas equally important in the prosecution of war: propulsion systems, aerodynamics and hydrodynamics, the explosive power of conventional ordnance, and the strength of armor.[23] Among military professionals most qualified to make experienced judgment, there is prudent caution about—tinged with healthy curiosity about the potential of—new technologies with direct or indirect military applications.

The major European Allies did not really counter American enthusiasm with skepticism. Rather, a general consensus among them that Europe needed to contribute more flexible and mobile forces to NATO's capabilities, both for the sake of genuine burden-sharing and of a stronger and more influential European pillar, ran up against the fact that none of them individually had the economic and technological base to pursue a national RMA, while any collective will to do so was tentative at best. Despite the enormous progress made in integration since the mid-1980s, the New Europe lagged well behind the United States in the exploitation of information technologies as well as in the adjustment to economic globalization.[24] The global commitments shouldered by the United States since the 1950s pushed Washington's defense planners to think instinctively about the application of new technologies to force mobility and flexibility. The narrower strategic horizons of post-Suez Europe and NATO's internal division of labor during the Cold War undercut any European need to do the same.

Still, to the extent that the development of post–Cold War doctrine in NATO stresses the development of highly mobile rapid reaction forces, European states with an expeditionary military tradition will be conversant with American strategic thinking and interested in acquiring certain new capabilities. A selective European abstinence from revolutionary technologies, meanwhile, is not of itself terminal to NATO effectiveness and unity. As long as a basic conceptual coherence is present, rooted in general agreement on the most probable adversaries and deployment scenarios—as well as on the most appropriate array of political and military means with which to act—allies can function in unison and yet disagree on the longer-term military implications of what they accomplish together.[25] The CFTFs developed in line with NATO's *New Strategic Concept* during the mid-1990s reflected such an agreement. Based on the assumption that non-Article V regional crisis-management scenarios on the European periphery as in Yugoslavia would be the alliance's most common deployment scenario of the future, the borrowing of "separable but not separate" NATO assets for missions from which the United States might want to abstain represented a commitment to flexibility in fashioning coalitions-of-the-willing for non-Article V missions.[26] Also implied was the notion that NATO might become involved in crises beyond Europe and would have to work together with non-NATO countries.[27] Although the CJTFs were intended for operations such as peacekeeping and crisis intervention, they could in principle be developed for a wider spectrum of contingencies, including large-scale power projection and high-intensity conflict. In theory, then, the requirements identified for effective CJTFs could focus attention on the specific RMA capabilities—and non-RMA capabilities—needed by the European allies in order to operate in coalition with each other and the United States. European forces would need greater flexibility and mobility for rapid deployment, along with the command and communications that would enable them to work with each other as well as with U.S. forces. The capabilities gap could be narrowed *à la carte*.[28]

Yet it is unlikely to satisfy the appetite of European capitals for either the symbol or the substance of greater European self-reliance. The Eurocorps, a Franco-German initiative dating to 1983 was made official by Chancellor Kohl and President Mitterrand in 1991 with the announcement that a European force would be built upon the foundation of the 4,200-strong Franco-German Brigade. French interest in the Eurocorps was linked to a genuine concern about over-reliance on the United States, while the German government viewed its integrative aspect as a worthwhile political end in itself rather than a step toward enhanced European capabilities.[29] Given the size of the Eurocorps, its value could be deemed primarily symbolic, but to leave it at this is to obscure important differences between French and German policy in the 1990s. Unapologetic for the commitment of considerable fiscal resources to robust military capability and determined to redress its military liabilities in the first half of the twentieth century, France has since de Gaulle maintained strong conventional and nuclear forces and has placed a premium on autonomy and freedom of independent action. The presidencies of Mitterrand and Jacques Chirac attempted to renegotiate France's relationship with NATO, in order to engage closely in Alliance affairs and exert influence on its strategic orientation in a post–Cold War environment while simultaneously promoting ESDI to reduce European reliance on the United States. Mitterrand's promotion of rapid reaction forces was a skilful but modest diplomatic exploitation of the European security crisis of the 1980s, characterized from the French perspective by Washington's confrontational stance with Moscow and the growth of the

German peace movement in response. His efforts to renew the Franco-German partnership, revitalize the Western European Union, and develop the Eurocorps were a corollary to his 1983 speech to the Bundestag supporting the Kohl government on the INF deployments. Stiffening West German resolve while developing a security partnership with Bonn was Mitterrand's contribution to the Gaullist tradition—a balance-of-power policy that was also revisionist in that it promoted greater European unity between the superpowers.[30]

His successor, Jacques Chirac, attempted a strategic revolution. He did this by building upon the Europeanization begun by Mitterrand but also by exploiting changed perceptions brought on by post–Cold War crises in the Persian Gulf and Yugoslavia. Simply put, French forces under Chirac "changed from focusing on territorial, nuclear deterrence to conventional force projections beyond the national territory."[31] The Gulf War was of cardinal importance in bringing this about. In 1991 France had 670,137 armed forces personnel (300,000 professionals and 240,000 conscripts) of whom 20,000 were involved in *Operation Desert Storm*. Yet their deployment was so awkward in the execution due to inappropriate equipment and inadequate logistics that the campaign has been cited as the moment when first-order military reform was placed on the national agenda.[32]

Certain trial-and-error initiatives, such as the gambit to place NATO's AFSOUTH under European command, failed spectacularly. But generally the Chirac reforms involved improvements to the conceptual vision of the 1994 White Paper on Defense prepared under the Mitterrand presidency. They were broadly in harmony with ESDI as well as the modular command structure and expeditionary mission of NATO's CJTF blueprint. Not least of all, the White Paper acknowledged explicitly that NATO represented the principal organization of Europe's defense and proposed a strengthened WEU for a complementary role. Although France initially opposed direct NATO involvement in Yugoslavia for fear that it would turn into a military confrontation with the Serbs and possibly antagonize Russia, by the summer of 1993 Paris had agreed to the deployment of a large peacekeeping contingent to Bosnia.[33] When progress on the reforms was stalled by Chirac's loss of a legislative majority in 1997, the Kosovo crisis of 1998–1999 permitted him to roll with the punches and realize new gains. To a considerable extent, *Operation Allied Force* in Kosovo, the subject of more detailed attention in Chapter 4, made the projects of French doctrinal reform and enhanced European defense capabilities one and the same undertaking.

In sum, the Chirac reforms were revolutionary because they placed a new stress on conventional force projection as opposed to national and nuclear priorities, sought a new relationship with NATO, and signaled a transition toward expeditionary warfare.[34] By the end of the decade France constituted in American eyes, a "pivotal security partner," with 46,000 military personnel outside its borders or in its territories, engaged diplomatically and militarily in NATO's Yugoslavian commitments.[35] The French government remained painfully aware of the capabilities gap and of the implications of the RMA for any ESDI worthy of the name, but on-the-ground changes were very significant. France remained officially committed to a unilateral capacity to secure national interests, but the renovation of its forces were increasingly focused on a smaller, professionalized army; the need to project and protect expeditionary forces; and the imperative to provide corresponding joint theater command resources to work with allied forces. In confronting operability problems, the French army stressed three areas of special attention: equipment, information systems, and procedures.[36] Projects such as the Helios satellite intelligence system were considered European investments; on the other hand, France's new nuclear-powered aircraft carrier, *Charles de Gaulle*, was designed to be compatible with U.S. Navy F/A 18s and had the same catapult and arresting gear as American *Nimitz*-class carriers.[37]

It is worth noting that Chirac's ambitions for military reform were influenced by the superior performance of British forces during the Gulf War. If France began in the 1990s to move its conventional forces in the direction of expeditionary warfare conducted by highly mobile, rapid-reaction forces in joint operations with NATO allies, the armed services of the United Kingdom provided much of the model for change. That being the case, the *Strategic Defence Review* completed by the government of Tony Blair in 1998 was among the most important national documents of the decade dealing with European security. Its chapter on Defence Missions and Tasks highlighted peacetime security, overseas territories, defense diplomacy, wider British interests, peace support and humanitarian operations, regional conflicts outside NATO, regional threats to NATO, and strategic attack on NATO.[38] The SDR planned for a new generation of military equipment by 2015, including attack helicopters; long-range precision munitions; digitized command-and-control systems; a new generation of aircraft carriers, submarines, and escorts; the Eurofighter, a successor to the Tornado bomber; and a replacement Short Take-off and Vertical Landing aircraft (STOVL) to replace the Harrier and Sea Harrier aircraft—the latter covered (as of January 17, 2001) by the U.S.-UK agreement on the Joint Strike Fighter.[39]

On the impact of new technologies, the SDR did not accept the RMA as a given in the sense common to American defense intellectuals. It noted that "there is a growing body of opinion, particularly in the United States, that we are approaching a Revolution in Military Affairs," and concluded that "leaving aside the academic debate on whether or not a revolution is underway," it is clear that exploiting new technologies will "lead to significant improvements in military capability."[40] Neither did the SDR focus on closing the transatlantic gap in defense capabilities. It advised instead that, if Britain and the European allies can "tap into" technology led by the United States, "the result will be more effective coalition operations."[41] The price of failing to do so intelligently could turn out to be high:

> There is a potential for multinational operations to become more difficult if compatible capabilities are not preserved. This could lead to political as well as military problems. Our priority must therefore be to ensure that we maintain the ability to make a high quality contribution to multinational operations and to operate closely with U.S. forces throughout the spectrum of potential operations. To do this

we need to be selective about the technologies we develop nationally or on a European basis, and be prepared to use U.S. technologies in other areas. . . .[42]

Selectivity between developing or purchasing new capabilities was at the root of what the UK Ministry of Defence called "smart acquisition." Smart acquisition was based on the notion that acquiring new capabilities rather than new weapons was the goal of defense investment. By "leaving the supplier greater freedom to determine how best to deliver the desired outcome," the customer could get more "value for money"—defined as the solution that meets the capability requirement at the lowest through-life cost.[43] In other words, the SDR was concerned primarily with acquiring new, even "revolutionary," capabilities without a dramatic increase in defense expenditure and was only secondarily interested in whether new technologies are American or European in origin. The market was to compete for Her Majesty's defense budget. Of equal importance to the strategic vision in the 1990s is the fact that Prime Minister Blair intended to redirect British policy on the EU away from the Euro-skepticism dominant in the Conservative governments of the Thatcher-Major years. The question of British membership in the European Monetary Union (EMU) had divided and weakened Conservative governments. It was over the issue of an American or European partnership for the ailing Westland helicopter manufacturer that the Thatcher government had lost its Defence Minister, Michael Heseltine, who unsuccessfully advocated the European option and later became a threat for the Tory leadership.[44]

On coming to office in 1997, furthermore, Blair had been dismayed by the lack of collective defense capacity among the EU's major powers. His summit meeting with President Chirac in Saint-Malô summit therefore represents a landmark event in that, after nearly fifty years of opposition to the idea, the United Kingdom consented in principle that the EU should have a role in defense and security. As Chirac put it, such a role would not be effective without "the two countries which are amongst those with a strong tradition, both diplomatically and militarily."[45] Beyond the possession of nuclear weapons, the common tradition to which Chirac referred was the maintenance of comparatively robust conventional forces with an expeditionary culture. The great virtue of the meeting at Saint-Malô was as a public expression of impatience. In a contest between the goals of European integration and the imperative of enhanced European military capacity, it was evident that any Anglo-French initiative genuinely serious about the latter could not wait for the EU's plodding multilateralism to deal with a challenge that could at least be engaged bilaterally. Two years after the Saint-Malô meeting a British parliamentary progress report on ESDI observed both that European defense budgets remained too modest for the EU to become less dependent on NATO and that France and the UK "have provided the driving force behind the reinvigorated search for a more capable European defence pillar."[46]. At the very least the summit reflected the Blair government's conviction that the United States would no longer underwrite European security as dutifully or as comprehensively as during the Cold War. Putting muscle on the bones of an ESDI—or a bilateral program dressed up as an ESDI—is a hedge against American disengagement from Europe.[47] By the late 1990s intensive Anglo-French cooperation constituted *the* critical factor in any measure of European self-reliance, for without it there could be no ESDI.

This is because Germany will for the time being remain more of a spectator than a participant in any effort to reconfigure European defense capabilities to the requirements of expeditionary warfare. In so far as the *Bundeswehr* was a political and military creature of the Cold War, constituted as a peoples' army and equipped for the territorial defense of Western Europe against Soviet invasion, it is singularly ill-suited to the challenge of mobile crisis management. In the mid-1980s the *Bundeswehr* constituted by far the most powerful conventional force among the eight armies that together composed NATO's central front in Europe. Its total strength stood at 700,000, the hard core of which organized 345,000 men into 36 fully manned brigades forming 12 divisions in 3 main army corps.[48] One particularly sound observation about post–Cold War Germany is that its armed forces have already been through a revolution of sorts. In addition to the heavy costs of national reunification, a good deal of the burden of reintegrating Eastern Europe into the liberal-democratic world has also been shouldered by Germany. This included the absorption of the East German *Nationale Volksarmee* and the contraction of its manpower strength from 495,000 to 340,000. The air force was reduced to 500 combat aircraft, well below its CFE ceiling of 900. In 1993, financial constraints were cited as the reason for still further reductions.[49] Collectively, the changes imposed on the *Bundeswehr* were the most radical since its creation by the Adenauer government of the 1950s.

What they did not constitute, however, was a structural transformation from territorial defense to expeditionary warfare. The verdict of *Bundeswehr Generalinspekteur* Harald Kujat as of March 2001 was that Germany's forces needed both revenue and revitalization "from the foundations up" to punch their weight among NATO allies.[50]

The most comprehensive recent review of the *Bundeswehr's* current condition and future needs is that of the commission headed by former *Bundespräsident* Richard von Weizsäcker. Released in the spring of 2000, the commission's recommendations were sweeping. They were based not only on the assumption that Germany's security circumstance has changed fundamentally but also that the change was likely to be durable, especially as it would take a recidivist Russian Federation a decade to again pose a credible danger to Germany's security.[51] The document maintained furthermore that the size, and to a certain extent the structure, of British and French conventional forces ought to be the benchmark goal of *Bundeswehr* reform, while acknowledging that Germany was presently in no position to approximate the capabilities of either country.

Nonetheless, the commission advised that reform should concentrate on building a rapid reaction capability to prosecute coalition warfare in two crises simultaneously.[52] While the report also featured the customary platitudes concerning Germany's Atlantic and European responsibilities—insisting that regional crisis management and Article V missions receive equal attention—the thrust of its substantive recommendations stressed the former: smaller and much more mobile forces featuring a much lower percentage of conscripts. While overall strength would be cut from 338,000 to 240,000 troops, the preference for a radically improved crisis-management capacity was most visible in the recommendation that operational strength jump from 60,000 to 140,000 troops.[53] The shopping list of procurement priorities was long. Integral to the logic of the report was that—barring an unlikely steep increase in defense expenditure—the proportion of new investment in the total defense budget should be increased through savings in personnel and maintenance costs.[54]

Defense Minister Rudolf Scharping and the *Bundeswehr* Inspector General found the report too radical. In defense review studies of their own they rejected the Weizsäcker recommendations on force strength and base closures, arguing that the *Bundeswehr* was the biggest employer in many of Germany's rural districts and that enabling conscripts to do their service close to home would preserve the military's relationship with civil society. Both reports favored the retention of a balance of collective defense and peace support capacities and shied away from the changes that would transform the *Bundeswehr* into a power projection force.[55] Although the Weizsäcker commission suggested a reconstitution of the draft into a system of selective service rather than outright abolition, Scharping opposed the change as inconsistent with the constitutional legitimacy of the *Bundeswehr* and had the support of the CDU-CSU opposition on this point. Because the retention of conscription limited the savings to be realized by force reductions—even though the Defense Ministry acquiesced in austerities on the defense budget imposed by the Finance Ministry—Germany found it difficult to meet the goals of the Scharping report and was further still from those proposed by the Weizsäcker study.[56]

Not surprisingly, the prediction of one of the most extensive scholarly studies of German security policy concluded that it "will continue to be marked by a degree of multilateralism, anti-militarism, and reticence that will make it exceptional for a country of Germany's size and resources."[57] To the politico-cultural limitations to radical change clearly evident in Sharping's thinking, however, must be added the significance of the structural changes a modern *Bundeswehr* would require, according to the Weizsäcker commission, and a national fiscal environment that prohibits them. The defense debate in Germany in the 1990s was *not* driven by the RMA and a national strategic vision of Germany's role within it. Rather, the issue of a restructured *Bundeswehr* was a continuation of post–Cold War downsizing running into a good deal of political resistance—and running well behind strategic reality.[58]

The more grotesque inconsistencies of Germany's post–Cold War adjustments were over by the late 1990s, and there was official recognition in principle that Germany and Europe had a responsibility to take on an equitable share of international security tasks. Still, any attempt to professionalize Germany's armed forces—as in France, Belgium, or the Netherlands—would be very sensitive politically. By the end of the decade, official American skepticism that the European NATO states were genuinely prepared to assume a greater military burden usually cited the case of Germany, the EU's largest economy, committing roughly 1.3 percent of its GDP to defense expenditure.[59] A robustly multilateral European effort also had little chance, and there was scarce evidence that this was about to change any time soon. Instead, there was a trend among the European states, due to the rationalizations brought on by modest defense budgets, toward differing degrees of defense national specialization and bilateral innovations based on regional interests or compatible capabilities—the UK/Netherlands Amphibious Force and the German/Netherlands Corp HQ representing two examples.

Of the major European allies most attractive militarily to the United States as coalition partners—France, Germany, and the United Kingdom—Germany is currently a poor candidate for anything beyond the most modest participation in RMA capabilities. For their part, France and the UK were strong promoters of the Helsinki Headline Goal (HHG) established at the 1999 EU summit a year after the Blair-Chirac meeting at Saint-Malô.

The issues of distinctly European defense and security robustness and the gap in alliance capabilities came to the fore of the Atlantic agenda in NATO's Defense Capabilities Initiative (DCI). The DCI was primarily concerned with the gap in a wide array of military capabilities between the United States and its European allies, many if not all of which are related to the RMA. By September 2001 the DCI had listed no fewer than 59 decision areas grouped into five categories: deployability and mobility; sustainability and logistics; effective engagement; survivability of force and infrastructure; NATO-level command, control, and communications (C^3). The HHG called for the creation by 2003 of a European force capable of undertaking the full range of "Petersberg Tasks,"[60] including the most demanding operations. In concrete terms this meant a force of 50–60,000 troops with provision for support and rotation, deployable within 60 days and sustainable for a year. The relationship between the DCI and the HHG is clear: In order even to approximate the latter, serious progress would have to be made through the long shopping list of the former. While virtually all of the DCI's five priority areas spoke to the requirements of CJTFs and were thus adjustments to the post–Cold War security environment from territorial defense to expeditionary missions, the last three—effective engagement, survivability of force and infrastructure, and C^3— were *necessarily* connected to the advanced technologies associated with the RMA. This meant in principle that both the cause of greater European self-reliance and the goal of narrowing the capabilities gap would be served by concentrating resources on those technologies critical to the effectiveness of CJTFs, for contingencies ranging from peacekeeping to coalition war fighting.

The DCI and HHG initiatives, influenced by the vision of NATO's *New Strategic Concept* and the concrete experiences of Bosnia and the Persian Gulf, concentrated overwhelmingly on narrowing the differential in capabilities between the United States and the European allies, both in pursuit of more effective coalition operations and of a higher degree of European self-reliance. The onset of the third stage of Yugoslavia's disintegration demonstrated again the validity of both concerns. But additionally, it broadened yet again the horizons of change for the

Atlantic Alliance by provoking debate on the legitimacy of waging "humanitarian war," its appropriate prosecution, and the sacrifices NATO states were prepared to accept in order to satisfy the humanitarian impulse.

HUMANITARIAN WAR

When events in Bosnia in 1992 introduced the term *ethnic cleansing* to the popular Western vocabulary, the Bush administration warned Belgrade that the United States would consider unilateral military action in response to similar atrocities carried out by the rump Serb-dominated Federal Republic of Yugoslavia (FRY) in its southern province of Kosovo. The warning might have been forgotten after Bush's departure from office, had it not been reiterated by the Clinton administration the following year. The fact that ethnic Albanian Muslims constituted 95 percent of the population in Kosovo meant that conflict there had a greater potential to involve neighboring states, among them NATO allies and hereditary foes such as Greece and Turkey, than was the case in Bosnia. Washington could not consider ethnic cleansing in Kosovo a purely Serbian affair.[61]

And yet the Dayton Accords of 1995 contributed indirectly to the probability of just such a contingency. The province had never been a republic of the Yugoslav federation but had nonetheless enjoyed a degree of self-governing autonomy—an autonomy of which it was stripped by the Serb nationalist government of Slobodan Milošević in 1989. Dayton's attention to ethnic consociational governing arrangements for Bosnia, and its comparative neglect of politically charged ethnic tensions in Kosovo, left the Albanian Muslims of the province a despised minority within the larger Serb republic. This undercut the position of the moderate federalists in Ibrahim Rogova's Democratic League of Kosovo and prompted the more militant Kosovo Liberation Army (KLA) to carry out assassinations of Serbian army and police personnel in 1996. Dayton told autonomists in Kosovo that the diplomatic metal was not hot enough to make the principle of self-determination work for them, so the KLA decided to make it glow. Events in the Drenica region of the province from February 28 to March 7, 1998—starting with small engagements between KLA units and Serb police and ending in retaliatory actions by the latter against the Albanian villages of Prekaz i Ulët and Llausha, in which whole families and clans were killed—transported Kosovo beyond the point where a peaceful settlement was likely.

A "Contact Group," initially composed of the United States, Russia, Britain, and France to deal with Bosnia but enlarged to include Germany and Italy, turned its attention increasingly to Kosovo during 1998. Britain and France then cosponsored negotiations between Serb and Albanian representatives under the auspices of the Contact Group at Rambouillet Castle near Paris in February 1999. More important, however, was a statement issued January 30 by the North Atlantic Council on NATO's behalf in which events in Kosovo were designated "a threat to international peace and security." The statement expressed NATO's determination

to avert a "humanitarian catastrophe," and demanded that the Milošević government reduce the Serb army and police presence in Kosovo or face NATO air
strikes.[62] The parallel development of plans for a 30,000-strong NATO-led implementation force to maintain peace in Kosovo reflected the lessons of Bosnia, in
terms both of skepticism that Belgrade could be trusted to hold to any agreement
or that the United Nations could enforce it. The Rambouillet talks may have been
interpreted in Belgrade as a partial climb-down from the intervention threats posted earlier by Bush and Clinton.[63] Whatever its reasoning, the Milošević government did not take Rambouillet seriously. It rejected outright any deployments of
NATO forces to Kosovo to monitor compliance with an agreement and was supported diplomatically by Russia in its rejection. Even as the talks proceeded, the
Milošević government made plans for a new round of repression in the province.[64]

The change in Western attitudes on Kosovo relative to Bosnia were quite striking. At Rambouillet it was not the EU but Britain and France, militarily the most
powerful West Europeans, whose governments most forthrightly represented the
viewpoint of the New Europe. Additionally, the Bosnian experience encouraged the
Clinton administration to be at the ready with threats of force, both unilateral and
through NATO, and to influence the proceedings at Rambouillet with such threats.
The memory of Bosnia still fresh, the scale of the suffering in Kosovo too was such
that the grounds for a justification for intervention were shifting. As the Rambouillet
talks failed, NATO eclipsed all other international organizations officially mandated with crisis management and peacekeeping and finally brushed aside the very
principle of sovereignty under the doctrine of humanitarian intervention.

NOTES

1. Carl C. Hodge, ed., *Redefining European Security* (New York: Garland, 1999); Arthur
   Denaro, "Introduction: The Ethical Minefield," in Patrick Mileham and Lee Willett,
   eds., *Military Ethics for the Expeditionary Era* (London: Royal Institute of Internation-
   al Affairs, 2001), 1–6.
2. David S. Yost, *NATO Transformed: The Alliance's New Roles in International Security*
   (Washington, D.C.: United States Institute of Peace, 1998), 8–9, 18. See also Ernst B.
   Haas, "Types of Collective Security: An Examination of Operational Concepts,"
   American Political Science Review 49, no. 1 (1955): 40–62.
3. Michael Mandelbaum, *The Ideas That Conquered the World: Peace, Democracy, and
   Free Markets in the Twenty-First Century* (New York: Public Affairs, 2002), 192–193.
4. Yost, *NATO Transformed*, 61–62, 243. See also John E. Peters and Howard Deshong, *Out
   of Area or Out of Reach? European Military Support for Operations in Southwest Asia*
   (Santa Monica, CA: RAND, 1995); Richard L. Kugler, *U.S.-West European Cooperation
   in Out-of-Area Military Operations: Problems and Prospects* (Santa Monica, CA: RAND,
   1995).
5. Lawrence Freedman and Efraim Karsh, *The Gulf Conflict, 1990–1991: Diplomacy and
   War in the New World Order* (Princeton, NJ: Princeton University Press, 1993), 346–349.
6. Ibid.
7. Ibid., 350–351; Trevor C. Salmon, "Europe, the EC, and the Gulf," in James Gow, ed.,
   Iraq, The Gulf Conflict, and the World Community (London: Brassey's, 1993), 94.

8. Karl Kaiser and Klaus Becher, quoted in Yost, *NATO Transformed*, 266.

9. Salmon, "Europe, the EC, and the Gulf," 94–95.

10. Susan L. Woodward, *Balkan Tragedy: Chaos and Dissolution after the Cold War* (Washington, D.C.: Brookings, 1995), 323–324; Sabrina Petra Ramet, *Balkan Babel: The Disintegration of Yugoslavia from the Death of Tito to the War for Kosovo* (Boulder, CO: Westview, 1999), 205–210.

11. Ivo H. Daalder, *Getting to Dayton: The Making of America's Bosnia Policy* (Washington, D.C.: Brookings, 2000), 187–188.

12. Ibid., 188–189.

13. Woodward, *Balkan Tragedy*, 398.

14. Col. Robert C. Owen, "The Balkans Air Campaign Study," Parts I and II, *Airpower Journal* 11, no. 2 (1997): 4–24 and 11, no. 3 (1997): 6–26, also available at <http://www.fas.org/man/dod-101/ops/docs/apj-sum97-owen.html>.

15. Fraser Cameron, *The Foreign and Security Policy of the European Union, Past, Present and Future* (Sheffield, UK: Academic Press, 1999), 32.

16. Yost, *NATO Transformed*, 76.

17. Ibid., 217; Lawrence S. Kaplan, *The Long Entanglement: NATO's First Fifty Years* (Westport, CT: Praeger, 1999), 208.

18. Andrew F. Krepinevich, "Cavalry to Computer: The Pattern of Military Revolutions," *The National Interest*, no. 37 (1994): 30.

19. Jeffrey McKitrick, et al., "The Revolution in Military Affairs," in Barry R. Schneider and Lawrence E. Grinter, eds., *Battlefield of the Future: 21st Century Warfare Issues*, Air War College Studies in National Security, no. 3 (Maxwell AFB, Alabama: Air University Press, 1998), 65.

20. See Colin S. Gray, *Modern Strategy* (New York: Oxford University Press, 1999), 200–205, and David C. Gompert, Richard L. Kugler, and Martin Libicki, *Mind the Gap: Promoting a Transatlantic Revolution in Military Affairs* (Washington, D.C.: National Defense University Press, 1999), 3.

21. Williamson Murray, "Thinking About Revolutions in Military Affairs," *Joint Force Quarterly* (Summer 1997): 103–110.

22. Colin S. Gray, "Weapons for Strategic Effect: How Important Is Technology?" Unpublished paper, Center for Strategy and Technology, Air University, Maxwell AFB, Montgomery, Alabama, 2000–2001.

23. Michael O'Hanlon, *Technological Change and the Future of War* (Washington, D.C.: Brookings, 2000), 26–30, 194.

24. Robbin F. Laird and Holger Mey, "The Revolution in Military Affairs: Allied Perspectives," *McNair Paper No. 60*, April 1999, Institute for National Strategic Studies, National Defense University, Washington, D.C.

25. Gray, *Modern Strategy*, 246–248; Martin Hoch, "Die 'Revolution in Military Affairs' — Zur Kritik eines Mythos," *Europäische Sicherheit*, August 2000, <http://www.gfw-sicherheitspolitik.de>.

26. Yost, *NATO Transformed*, 200; also Simon Duke, *The Elusive Quest for European Security from EDC to CFSP* (New York: St. Martin's, 2000), 296.

27. Ibid.

28. Gompert, Kugler, Libicki, *Mind the Gap*, 83.

29. John S. Duffield, *World Power Forsaken: Political Culture, International Institutions, and German Security Policy After Unification* (Stanford, CA: Stanford University Press, 1998), 134.

30. Sten Rynning, *Changing Military Doctrine: Presidents and Military Power in Fifth Republic France, 1958–2000* (Westport, CT: Praeger, 2002), 128.

31. Ibid., 168.

32. Ibid., 142; also Louis Gautier, *Mitterrand et son armée* (Paris: Grasset, 1999); Philippe Masson, "La Marine de 1945 à 1992: Redressement, virage nucléaire, action extérieure,"

in André Corvisier, ed., *L'Histoire Militaire de la France: de 1940 à nos jours* (Paris: PUF, 1994).

33. Michael Meimeth, "France and the Organization of Security in Post–Cold War Europe, in Carl C. Hodge, ed., *Redefining European Security* (New York: Garland, 1999), 152–155.

34. Rynning, *Changing Military Doctrine*, 140; R. E. Utley, *The French Defence Debate: Consensus and Continuity in the Mitterrand Era* (London: MacMillian, 2000), 156–158, 207–208; Charles G. Cogan, *The Third Option: The Emancipation of European Defense, 1989–2000* (Westport, CT: Praeger, 2001), 104–107.

35. Jeffrey B. Jones, "French Forces for the 21st Century," *Joint Force Quarterly* (Summer 2000): 31–38.

36. Ibid., 32–35; Ronald Tiersky, "French Military Reform and NATO Restructuring," *Joint Force Quarterly* (Spring 1997): 95–102.

37. Ibid., 34–37.

38. Ministry of Defence, *Strategic Defence Review, 1998*, Ch. 3, available at <http://www.mod.uk/issue/sdr>.

39. Ibid., Ch. 11.

40. Ibid.

41. Ibid.

42. Ibid.

43. Ministry of Defence Policy Papers, No. 4, *Defence Acquisition*, 14.

44. Hugo Young, *This Blessed Plot: Britain and Europe from Churchill to Blair* (New York: Overlook, 1999), 484–495; Michael Crick, *Michael Heseltine: A Biography* (London: Penguin, 1997), 267–292.

45. Cogan, *The Third Option*, 147; Foreign & Commonwealth Office, British-French Summit: Press Conference 4/12/98.

46. House of Commons, Research Paper 00/84, 31 October 2000, *Common European Security and Defense Policy: A Progress Report*, 35–36.

47. Jolyon Howorth, "Britain, France and the European Defence Initiative," *Survival* 42, no. 2 (2000): 33–55.

48. See David Clay Large, *Germans to the Front: West German Rearmament in the Adenauer Era* (Chapel Hill, NC: University of North Carolina Press, 1996), and Stephen Szabo, ed., *The Bundeswehr and Western Security* (London: Macmillan, 1990). The figures on troop strength date to 1986 and were taken from "The Sentry at the Gate: A Survey of NATO's Central Front," *The Economist*, August 30, 1986.

49. John S. Duffield, *Power Rules: The Evolution of NATO's Conventional Force Posture* (Stanford, CA: Stanford University Press, 1995), 272.

50. *Handelsblatt*, March 6, 2001; also Harald Kujat, "Die Bundeswehr auf ihrem Weg der Erneuerung von Grund auf," *Europäische Sicherheit*, January 2001, 30–40.

51. Bundesministerium der Verteidigung, *Gemeinsame Sicherheit und Zukunft der Bundeswehr: Bericht der Kommission an die Bundesregierung*, May 23, 2000, 23.

52. Ibid., 52–53.

53. Ibid., 53–55.

54. Ibid., 137–140.

55. *Eckwerte fur die konzeptionelle und planerische Weiterentwicklung der Streitkräfte*, May 23, 2000, and *The Bundeswehr—Advancing Steadily into the 21st Century: Cornerstones of a Fundamental Review*, June 2000; Franz-Josef Meiers, "The Reform of the Bundeswehr: Adaptation of Fundamental Renewal?" *European Security* 10, no. 2 (2001): 8.

56. Meiers, "The Reform of the Bundeswehr," 16–19; Hans-Dieter Lemke, "Bundeswehrreform: Schwachpunkt Krisenfähigkeit," *SWP-aktuell*, no. 66 (November 2000).

57. Duffield, *Power Rules*, 241–242; also Robert H. Dorff, "Germany and the Future of European Security," *World Affairs* 161, no. 2 (1998): 59–69.

58. *McNair Paper No. 60*; Hans Rühle, "Das Ende der Wehrpflicht in Deutschland," *Neue Zürcher Zeitung*, March 5, 2002, 1. See also Reiner K. Huber, "Umfangsreduzierungen der Bundeswehr zum Abbbau des Investitutionsdefizits," *Europäische Sicherheit*, October 1998, 43–47.

59. See, for example, the testimony of Jeffrey Gedmin, Resident Scholar of the American Enterprise Institute, before the European Subcommittee of the U.S. Senate Foreign Relations Committee, *FDCH Political Transcripts*, March 3, 2000, available at <http://www.jsonline.com/news/nat/ap/oct99>.

60. Meaning humanitarian and rescue operations, peacekeeping and crisis management, including "peacemaking," approved in 1992 by the WEU as integral to ESDI. Helsinki European Council, December 10–11, 1999, *Presidency Conclusions*, Annex I–IV.

61. Constantine P. Danopoulos, "Turkey and the Balkans: Searching for Stability," in Constantine P. Danopoulos and Kostas G. Messas, eds., *Crisis in the Balkans: Views from the Participants* (Boulder, CO: Westview, 1997), 215.

62. Quoted in Tim Judah, *Kosovo: War and Revenge* (New Haven, CT: Yale University Press, 2000), 195.

63. Ibid., 73–77, 137–140; Stefan Troebst, *Conflict in Kosovo: An Analytical Documentation, 1992–1998* (Flensburg: European Center for Minority Issues, 1998), 1–3, 105.

64. Marc Weller, "The Rambouillet Conference on Kosovo," *International Affairs* 75, no. 2 (1999): 211–251.

SMART WAR AND RESPONSIBLE STATECRAFT

When is smart war wise statecraft? In light of *Operation Allied Force*, NATO's air campaign to force an end to the ethnic cleansing of the Albanian population of the Serb province of Kosovo, this question represented one of the more interesting facets of the broader controversy of humanitarian intervention in the 1990s. If we define humanitarian intervention as *military intervention in order to protect the human rights of a state's inhabitants that does not have the authority of its government,*[1] NATO's war in Kosovo stands as a particularly robust example. International intervention in Bosnia had enjoyed the consent of the newly independent Bosnian government as its sovereignty was assaulted by Croatian and Serbian secessionists. In the case of Kosovo, by contrast, NATO marked the fiftieth anniversary of its existence by the transformative act of going to war for the first time in its history, not in the kind defensive contingency for which it was created, but in a humanitarian cause. The Alliance was not only denied the acquiescence of the Yugoslav government but also acted in violation of the basic norms of the UN Charter and in the absence of Security Council mandate. The intervention really began with the Rambouillet conference, in which a select group of NATO states attempted to dictate political terms profoundly affecting Yugoslavia's internal affairs; that attempt and the threat of force that accompanied it, moreover, were influenced by the experience and cost of collective vacillation in Bosnia. Kosovo was therefore a watershed.[2] The features of the intervention reflect NATO's sense of proprietary interest in the former Yugoslavia as well as the continuing military transformation of the Alliance from a defensive coalition to an expeditionary instrument of coercion.

Additionally, Kosovo raised issues concerning the ethics and political prudence of humanitarian intervention, both in principle and in its NATO iteration of 1999. In strictly military terms the effectiveness of *Allied Force* was circumscribed by the priority given to casualty avoidance in a conflict where vital national interests were not directly engaged. The technologies that facilitated a surgical application of force and helped to minimize civilian and military deaths also served to legitimate the intervention in spite of its violation of international norms. Yet they simultaneously undermined the sense of collective European responsibility for regional security through the employment of military capabilities possessed solely or preponderantly by the United States. A lower-tech alternative to *Allied Force*, using European ground troops, might have come closer to meeting the humanitarian rescue challenge and made the operation a catalyst for greater European unity. A crisis, after all, is an opportunity for creative innovation; once it has passed, governments revert to old habits. The opportunity to make Kosovo a project of collective European crisis-management was passed up, and the responsibility of the United States for peace in the Balkans was increased in proportion to American dominance in *Allied Force*.

The Kosovo campaign, lastly, represented another episode in post–Cold War NATO *Ostpolitik*, begun with Germany's reunification, extended in the application of CFE standards in the former Warsaw Pact and the offer of NATO membership to the Czech Republic, Hungary and Poland, and expressed in the form of political trusteeship for Bosnia after the Dayton Accords. Kosovo broadened and deepened this trusteeship. It also posed questions about the limits of American responsibility for peace-support and political trusteeship in the former Yugoslavia specifically and for European security generally. As the decade drew to an end and the struggle to succeed Bill Clinton in the White House got underway, the domestic sense of these limits inside the United States raised issues of enormous potential consequence to the Atlantic Community.

THE HIGH TIDE OF INTERVENTIONISM

The Alliance's involvement in the former Yugoslavia resonated with a broader international trend of the decade, favoring humanitarian intervention on behalf of populations suffering famine, domestic political anarchy, or violent repression. Haiti, Rwanda, and Somalia figured prominently alongside Bosnia and Kosovo as targets of a humanitarian impulse exercised not only by the nongovernmental organizations traditionally active in humanitarian relief but also by states whose governments attempted to integrate humanitarian concerns into their official foreign policy missions.[3] At the same time, a new enthusiasm for multilateral peacekeeping as a means of conflict prevention and containment—often in combination with humanitarian missions and rechristened "peace support"—reflected the hope of many that ideas of collective security and supranational regulation of conflict would at last be given the fair test they deserved after the "false start" of the 1950s.[4]

There was some justification for this enthusiasm. True, the principle of self-determination was as controversial and demonstrably unpredictable in its consequences as ever, while the cause of arms-control had a poor decade in light of the proliferation of weapons of mass destruction (WMD). But the growth of free markets and borderless commerce in the 1990s was in many cases truly transformative, while the notion that international organizations could underpin conditions favoring the spread of democracy was not without merit and notable successes. Indeed, precisely this was happening in one fashion or another all over Europe, the continent whose wars had inspired the ideas in the first place. The world was more democratic and free trading than ever before. Looking back on the century, it was not unreasonable to conclude that Woodrow Wilson had been more of a prophet than a statesman.[5]

The trouble with the humanitarian impulse was its very impulsiveness. Between 1988 and 1994 the United Nations took on almost double the total of its peacekeeping missions of the previous forty-three years, a hyperactivity with little regard for pragmatic selectivity that by mid-decade had produced as many disappointments as successes due to the number of missions and the variety of circumstances into which they were cast.[6] The 1992–1993 Somalia intervention was disastrous. The mixed scorecard of interventionism elsewhere was in part the result of the UN's resources being stretched beyond capacity by a confusion of universalism with nondiscrimination — the imperative that intervention be demonstrably effective somewhere with a desire to make it decisive everywhere.[7] It was additionally limited by the commitment member-states were prepared to make to the enforcement of international peace beyond resort to lofty rhetoric. Short-circuited by forty years of Cold War polarization, the development of an authentic sense of international community in the 1990s was hobbled not by a struggle of superpowers but by the demonstrated heresy of the community's members. "Assertive multilateralism" expressed the hopes that the Clinton administration cherished concerning the evolution of international affairs but in the application was logistically challenging and usually much less multilateral than Clinton had hoped. In Somalia parallel command-and-control structures under the United Nations led to operational confusion, which impressed upon Clinton the potentially high cost of failing to establish American leadership in multilateral efforts. Clinton was rightly criticized for his "tentative" attitude to intervention and his reluctance to back it with robust force, but he was also justly skeptical about the substantive commitment of other states to the humanitarian ethos. In 1994 his administration issued Presidential Decision Directive 25 (PDD-25) dealing specifically with "multilateral peace operations," a document that indicated to some observers that an American willingness to engage in unilateral action might be the near-term response to the failure of emergency multilateralism.[8]

Growing American skepticism concerning the viability of multilateral operations was valid in light of the fact that comparatively wealthy powers fond of advocating multilateral intervention were often able, due to modest defense budgets, to offer only limited military resources to the collective effort. By the 1990s NATO had only partially accepted, through the *New Strategic Concept* and the Bosnian experience, the conversion to an expeditionary ethos. Moving from the global challenge confronting the United Nations to the regional European context, the most valid generalization of the time was that "the political will to deal decisively with the ethnic violence percolating within NATO's territory and on its periphery is not in great evidence."[9] The Alliance's underachieving "middle powers" reflected the differential between principle and practice. The Canadian government, to cite a non-European example, was rarely short on sanctimony regarding the duties of the international community, yet reduced its own service personnel from 87,000 in 1990 to 58,000 in 2000, even as it increased its overseas peace-support commitments. The combination of over-tasking with stingy defense budgets resulted in morale, equipment, and readiness problems that hampered Canada's ability to contribute in proportion to its national fiscal capacity and in harmony with its multilateral enthusiasms.[10]

An additional shortcoming of the interventionist impulse of the 1990s was its apolitical quality. The rush to rescue victims in reaction to their suffering alone built erroneously "on the metaphor of saving a drowning stranger" and distorted the context surrounding the stranger's dilemma.[11] In Yugoslavia, as elsewhere, international consensus on the desirability of intervention had no sooner emerged than it was subject to a debate on the appropriate "exit strategy," which divorced the moral imperative of rescue from the sober contemplation of the self-interested reasons for intervening . . . or not. In Yugoslavia the idea that intervention was based on humanitarian principles applicable anywhere glossed over the fact that both geopolitical proximity to Western Europe and the availability of institutions such as NATO, the EU, and the OSCE made the region a comparatively attractive candidate for intervention in terms of distance, access, military logistics, and available infrastructure. This oversell of the intervention as an inherently altruistic action—and the under-sell of the economic, historic strategic reasons for absorbing fragments of the Yugoslav federation into Western Europe—involved a less-than-honest evasion of the wholesomely self-interested reasons for intervention on the one hand and a public admission of the likely open-ended commitment to occupy the territory indefinitely on the other. Intervention here was not a discrete act of assistance but rather a new chapter in the ongoing relationship between Yugoslavia and the rest of Europe since the federation's invention by the victors of 1919. History, culture, and power made the attempt to impose a democratic peace more realistic and less idealistic than the governments advocating it would acknowledge.[12]

The third stage of the wars of the Yugoslav succession, civil war in Kosovo, came late in the decade at a time when humanitarian intervention had already lost a good deal of its perceived legitimacy. The intervention was largely successful in terms of consolidating post–Cold War territorial and political change, but it succeeded on terms that did damage to the prestige of the humanitarian ideal and again exposed fissures in NATO. This might not have been so, had the Clinton administration not chosen to brush aside the principle of sovereignty in order to redeem the humanitarian ethos at minimal political exposure to itself and the governments of its Allies.

RIGHTEOUS MIGHT AND CASUAL WAR

The abridgement of any state's sovereignty constitutes a very serious action. The Alliance's Kosovo intervention can be viewed from the perspective of a long history of interventions by strong states into the affairs of weaker neighbors, and any charge against NATO for reckless endangerment of hallowed custom would be compelling

THE FORMER YUGOSLAVIA

least of all in the case of the Balkan region, where compromised sovereignty has historically been closer to the norm than to the exception. Still, the great virtue of the "organized hypocrisy" of sovereignty is that it has, after all, organized and served international peace well enough that it should not be tampered with blithely. Peace, Michael Howard reminds us, is "the order, however imperfect, that results from agreement between states."[13] And NATO was clearly guilty of a form of recklessness in Kosovo. The violation of Serbian sovereignty involved a sharp contrast between the imperatives invoked to legitimate it and the means brought to bear in pursuit of an acceptable outcome—what was promptly judged as a "disconnection between the high moral language of the cause and the essentially limited character of the war itself."[14]

Critics of the war blamed the "human rights prism" for a Western inability to understand the nature of political conflict in the former Yugoslavia that would frustrate NATO and the European Union from playing a constructive role in regional peace.[15] But it is difficult to believe that Western governments were genuinely deluded about the chances of durable peace in Kosovo after their experience in Bosnia, both before and after Dayton. The human rights imperative and RMA technologies worked together to facilitate not an optimal diplomatic or humanitarian outcome in Kosovo but rather an acceptable short-term political outcome for NATO's member-states. Due to the precision of which contemporary weapons are capable, options were available to them that had never before accompanied a military conflict. They exploited these options and accorded secondary priority to the security of the civilian population of Kosovo. This was evident from the outset of military operations. When *Operation Allied Force* was launched on March 24, 1999, President Clinton insisted that "ending this tragedy is a moral imperative," yet cautioned almost in the same breath that "I don't intend to put our troops in Kosovo to fight a war."[16] As an indirect result, the inauguration of NATO bombing was accompanied by an *intensification* of ethnic cleansing in Kosovo. A report tabled by the OSCE catalogued in some 900 pages of detail a litany of rape, torture, and killing. The details were prefaced by the observation that "violations inflicted on the Kosovo Albanian population on a massive scale after March 20 were a continuation of actions by Serbian forces that were well-rehearsed, insofar as they were taking place in many locations before that date."[17] Whereas some 69,500 Kosovars were displaced from the province by March 23, the number ballooned to an estimated 862,979 by June 9. Because no NATO army invaded either Kosovo or the Serb Republic itself, Serb forces were able to accelerate the ethnic cleansing that had, since 1991, been integral to the goal of patching together a Greater Serbia from the fragments of federal Yugoslavia.

Determined from the outset to hold its losses to the absolute minimum, the Alliance restricted its aircraft to operations above 15,000 feet. The "moral arithmetic here became perverse," noted one critique, "we were unwilling to risk many American casualties in air or ground combat but, given the rightness of our cause, we felt justified in a high-altitude bombing campaign that inevitably killed civilians."[18] Javier Solana, NATO Secretary General, spoke in terms of a "moral duty" to "stop the violence and bring an end to the humanitarian catastrophe now taking place in Kosovo." He stressed further that the Alliance had no quarrel with the Yugoslav people,[19] who must have been surprised when NATO's first bombs and missiles slammed into targets in and around Belgrade rather than into Serb tanks, trucks, and troops in Kosovo. NATO's political leadership essentially contrived to punish Serbia's infrastructure—"degrading its war-making capacity" was the favored phrase of press briefings in the first phase of the war—for crimes its soldiers had committed, and continued to commit, in Kosovo. Tragic as the civilian casualties were, they represented only one half of the perverse equation. Seventy-two days of bombardment ultimately compelled Serb forces to withdraw from Kosovo. An enormous quantity of Serb military equipment was pulled out of Kosovo after the cease-fire,[20] spared by the absence of NATO troops in the ravaged province but also by the fact that, even at its height, NATO's air campaign was notable neither for its ferocity nor for its precision but rather for its circumspection. Apache helicopters from the U.S. Army were never committed against Serbian tanks,[21] while the Hercules AC-130 gunships available were subject to such operational restrictions as gave them scant opportunity to fulfill the role of scourge from the sky expected of them. Columnist Charles Krauthammer, no friend of humanitarian intervention even in principle, nevertheless restricted himself to ridiculing NATO's mission on its own terms. While the achievement of its primary humanitarian objective was hampered by its less-than-robust military measures, he maintained, the secondary mission of preventing instability in neighboring states too was compromised by the accelerated rate at which Kosovar refugees were flooding into Albania, Macedonia, and Montenegro. In the early phase of the air campaign, additionally, two Serbian MIGs were shot down attempting to attack NATO peacekeeping forces in Bosnia; later there were reports of incidents involving Serb forces on the borders of Albania, Croatia, and Montenegro.[22]

Among NATO governments, that of Tony Blair in Britain was most insistent on the need for an invasion of Kosovo. But Blair was out of phase with the other NATO states. From the outset, both the bombing campaign and the war of words crafted by Alliance spokesmen were designed to reflect the center of gravity of *existing* public opinion in the Alliance rather than to prepare the public for the possibility of greater sacrifice with frankness about a ground war. The tension between the declared goal of saving the Kosovars and the domestic political exposure inherent for NATO governments of committing ground troops was artfully triangulated with the air power–only approach. Neither France nor Italy was prepared to contribute as many troops as Britain, but both were willing to provide troops if a ground war were approved. At one point British Defense Secretary George Robertson speculated that sending in ground troops might appear as an act of war against Yugoslavia rather than the regime of Slobodan Milošević, while German Chancellor Gerhard Schröder opposed a ground war and went so far as to suggest that Germany would block authorization for an invasion.[23]

But it was the political timidity of the Clinton administration that vetoed the ground option altogether, even in the face of the preference of Supreme Allied

Commander in Europe (SACEUR), General Wesley Clark, for a force of 175,000, using Albania as the principal invasion route. Having decided against the two extremes, washing its hands of the crisis or facing the risks of outright invasion, the administration opted for a "bomb and pray" reliance on air power alone to achieve its military ends. The dissonance between an ostensibly humanitarian mission and the less-than-heroic means used to achieve it made this policy controversial; equally, it threatened to be ineffective until the Alliance broadened its array of targets and intensified the bombing of them.[24]

In a press conference given by General Klaus Naumann, Chairman of NATO's Military Committee, on May 9, 1999, a succession of reporters asked why the Alliance conceded no need to change its approach to the war despite the fact that the air campaign had not stopped ethnic cleansing inside Kosovo. Naumann's answer dealt adroitly with the dilemma of defending a policy with which he was clearly uncomfortable:

> You are asking a moral question, I understand you fully and from a moral point of view I also hate to see this news, but on the other hand, you can only do what is achievable and what is acceptable by our nations in this Alliance. And for that reason I have to tell you once again that we have no reason at this point in time to change the strategy which is focused to some extent on the philosophy of our democracies that we should avoid casualties, we should avoid the loss of life.[25]

Both Naumann and the reporters understood the deeper reason why *Allied Force* was being conducted in a way that nobody found very edifying. While considerable scholarly attention has been given to explaining why Western publics have become distrustful of their elected representatives, the mounting evidence that this sentiment is reciprocal has had little attention. The governments of the mature democracies have acquired a low regard for the character of their electorates and are inclined to undertake foreign policy initiatives, to the extent possible, on the political cheap. The war was being prosecuted with a mind to keeping casualties to zero, while minimizing Serb civilian casualties and attacking military and industrial infrastructure. War waged in this fashion enabled NATO governments to insure themselves against popular outrage when the outcome of the conflict was less than optimal.[26] During the dark days of the Cold War Michael Howard speculated as follows:

> Even in the nuclear age, the obligation on the citizen to fight in defense of the community that embodies his values seems to me to be absolute, and the more fully he is a citizen, the more total that obligation becomes. The ugly skeleton of military obligation for the preservation of the state can become so thickly covered with the fat of economic prosperity and under-exercised through the skillful avoidance of international conflict that whole generations can grow to maturity, as they have in Western Europe today, without even knowing it is there."[27]

The charge that *Allied Force* resulted in a victory worthy only of cowards is harsh in view of the very high level of professionalism to which Western militaries are held. The professional military of the NATO states in the 1990s operated in a political environment in which enthusiasm for humanitarian intervention was often strong in proportion to the absence of direct sacrifice from the public—a public for whom any sense of the connection between the right to security and the duty to serve was lost and the ethos of the citizen-soldier dead. Such support could prove suddenly ephemeral when intervention involved casualties, cost, and inconvenience. In the case of *Allied Force*, NATO's political and military leadership was forced to give as much attention to the unpredictable shoals of contemporary democracy as it did to the difficult terrain of Kosovo and the tragedy unfolding there.

What did *Allied Force* mean for the Atlantic Alliance as Europe's premier security organization? Because air operations initially witnessed an acceleration of the atrocities visited upon the population of Kosovo, its reliance on air power was prominent among the reasons cited by critics who judged the operation a perfect failure. In addition, NATO's policy going back to Rambouillet was ridiculed as self-contradictory, in so far as the Contact Group did not support Kosovo's secession from Yugoslavia yet had militarily aided the side of the secessionists—more forcefully put, "had intervened in a civil war and defeated one side, but embraced the position of the party it had defeated on the issue over which the war had been fought."[28] In response its advocates conceded the humanitarian shortcomings of *Allied Force* but rejected the notion that Wilsonian idealism, or the abuse thereof, had paved a path to hell with good intentions. The war had put NATO's very credibility on the line yet had reaffirmed American leadership of the Alliance militarily, politically, and morally. "Today may not be the Wilsonian moment in the sense that all the world is ready to adopt Western values and institutions," claimed one review, "but it is a period in which unprecedented power can be used to promote human rights and democratic government in circumstances where the terrain is favorable."[29] General Wesley Clark, as Supreme Allied Commander in Europe responsible for implementing militarily the political will of the NATO governments, later referred to the "brave talk" about "the so-called Revolution in Military Affairs" yet conceded that the operation achieved "a military success at remarkably little cost in Allied lives and resources," despite the fact that its prosecution violated almost every basic principle of the conduct of war.[30] *Allied Force* turned out to be a testimony to American power that would radiate well beyond the Balkans.

Between these two views there is a more sober interpretation that, looking back from 1999 to 1989, *Allied Force* was the most ambitious manifestation of post–Cold War *Ostpolitik* involving the liquidation of East European communist systems and the incremental extension of Euro-Atlantic democracy eastward.[31] Since the initial phase of Yugoslavia's disintegration, the Alliance had acted progressively as an anti-Serb coalition whose diplomacy and military power had supported the self-determination claims of Croats, Slovenians, Bosnians, and Albanian Kosovars *against* the Yugoslav rump-state headquartered in Belgrade. An analyst in Belgrade observed with some justice that the campaign in Kosovo "was like the final battle of the Cold War."[32] Admittedly this was not the intended outcome, but it was what the sum of NATO's actions represented. In Yugoslavia the Alliance had pushed aside the United Nations and the accepted conventions of international relations, yet had done so ostensibly to redeem a more ambitious definition of "international community," even as it consolidated the Atlantic community's Cold War victory.

THE HOLLOW SHELL OF BURDEN-SHARING

The claim that *Allied Force* reasserted American leadership merits closer examination, not because it is wrong but rather because the articulation of American leadership in the campaign limited its contribution to the cause of European self-reliance. Having decided to take on the humanitarian mission, the Clinton administration passed on the ground war option and with it the opportunity to involve America's European allies more intensely in a European security crisis. Rare indeed is the occasion when Britain is eager to commit troops to a continental conflict. In achieving the mission using advanced weaponry plus integrated command-control and communications capabilities possessed almost exclusively by the United States, the administration made *Allied Force* an American affair and undercut the ability of European allies — quite apart from the issue of their willingness — to contribute more to the overall military effort.

Almost alone, American air power broke the Yugoslav military and forced the Milošević government to yield to the Alliance's demands. This may have been its most fortunate aspect, skeptics of the RMA have pointed out, because NATO's new technologies did not permit its aircraft either to attack Serbian armored forces in poor weather or to distinguish military from civilian vehicles without the aid of a pilot's eye.[33] If one holds that the Clinton administration and most of the NATO allies chose an airpower-only campaign due to a fear of casualties, then *Allied Force* was a success, above all because the RMA was never subjected to a thorough test.[34] To the contrary, the campaign was a mixture of competing political impulses and military imperatives, the sum of which placed egregious limitations on the conduct of coherent operations. A principal criticism of *Allied Force* is that the manner in which it was launched "violated two of the most enduring maxims of military practice: the importance of achieving surprise and the importance of keeping the enemy unclear as to one's intentions."[35] Each weakness was in its own way either a by-product of coalition warfare or of political micromanagement of a military campaign — or both. By ruling out altogether a ground campaign, let alone an invasion, the Clinton administration revealed so much of NATO's hand to Belgrade that Serb forces in Kosovo could adapt themselves to the certainty of a one-dimensional threat. The politics of coalition warfare meanwhile further intensified the political scripting of the campaign. French President Jacques Chirac opposed any attack on Belgrade's electrical power grid that would leave the Serb capital in the dark for any length of time. Ultimately, CBU-104 (V)2/B cluster munitions were used to deposit carbon-graphite on the grid and thus shut it down for only a few hours. The point here is that neither weather nor terrain, neither Serb guile nor NATO interoperability problems, made *Allied Force* initially a close-run thing. Rather, it was the strategy chosen by the Alliance's political leadership that "risked frittering away the hard-earned reputation for effectiveness that U.S. air power had finally earned for itself in *Desert Storm* after more than three years of unqualified misuse over North Vietnam a generation earlier."[36] To a significant extent, the promise of RMA technologies encouraged NATO's political leaders to impose limitations on the campaign, but those very limitations meant that other aspects of the RMA and of NATO's concept of Combined Joint Task Forces (CJTF) were not tested at all.

Among the less publicized problems of the war for Kosovo was the interoperability of NATO air forces. Of all the European allies, France's contribution of deployed aircraft and total sorties flown was the largest—more than 100 aircraft in a total of 2,414 sorties. France's possession of precision-guided munitions (PGMs) permitted its pilots to participate in the strike phase of operations involving restrictive rules of engagement, prevailing weather conditions, and challenging terrain. France also contributed a larger number of support aircraft than other European allies for combat air patrol (CAP), electronic warfare (EW), airborne warning and control (AWAC), intelligence-surveillance-reconnaissance missions (ISR), and aerial refueling.[37] The United Kingdom provided the second largest allied force, the Royal Air Force accounting for 1,008 strike missions. Because the RAF was supplied with PGMs it was able to offer a strike capacity similar to that of France. The RAF also flew CAP, AWAC, and ISR missions. However, the combined Anglo-French punch was limited by the fact that it lacked all-weather munitions capable of dealing with the adverse conditions that lasted for the duration of the campaign.[38]

Italy was the third largest allied contributor overall. Its aircraft accounted for 1,081 sorties, but Italy's contribution did not include any traditional support aircraft. One of the great merits of the Italian effort was the fact that, like the German *Luftwaffe*, Italy's Tornado electronic and combat reconnaissance aircraft (ECRs) were equipped with HARM anti-radiation missiles and advanced electronic countermeasures, permitting them to play a role in suppression of enemy air defenses (SEAD) missions. German and Italian Tornados jointly accounted for 37 percent of all HARM shots taken during *Allied Force*. Proportional to its size, a remarkable contribution was made by the Royal Netherlands Airforce, which chalked up 1,252 sorties in strike and CAP roles. Additionally, Dutch aircraft were equipped with forward-looking infrared (FLIR) and were therefore able to undertake strike missions at night. Yet because these aircraft did not carry PGMs, their night capabilities were reduced as the rules of engagement became more restrictive.[39]

Yet the collective effort of the European NATO states represented a supplementary contribution to the prosecution of *Allied Force*. The United States supplied more than 700 of the total 1,055 aircraft deployed and flew more than 29,000 sorties. The USAF provided fighters, bombers, ISR aircraft, SpecOps/Rescue aircraft, and intra-theater airlifters. The EA-6 Prowler accounted for most of the SEAD missions, providing stand-off jamming for allied sorties. American aircraft also delivered far and away the largest number of PGMs and all-weather weapons, ranging from JDAM, JSOW, the Paveway II and III also used by the British and French airforces, Maverick AGM-130, to air- and sea-launched cruise missiles. This array of capabilities was ultimately crucial to the success of the air war, given that the restrictive rules of engagement and adverse weather conditions made precision bombing indispensable. The United States provided almost all of the aerial intelligence employed and selected virtually every target.

Commenting on the discrepancy between U.S. and European contributions to the air campaign, one study noted that the "capabilities gap" was both quantitative and qualitative, characterized by *asymmetry* on the one hand and *interoperability* problems on the other. There were particular problems with rapid and secure communications given that many European fighters lacked Have-Quick-type frequency-hopping UHF and KY-58-like radios for encrypted communications. American command and control aircraft were often required to transmit target and aircraft position data "in the clear," running the risk of giving away tactical intelligence to Serb forces. Neither was the STU-3 secure phone system common to U.S. forces available to the allies. At worst, classified communications had to be passed by hard copy. The absence of a common identification friend or foe system (IFF); a variable ability to detect which Serb SAM installations were tracking coalition aircraft; and the small number of non-U.S. aircraft capable of laser target identification all complicated the work of AWACs operators.[40]

Possibly a more telling fact of NATO dependence on U.S. capabilities, however, is that some 70 percent of the American aircraft deployed for *Allied Force* were in a support role. The United States supplied over 90 percent of aerial refueling and virtually all of the tactical jamming for SEAD missions. Its C-17s and C-130s also furnished the bulk of airlift requirements. The C-160 Transall used by the European allies was perfectly capable but was not available in sufficient numbers to support a mission as extensive as *Allied Force* became. It is tempting to speculate that the transatlantic gap in support capabilities visible in Kosovo could well turn out to be more critical than any difference in combat firepower, because their role in *Allied Force* "reflects the growing importance of these assets in the types of operations NATO could face in the future."[41] Indeed, they are assets central to the CJTF concept developed in the mid-1990s.

Both during and immediately after *Allied Force* much was made of the capabilities gap and the absence of European self-reliance in coping with a European crisis. General Naumann confessed in testimony before the Senate Armed Services Committee that "as a European, I am ashamed we have to ask for American help to deal with something as small as Kosovo."[42] The defense press observed that the Balkan operation had reinforced both the idea that all future wars will be coalition wars and that interoperability with U.S. forces will be the key to coalition success. Yet the more NATO relied on high-tech systems, it went on, the more the alliance would depend on the nations willing to buy them. In the face of these facts, retired RAF Air Vice Marshall R. A. Mason noted that "we fear that we will end up as spear carriers to the United States" and "burden-sharing will become no more than a hollow shell."[43] This perception of the Kosovo experience was reinforced from the other side of the Atlantic, in statements from the U.S. Deputy Secretary of Defense concerning the "visible antiquity" of European systems, and from Congress that the Europeans "are slipping one or two generations behind the USA."[44]

Post-Kosovo reports by the two most militarily capable European allies, France and the UK, focused on the capabilities gap. Not surprisingly, the French report was more concerned with closing the gap as much in the pursuit of greater European autonomy from the United States as in the name of enhanced European military effectiveness itself. The British report acknowledged European reliance on the United States and noted five areas of deficiency: precision all-weather strike; strategic lift; intelligence, surveillance, reconnaissance; suppression of enemy air defense/electronic warfare; and air-to-air refueling. The British report was also less concerned with European autonomy than with responsible burden-sharing. Consistent with the 1998 *Strategic Defence Review* and its value-for-money spirit, it highlighted the tension between preferences and limitations. Where it cited "the alarming deficit in European capabilities for suppressing and destroying even relatively unsophisticated air defenses," it recommended that Europe should "accept that its scope for action independent of the United States is very limited" or undertake to improve its capabilities "sufficiently to act independently."[45] Under *Command, Control and Coordination* it dealt directly with European dependency on U.S. capabilities, stating that American dominance in NATO could be viewed either as a vehicle for Washington to push the Alliance in directions for which there is less than full consensus or as self-imposed constraint on American military might, enabling European views to carry more weight than they would otherwise. The report stated "we favor the latter view."[46] Where the French report turned to the non-RMA dimension of the need for greater European autonomy, it called for the Eurocorps to be transformed into a projectable rapid reaction force, whose headquarters could command a multi-national force.

For all their differences over Europe's security relationship with the United States, in other words, the reports jointly catalogued a trans-Atlantic capabilities gap stretching from the most exotic war-making hardware to the most traditional skills. German defense and security analysts agreed but drew additional attention to the systemic problem of European defense spending. "The situation would be hilarious if it weren't so tragic," observed Holger Mey of the Institute for Strategic Analysis, "We come out of the Washington and Cologne NATO and [European Union] meetings with strong statements of how Europe has learned its lesson from Kosovo, but the defense budget shows that we haven't learned a thing."[47] Far from providing a catalyst for greater European self-reliance, the prosecution of *Allied Force* was testimony to the remarkable and continuing dependence of a club of the wealthiest nations of Europe on the military capacity of the United States. One of the more thoughtful promoters of European unity, former Swedish Prime Minister and UN Special Envoy to the Balkans, Carl Bildt, observed that the United States is "as much a solo player as ever."[48]

Bildt's statement was in diplomatic terms something of an exaggeration. The campaign took place, after all, against the backdrop of the Anglo-French Summit at Saint-Malô the previous year. The Chirac and Blair governments assumed a more prominent diplomatic role at Rambouillet than had been the case in Bosnia, their respective foreign ministers, Hubert Védrine and Robin Cook, working well together despite the fact that Védrine held Cook's position to be too anti-Serb.[49] The reluctance of the Clinton administration to consider the use of American ground troops prior to a settlement gave a sense of urgency to the Anglo-French initiative.[50] Furthermore, the Europeans together exerted a political influence on the conduct of *Allied Force* that was, on occasion, in excess of their military contribution—an influence occasionally resented by a U.S. military shouldering the lion's share of the load. Along with the United States, lastly, Britain, France, Germany, and Italy were leading participants in the postwar occupation force for Kosovo (KFOR).[51] The higher European diplomatic profile before, during, and after the campaign in Kosovo, however, did little to mitigate the fact that it would not have taken place at all without U.S. leadership and precision firepower.

That being the case, the Clinton administration's reception of the European effort to narrow the capabilities gap was not always consistent with Washington's recurrent concerns about burden-sharing. As the Clinton administration drew to a close, Defense Secretary William Cohen engaged in some frank exchanges with European allies about the Anglo-French initiative for a European defense force. Cohen's remarks included the blunt warning that a European rapid reaction force could make NATO a "relic of the past."[52] In light of the Kosovo experience, it was an odd and somewhat contradictory statement. If its intention was to caution London that a new partnership with France could undermine the "special relationship," it came from an administration that rejected Prime Minister Blair's entreaties for ground war and opted to achieve its military goals with air power alone. It suggested that the United States wanted more defense spending from European governments but not the kind of European self-reliance that would inevitably involve a measure of independence. It was, in effect, a non-policy and at odds with a long-held American conviction that European integration and the Atlantic Alliance were entirely compatible. It is worth recalling that in mid-1950s the Eisenhower administration had considered the NATO solution to European security in some respects second-best to that of a European Defense Community. Eisenhower would have been near euphoric at the prospect of an integrated and effective European force.[53]

A DECADE'S DIVIDEND

This leaves aside the issue as to whether it was prudent in the first place to intervene in a conflict within a sovereign state and in a fashion that essentially interrupted rather than resolved a domestic power struggle.[54] As for NATO's present role in the former Yugoslavia such considerations are academic; the Alliance crossed a threshold in Kosovo that it is by no means obliged to cross elsewhere, but it cannot withdraw prematurely from the role of political trusteeship it has taken on in increasing increments since the failure of the UN and the EU in the secessionist crises of the early 1990s. By the end of the decade the anticipation of an American presidential election served to enliven debate on the scorecard of the post–Cold War era. Humanitarian intervention in general and the Balkan experience in particular prompted critics of the Clinton administration to charge that it had "lurched prematurely toward the mirage of political globalization, conflating American leadership with multilateralism, committing the United States to humanitarian activism ambitious in aims but limited in action."[55] Even the skeptics, nonetheless, noted that the United States had taken on responsibilities in the Balkans that it could not responsibly abandon. They insisted with some justification that a Europe whose unity was worth anything really *ought* to be able to take over entirely while conceding that its governments would likely "scream bloody murder" if actually challenged to do so.[56]

At the end of the 1990s, in other words, the asymmetry in military capacity and the attendant issue of a more just burden-sharing remained a central issue for the expanding Atlantic community. By most measures it had been an extraordinarily successful decade, beginning with German reunification and moving on to the first round of eastern enlargement. It had also involved the formal embrace of an entirely new strategic perspective and its application, however imperfect, to regional crisis-management. In the mid-1990s the Alliance sought to integrate Russia, to the extent that this was possible, rather than to ostracize it. But just as the observation that NATO exhibited a reluctance to lead humanitarian missions and preferred "to act as a subcontractor for the military tasks assigned to it by the UN Security Council" turned out to be premature and was refuted by *Allied Force*, so too did the intervention in Kosovo demonstrate that relations with Moscow were of secondary importance to the consolidation of NATO's position in the Balkans.[57] The Alliance sought neither to alienate nor to appease Moscow. Its members were highly critical of Russia's suppression of revolt in its southern province of Chechnya in 1994; when Russia attacked again in 1999 their response was more muted, but concern over Moscow's vocal objection to *Allied Force* was, with few exceptions, nonexistent.

In the United States a certain fatigue with the role of world leadership was unmistakable. On the political left, the globalization of the international economy came under assault as a plot to exploit Third World labor, export jobs, and subvert environmental protection. After eight years in power, support for the Clinton agenda was eroding in the Democratic camp. On the right, the thematic thrust of the Republican presidential aspirant George W. Bush began to emerge in late 1999. In foreign policy it fastened upon the "Wilsonian overreaching" of the Clinton administration, citing Haiti as an improper use of American military power and pondering the prospects of withdrawing U.S. forces from Kosovo. The best evidence that NATO was headed for troubled waters came in a December meeting of defense ministers in Brussels, where Secretary Cohen again impressed on European governments the need for increased defense spending. It also appeared in the vain attempt by Deputy Secretary of State Strobe Talbott to get NATO Allies to take seriously the need to amend the 1972 ABM Treaty to permit the creation of a limited ballistic missile defense in response to the proliferation of missile technology in the Third World. President Chirac rejected any questioning of the ABM that might upset "strategic equilibria" and trigger a new arms race.[58] In retrospect it might have been prudent to welcome, differences notwithstanding, the outgoing administration's attention to Atlantic affairs. In the camp of presidential candidate Bush, the Alliance hardly figured at all.

NOTES

1. Adam Roberts, "The Changing Form and Function of the Laws of War," in Patrick Mileham and Lee Willett, eds., *Military Ethics for the Expeditionary Era* (London: Royal Institute for International Affairs, 2001), 21.
2. Robert Jackson, *The Global Covenant: Human Conduct in a World of States* (New York: Oxford University Press, 2000), 277–280; Nicholas J. Wheeler, "Reflections on the Legality of NATO's Intervention in Kosovo," *International Journal of Human Rights* 4, no. 3/4 (2000): 145–163.
3. Amir Pasic and Thomas G. Weiss, "The Politics of Rescue: Yugoslavia's Wars and the Humanitarian Impulse," *Ethics & International Affairs* 11 (1997): 105–131.
4. Charles W. Kegley, Jr., "International Peacemaking and Peacekeeping: The Morality of Multinational Measures," *Ethics & International Affairs* 10 (1996): 25–26.
5. Tony Smith, "A Wilsonian World," *World Policy Journal* (Summer 1995): 62–66; Michael Mandelbaum, "Bad Statesman, Good Prophet: Woodrow Wilson and the Post–Cold War Order," *The National Interest* (Summer 2001): 31–41; Robert S. McNamara and James G. Blight, *Wilson's Ghost: Reducing the Risk of Conflict in the Twentieth Century* (New York: Public Affairs, 2001).
6. Adam Roberts, "The Crisis in UN Peacekeeping," *Survival* 36, no. 3 (1994): 93–120.
7. Kegley, "International Peacemaking and Peacekeeping," 44.
8. Roberts, "The Crisis in UN Peacekeeping," 108–109; Christopher M. Gacek, *The Logic of Force: The Dilemma of Limited War in American Foreign Policy* (New York: Columbia University Press, 1994), 313–336; Mark T. Clark, "The Trouble with Collective Security," *Orbis* 39, no. 2 (1995): 237–259.
9. Kegley, "International Peacemaking and Peacekeeping," 35.
10. Brian Finlay and Michael O'Hanlon, "NATO's Underachieving Middle Powers: From Burdenshedding to Burdensharing, *International Peacekeeping* 7, no. 4 (2000): 145–160; also Nicholas Gammer, *From Peacekeeping to Peacemaking: Canada's Response to the Yugoslav Crisis* (Montréal: McGill-Queen's University Press, 2001).
11. Pasic and Weiss, "The Politics of Rescue," 106–107.
12. Ibid., 130–131; Tony Smith, "Morality and the Use of Force in a Unipolar World: The Wilsonian Moment?" *Ethics & International Affairs* 14 (2000): 11–22.
13. Stephen D. Krasner, *Sovereignty: Organized Hypocrisy* (Princeton, NJ: Princeton University Press, 1999), 84–90, 98–103; Michael Howard, *The Invention of Peace: Reflections on War and International Order* (New Haven, CT: Yale University Press, 2000), 103.
14. Michael Ignatieff, "The Virtual Commander," *New Yorker*, August 2, 1999, 36. From the same author, see *The Warrior's Honor: Ethnic War and the Modern Conscience* (London: Chatto & Windus, 1998), 6.
15. David Fromkin, *Kosovo Crossing: American Ideals Meet Reality on the Balkan Battlefields* (New York: Free Press, 1999); John A. Gentry, "The Cancer of Human Rights," *Washington Quarterly* 22, no. 4 (1999): 95–112.
16. *New York Times*, March 25, 1999.
17. OSCE, *Human Rights in Kosovo: As Seen, as Told*, Background 3.

18. Elliot Abrams, "To Fight the Good Fight," *The National Interest*, no. 59 (2000): 70–78. For an expert dissenting view on this issue, see Benjamin S. Lambeth, *NATO's Air War for Kosovo: A Strategic and Operational Assessment* (Santa Monica, CA: RAND, 2001), 140–143.
19. *NATO Press Release* (1999) 041, 24 March 1999.
20. Philip Towle, Cambridge University, "NATO's Strategic Bombardment Campaign against Serbia in 1999," paper presented to the Annual Conference of the Committee on Atlantic Studies, American University of Paris, October 15–17, 1999, 3.
21. Pentagon resistance to using the Apaches was in fact a source of frustration to the SACEUR, General Wesley Clark, in his effort to escalate the campaign against Serb ground forces and thus bring the operation to closure. See *Waging Modern War: Bosnia, Kosovo, and the Future of Combat* (New York: Public Affairs, 2001), 228–242, 278–292.
22. "The Road to Hell: Clinton, Kosovo and Good Intentions," *Washington Post*, April 2, 1999, A29; *Financial Times*, March 27/28, 1999, 1; *Financial Times*, April 22, 1999, 2.
23. *Financial Times*, March 30, 1999, 2.
24. Clark, "The Trouble with Collective Security," 301–302; Ivo Daalder and Michael O'Hanlon, *Winning Ugly: NATO's War to Save Kosovo* (Washington, D.C.: Brookings, 2000), 99–100, 117–125, 130–136, 155–165, 204; Carl Cavanagh Hodge, "Casual War: NATO's Intervention in Kosovo," *Ethics & International Affairs* 14 (2000): 39–54.
25. Transcript of Press Conference given by General Klaus Naumann, Chairman of the Military Committee, NATO HQ, May 4, 1999, <http://www.nato.int/docu/speech/1999/s990504c.htm>.
26. Eliot A. Cohen, "What's Wrong with the American Way of War?" *Wall Street Journal*, March 30, 1999.
27. Michael Howard, "Empires, Nations, and Wars," Yigal Allon Memorial Lectures, University of Tel Aviv, March 1982, reprinted in *The Lessons of History* (New York: Oxford University Press, 1991), 48.
28. Michael Mandelbaum, "A Perfect Failure: NATO's War against Yugoslavia," *Foreign Affairs* 78, no. 5 (1999): 2–8.
29. Smith, "Morality and the Use of Force in a Unipolar World," 22.
30. Clark, *Waging Modern War*, 124, 423–426.
31. Smith, "Morality and the Use of Force in a Unipolar World," 18.
32. *Financial Times*, April 22, 1999, 2.
33. Michael O'Hanlon, *Technological Change and the Future of Warfare* (Washington, D.C.: Brookings, 2000), 28.
34. Grant Hammond, "Myths of the Air War over Serbia," *Aerospace Power Journal* 14, no. 4 (2000): 78–87.
35. Lambeth, *NATO's Air War*, 231.
36. Ibid., 250.
37. John E. Peters, Stuart Johnson, Nora Bensahel, Timothy Liston, Traci Williams, *European Contributions to Operation Allied Force: Implications for Transatlantic Cooperation* (Santa Monica, CA: RAND, 2001), 18–21.
38. Ibid., 22–23.
39. Ibid., 21–22; Lambeth, *NATO's Air War*, 169.
40. Lambeth, *NATO's Air War*, 166–170.
41. Peters, et al., *European Contributions*, 24. For detail on Kosovo airlift requirements, see Lt. Col. Rowayne A. Schatz, USAF, "Theater Airlift Lessons from Kosovo," *Aerospace Power Chronicles*, July 10, 2000, available at <http://www.airpower.maxwell,af.mil/airchronicles/cc/schatz.html>.
42. Quoted in *Air Force Times* 60, no. 15 (November 15, 1999): 29.
43. *Aviation Week & Space Technology*, August 9, 1999, 32; *Aerospace Daily*, August 17, 1999, 252.

44. Deputy Secretary of Defense John Hamre and Senator John Kyl, cited in *Defense Week*, July 19, 1999, 1, 14.
45. House of Commons Select Committee on Defense, Fourteenth Report, *Kosovo: Lessons from the Crisis*, Annex A Summary, Paras. 110–111; Charles G. Cogan, *The Third Option: The Emancipation of European Defense, 1989–2000* (Westport, CT: Praeger, 2001), 104–110.
46. Ibid., Para 202.
47. Douglas Barrie and Jack Hoschouer, "Bundeswehr's Unclear Role Underlies Budget Conflicts," *Defense News*, August 9, 1999, 1.
48. Quoted in Simon Duke, *The Elusive Quest for European Security: From EDC to CFSP* (New York: St. Martin's, 2000), 234. See also Daalder and O'Hanlon, *Winning Ugly*, 147–150, 217–218.
49. *Financial Times*, February 20/21, 1999, 2
50. Cogan, *The Third Option*, 98–99.
51. Ibid., 102–103.
52. *Wall Street Journal*, December 7, 2000, <http://interactive.wsj.co>.
53. See Marc Trachtenberg, *A Constructed Peace: The Making of the European Settlement, 1945–1963* (Princeton, NJ: Princeton University Press, 1999), 95–145.
54. Edward N. Luttwak, "Give War a Chance," *Foreign Affairs* 78, no. 4 (July–August 1999): 36–44.
55. Richard Betts, "The Lesser Evil: The Best Way out of the Balkans," *The National Interest*, no. 64 (2001): 64.
56. Ibid., 63.
57. Kegley, "International Peacemaking and Peacekeeping," 35.
58. *New York Times*, December 3, 1999.

THE DECLINE OF NATO

Whereas *Operation Allied Force* tested Atlantic unity, the international diplomacy leading to *Operation Iraqi Freedom* broke it. Serious consideration of the future of Atlanticism is necessarily concerned with change in the foreign relations of the United States. Though the idea of an Atlantic Community dates to the nineteenth century, official Atlanticism as we have known it was begun by the presidencies of Woodrow Wilson and Franklin Roosevelt and elaborated into an extensive institutional edifice by the succession of Cold War presidents. The future vitality of Atlantic community is likely to depend on American enthusiasm for a broader, unofficial club of like-minded states less centered on cohesion between North America and Western Europe.[1] As a co-author of the Atlantic Charter and architect of much of the post–1945 international order, Franklin Roosevelt is said to have sought two things with regard to Europe. In answer to the failure in the first half of the twentieth century either to insulate the United States from European conflict or to influence European affairs decisively from a distance, his policy was first to bring about Europe's retirement from global affairs. Because he did not want to preside over a patched-up peace and yet was more skeptical than Wilson about the prospects of permanence, he suggested in words as prophetic as they were pragmatic that the United States secure the peace for fifty years "and leave the rest to posterity."[2] The long peace of superpower confrontation over Europe began to unravel in the mid-1980s, after having produced one of the longest periods of great power stability in modern history,[3] and within a decade it was apparent that Europe had indeed been retired as an arbiter of international order.

Today, Washington and many of its traditional European allies exhibit increasingly divergent views about the nature of international society and their respective roles in it. This divergence has been the dominant theme of trans-Atlantic affairs since the events of September 11, 2001, but it bears repeating that its source is not to be found in differing interpretations of the meaning of that day; nor did it begin with the inauguration of George W. Bush in January 2001 as president of the United States. The unassailable fact of the Atlantic Community is that its primary institution, NATO, achieved its historic mission on November 19, 1990, when the *Charter of Paris* formally ended the conflict with the Warsaw Pact on terms wholly favorable to the West. It has since expanded and changed its strategic objectives radically, partly in response to an internal discussion of Europe's future security needs in theory, but much more directly as an answer to the Western aspirations of former Soviet-bloc states, as well as to the serial wars of the Yugoslav succession. An enlarged NATO will continue to play a role in European integration, but its contribution is likely to be tertiary to that of the European Union. The Alliance is furthermore unlikely to maintain its place of privilege among the overseas commitments of the United States. Those commitments are today less conditioned by the etiquette of multilateralism as a principle of diplomacy generally, and are in open conflict with the often sclerotic effect of multilateral institutions in particular.

The administration of George W. Bush initially based its foreign policy on conclusions drawn from the successes and the misadventures of U.S. foreign policy 1990–2000 in Europe, the Middle East, and Asia. The terrorist attacks on the World Trade Center and the Pentagon of September 11, 2001, produced a national security strategy widely touted as a radical departure both from American diplomatic tradition and from the initial priorities of the administration. Indeed, among the more thoughtful critiques of the Bush administration since that day is that it has returned the United States to Wilsonian internationalism with imperial overtones. The United States is today a much closer approximation of the "imperial republic" described by Raymond Aron in the 1970s, its decade of relative decline.[4] Allowing for national differences, however, the diplomacy of contemporary West European governments is as Wilsonian as that of Washington; the United States and its NATO allies disagree on which aspects of the Wilsonian heritage have stood the test of experience and therefore which principles are ascendant. And these principles have been so thoroughly incorporated into and adapted by Euro-Atlantic political and diplomatic culture that tracing them to the twenty-eighth president of the United States is not very useful in understanding the current crisis of Atlanticism.

The crisis is partly the product of assumptions about the erosion of American international dominance that turned out to be spectacularly wrong. The debacle of Vietnam conditioned these assumptions, but so too did assertions of European unity such as the creation of the first EMS in 1978 and the diplomatic prestige enjoyed in the counsels of the G-7 by mature economies such as Germany and Japan. For a time, these developments made the Western camp akin to a community of equals and, simultaneously, produced a substantial literature on the sunset of American hegemony.[5] Among the most popular was the thesis of Paul Kennedy that "imperial over-stretch" had forced the United States to spend too much on military capacity while devoting insufficient investment to such civilian research and development as would permit it to maintain its superiority over competitors like Germany and

Japan.[6] Authors such as Henry Nau and Joseph Nye countered—rather coura-
geously at the time—that American decline was a myth constructed on specious arguments.[7] By the end of a decade in which the Cold War ended and American
national confidence produced growth rates that left Germany and Japan far behind, the trend of the literature had reversed. Best-selling historian Niall Ferguson
asserted that a threat to world peace resided with American "imperial under-stretch"
and "that the leaders of the one state with the economic resources to make the
world a better place lack the guts to do it."[8]

"Any international moral order," wrote E. H. Carr in 1939, "must rest on some
hegemony of power." He hastened to add that such hegemony "is itself a challenge
to those who do not share it and must, if it is to survive, contain an element of give-
and-take, of self-sacrifice on the part of those who have, which will render it toler-
able to the other members of the world community."[9] The give-and-take of
multilateral international institutions established under American leadership after
1945 facilitated the widespread, if not universal, acceptance of the policies that secured Western unity and victory in the Cold War. That victory made liberal internationalism the hegemonic, if not universal, principle of international affairs in
the 1990s.[10] A related phenomenon was the continuing development of multilateral institutions and of multilateral*ism* as an organizing principle of international
affairs. Whether adherence to the principle has mitigated the need for hegemonic power headquartered in Washington is an issue to be dealt with later. A more immediate concern is with the charge that the post–Cold War United States has in fact
failed to be appropriately hegemonic and has, with a foreign policy of half measures,
contributed to an erosion of international order.[11]

A Distinctly American Internationalism

Certainly the Republican candidate for the presidency in election year 2000, George
W. Bush, assumed the need for a course correction of the Clinton years. In November 1999, candidate Bush gave a speech at the Reagan Presidential Library in
Simi Valley, California, in which he advocated a "distinctly American internationalism" and stressed that the goal of his administration would be "to turn this time of
American influence into generations of democratic peace."[12] He then pledged that
this would be achieved by concentrating on enduring national interests and working with democratic allies in Europe and Asia to "extend the peace." The international community made no appearance, except where Bush noted the need for
reform of the United Nations, the World Bank, and the International Monetary
Fund. The NATO alliance made only one appearance. Bush conceded that in order
to be relied upon when needed, "our allies must be respected when they are not."
He cautioned, however, that the United States needs strong European allies who recognize "that sharing the enormous opportunities of Eurasia also means sharing the
burdens and risks of sustaining the peace."[13] The speech devoted much more attention to the future of American relations with China, India, and Russia, possibly

indicating an appetite for great power cooperation over multilateral diplomacy. During the presidential campaign these themes were developed further by Bush's foreign policy advisor, Condoleezza Rice, who chided the Clinton administration for prosecuting the war in Kosovo incompetently; failing to apply military force decisively while burdening the U.S. military indiscriminately with humanitarian missions; and neglecting the national interest in the name of "an illusory international community."[14]

During his first year in office Bush demonstrated a determination to set down clear markers on foreign policy with a populist frankness similar in style to the early months of the Reagan administration. In policy terms, his administration's withdrawal of consent to the 1997 United Nations Kyoto Treaty on Climate Change and its announcement of plans to develop a ballistic missile defense system (BMD) had a troubling effect on trans-Atlantic relations. The Kyoto decision was met with consternation, in part because European governments had been working on revisions to the treaty in response to a demand for more flexibility made by the Clinton administration. But their collective expression of shock was surprising in light of the fact that, at the time, only one of Kyoto's signatories had ratified the treaty, while the U.S. Senate had voted 95–0 against it in the year of its signing. These facts did not stop European governments from registering dismay nor dissuade editorial pages from predicting with more than a dash of hysteria that "nobody has explicitly remarked that Bush's policies could lead to as many deaths as Stalin's or Mao's; but the comparison would not be wholly fanciful."[15] The fact that China and the Asia-Pacific region figured prominently in the administration's view of ballistic missile proliferation and the role BMD assumed in its security policy reflected the diminished importance of Europe. At the Munich Conference on European Security in February 2001, Secretary of Defense Donald Rumsfeld explained to his European audience in characteristically blunt terms that his president approached BMD "as a matter of the President's constitutional responsibility"; no president, he maintained, could "leave the American people undefended against threats that are known to exist."[16] The remarks revived the moral and strategic argument for defense over deterrence initiated by President Reagan when he unveiled the Strategic Defense Initiative (SDI) in March, 1983.[17] The NATO allies were welcome to participate in missile defenses, but the United States would go forward with or without them. In his confirmation hearings before the Senate Armed Services Committee, Rumsfeld had called the ABM Treaty "ancient history."[18] Blunt language aside, the administration's policy was less of a radical departure than its critics claimed. In October 1999, after all, the U.S. Senate had rejected the Comprehensive Test Ban Treaty (CTBT) partly due to the international proliferation of weapons of mass destruction (WMD) and the perception that the new strategic environment favored defense or counter-deployment over deterrence.[19]

Initial European reaction to BMD was less than thoughtful. On the occasion of Bush's first trip to Europe, prominent dailies worried about the possible long-term damage to trans-atlantic relations done by Bush's perceived arrogance and unilateralism, while President Chirac and Chancellor Schröder spoke reflexively of the

ABM Treaty as a "pillar" of the "architecture" of the international strategic balance in a way that was reminiscent of early European reactions to Reagan's SDI.[20] Yet the balance of mutual deterrence underlying superpower relations—ever since the doctrine of massive retaliation articulated by the Eisenhower administration in the 1950s evolved into mutual assured destruction under conditions of nuclear parity in the 1960s and was sanctified in 1972 by the ABM Treaty—was gone. The international strategic environment of United States and allies was now completely different. The existential threat posed by the nuclear and conventional might of the Soviet Union and the Warsaw Pact had been replaced by one in which Europe and North America faced less powerful yet less predictable threats from "rogue" states such as North Korea, Iran, Iraq, and Libya, suspected of developing ballistic missiles armed with WMD. The ABM Treaty had been under attack in the United States ever since President Reagan broached the idea of a Strategic Defense Initiative in 1983.[21] From the outset, mutual deterrence had made a perverse virtue of necessity because an effective defense against nuclear attack did not exist. However, by the mid-1990s the Pentagon was able to report on the emergence of a half-dozen interceptor technologies, preponderantly in theater missile defense (TMD)—for the protection of forward-deployed elements of the United States and allies armed in peace-support operations, for example—that collectively rendered the superpower ABM regime anachronistic. On the one hand, the advance of technology had made Reagan's vision more plausible; on the other, the acquisition of missile technology by a variety of potential adversaries meant that the stable nuclear terror maintained by the United States and Soviet Union was no longer possible.[22]

The missile defense issue also touches on differences in strategic culture. Whereas American and European assessments of the threat of WMD are broadly similar, the United States has traditionally defined threats in terms of a potential adversary's *capabilities* while European governments tend to look to the *intention* of a hostile regime. History and geography have brought Europeans to accept a degree of inescapable vulnerability in which the capabilities of rogue states in Northern Africa and the Middle East constitute an ever-present worry along with terrorism and the spillover effects of regional conflicts. In his first formal attempt to secure support for missile defense from NATO, Secretary of State Colin Powell predictably came up against Franco-German skepticism concerning both the nature of the missile threat to Europe and the irrelevance of the ABM Treaty. However, the assembled European ministers agreed to continue assessing the level of threats, while welcoming from Powell an assurance that the United States did not intend to pull its peacekeeping troops out of the former Yugoslavia.[23] The meeting reflected, in other words, differing security perceptions and priorities, and both sides heard what they wanted to hear.

Beyond the timeless European worry over American disengagement from Europe, there was a deeper concern about the animating spirit of Bush's foreign policy. A recurrent feature of Atlantic relations during the H. W. Bush and Clinton presidencies had been the uses and limits—more critically, the operative definition—of multilateralism. This was somewhat surprising insofar as, after 1945, the United

States had been a primary agent in founding multilateral institutions and promoting multilateral cooperation. Yet to assert that "multilateralism is the calling card of American internationalists, much as unilateralism is of nationalists"[24] is to impose polarities on serious thinking about the conduct of American foreign relations. The United States regards multilateral institutions primarily as *instruments* for accomplishment of specific goals in the international arena, enhancing the legitimacy of actions taken through shared responsibility while mitigating direct cost through shared burdens. The states of Western Europe, by contrast, have been immersed for nearly a half-century in a project of supranational integration in which the institutions of the European Union are regarded as achievements in themselves; because the elaboration of EU institutions and practices are signposts in the work of "building Europe," the procedures and processes by which policies are made are often considered as equal in importance to the thrust of emerging policies.[25]

It should be remembered that the first generation of post-1945 European integrationists regarded the nation-state as a failure and looked to European institutions as a means of restraining national governments from taking the kind of arbitrary self-serving actions that led to two world wars. For West Europeans multilateralism is therefore "hard-wired," insofar as multilateral institutions and processes at the European and international level are arbiters of the content and legitimacy of policy. Symptomatic of these differing approaches to multilateral diplomacy was the transformation of the Conference on Security and Cooperation in Europe (CSCE) into the Organization for Security and Cooperation in Europe (OSCE) in 1995. Whereas the United States and Canada favored the retention of the CSCE, along with the flexibility they deemed inherent in a loose institutional structure, the Europeans prevailed. This outcome was in part an acknowledgement of the EU's enhanced prestige relative to NATO, but it was also a product of the EU bloc's "pronounced penchant for bureaucratization of interstate issues."[26] This bureaucratization is not merely a bi-product of European integration. Rather, attention to the process by which interstate problems are addressed is a core principle of the political ethos of Europeanism. This "masque of institutions" is a diversion from direct discussion of national interests in large part because it was always meant to be.[27] To outsiders the policy dividend of integration initiative seems inversely proportional to the edifice of verbiage and institutional "architecture" erected in its name, but in the history of European integration, "process" has always been a legitimate and often a primary concern.[28]

After the collapse of the Soviet Union, Europeans expected American diplomacy to evolve toward greater reliance on multilateralism.[29] Initially it did, most notably in the massive international coalition Washington put together in 1990–1991 in order to eject Iraqi forces from Kuwait in the name of international law and with the blessing of the United Nations. But Washington came to regard that war as a failure because it did not disarm Iraq, just as it regarded the EU as a security failure for its reliance on American arms to impose peace in Yugoslavia. For the Clinton administration these episodes were evidence that the United States alone possessed the will and capacity to act effectively. The notice given in Clinton's PDD-25, that multilateral operations were to be "placed in proper perspective among the instruments of U.S. foreign policy" and could not be permitted to impair national military strategy, was echoed in Bush's Simi Valley pledge to restore the morale of the U.S. military, "squandered by shrinking resources and multiplying missions," with a foreign policy based on "enduring national interests."[30]

Bush's foreign policy was thus pitched as an alternative to that of his predecessor, but it had drawn formative instruction from Clinton's experience as well as from that of the president's father on the evolution of post–Cold War global affairs. The prosecution of *Operation Desert Storm* and the dispatch of the U.S. military to Somalia in *Operation Restore Hope* were attempts to render service to the international community for which the United States and others paid a high price. The 1991 war against Iraq came at a unique juncture that facilitated the senior Bush's extraordinary effort to fashion an international coalition against Iraq. In another time it would have been called "the organization of world opinion." Washington secured a series of resolutions from the UN Security Council, including *UNSC Resolution 687* authorizing the use of "all necessary means." The White House accorded higher priority to the succession of UN resolutions than it did to congressional approval for going to war.[31] At the point of Iraqi military collapse the United States adhered to the letter of the UN mandate and resisted the temptation to drive on to Baghdad to topple the regime of Saddam Hussein. The resulting paradox—that "an enormous military effort had been undertaken, and yet there was Saddam, still thumbing his nose at the international community"—was entirely the result of a campaign waged on behalf of the international community and according to its express standards. It violated the American military tradition of unconditional surrender and the removal of the political source of aggression.[32] In Somalia the United States again looked beyond its national interest so as to burnish the prestige of the United Nations. When the mission there collapsed in disaster the Clinton administration's perspective on the former Yugoslavia, where by 1999 its European NATO allies were no more self-reliant in the Kosovo crisis than they had been for Bosnia in 1995, adjusted accordingly. Clinton was prepared to dictate *in detail* the terms of NATO's military intervention.

Such was the state of drift between the United States and its European Allies prior to the horrific events of September 11, 2001. Before that day Bush's early months in office occasioned a more assertive rhetoric, yet were nonetheless judged by some as otherwise notable for their continuity with the Clinton years.[33]

WORLD ORDER AND IMPERIAL POWER

To say that all this was changed radically by the unprecedented terrorist attacks in New York City and Washington D.C. that targeted and killed more than 3,000 civilians is an understatement. The day after the attacks, NATO invoked Article V of its founding treaty, the collective defense article, for the first time in its history. The symbolism of collective support was more significant than anything substantive the Alliance could bring to the course of action the United States was about to take in response to its national trauma. That the trauma was deep and enduring was evident in press briefings on the Bush administration's early responses to the attacks. Secretary of State Colin Powell was asked whether the administration's use of the "language of war" carried with it any specific guidelines concerning what the United States was about to do. Powell responded that "the President is speaking about war as a way of focusing the energy of America and the energy of the international community." He added that under the label of "war" the administration would feel free to take a variety of political, diplomatic, economic, financial, and military actions and to use every "tool" and "weapon" at its disposal.[34] What was taking place was a shift in the normative dialogue of international affairs. The jargon of the carefully organized insincerity of the 1990s was being forced to cohabit a sentence with words expressing both the mood of the administration and the policy to which it was now compelled.[35] In the following weeks the administration's diplomatic efforts to build international support for military action against al-Qaeda terrorist bases and the Taliban regime in Afghanistan made the governments of Pakistan, Uzbekistan, Saudi Arabia, and Egypt more important than any Atlantic ally. In early October, nonetheless, NATO Airborne Warning and Control Systems (AWACS) aircraft from Geilenkirchen, Germany, were sent to Oklahoma to assist in the defense of North American airspace in order to free U.S. aircraft for deployment abroad. Britain was participating in air strikes in Afghanistan, while Australia, Canada, France, and Germany had pledged forces for operations there.

Germany's parliamentary debate on Afghanistan was revealing. On November 6, 2001, Chancellor Gerhard Schröder announced that Berlin would be putting 3,900 *Bundeswehr* troops, including commando units, at the disposal of the American-led war against terrorism. With this historic decision, he observed, his government was taking a step critical to Germany's future role in international affairs.[36] To the assembled parliamentarians Schröder argued that the preliminary steps in Germany's military engagement had already been taken in United Nations *Resolution 1368*, acknowledging the American right of self-defense based on Article 51 of the UN Charter, as well as in the NATO Council's invocation of Article V of the North Atlantic Treaty. The decision to place German troops at the disposal of the war effort flowed as a natural material consequence of those principles and commitments. He observed further that alliance solidarity, of which the Bonn republic had for decades been a principal beneficiary, was not a one-way street; he heaped scorn on critics of the American effort in Afghanistan who implied that European support ought to be conditioned on the chances of success; and he denied a direct relationship between Al Qaeda's terrorist activities and the decades-long Middle East conflict.[37]

Schröder's foreign minister, Joschka Fischer, then argued that the critical investment Germany had now to make was in a multilateral diplomacy of responsibility for Afghanistan's future, the first installment of which would necessarily be military. German nonparticipation could only weaken Europe's collective influence. But more important still was the fact that, whereas the Bush administration had been on a "step by step" course of unilateralism before September 11, the war against terrorism had shunted Washington back onto a multilateralist track. "For me," said Fischer, "one of the great lessons of September 11 was that we cannot permit the United States to be pushed back toward unilateralism."[38] Germany had an obligation to the United States that could not be shirked, but the crisis was also an opportunity for Europeans to steer the Bush administration away from the unilateral temptations inherent in American hegemony. Four days later Fischer pledged German support for a strengthened United Nations to the General Assembly and cited "cooperation, solidarity, and multilateralism" as the key principles for the fight against terrorism; eight days later the Schröder government made its policy on Afghanistan a question of the confidence of the German parliament and survived by ten votes.[39]

The speed and outcome of the Afghan campaign, however, showcased the unavoidable *fact* of American hegemony. The only significant help from a NATO ally in the military campaign came, not surprisingly, from Britain. The Bush administration otherwise sought to maximize its flexibility of action by not seeking an explicit mandate from the UN Security Council and by keeping military units from allied countries to a minimum. To the extent that Britain offered SAS troops, Tornado bombers, and useful intelligence while the cooperation of neighboring states facilitated operations inside Afghanistan, the campaign was not strictly unilateral. Still, the mission determined the coalition in an American military effort featuring select allies. The rapid collapse of the Taliban regime in a campaign scrupulously mindful of civilian casualties—aided by the use of weaponry capable of unprecedented discrimination—demonstrated again the surgical power projection of which the U.S. military is capable. The war occasioned from Paul Kennedy the concession that, far from "overstretch," the relationship of the United States to the world around it was one of dominance that even Imperial Rome had never approached.[40] Unlike NATO's "virtual war" for Kosovo, moreover, the Afghan campaign defined expeditionary warfare for the new century. It involved precision weapons and men on horseback; it incorporated ground troops as an invasion and occupation forces to root out the vestiges of al Qaeda and the Taliban and to protect the fledgling government of President Hamid Karzai from terrorists and warlords. Gone was the injunction against "nation-building" under the Clinton administration, but gone too was the deference for traditional multilateral institutions. "We are a long way down a path," noted an interpretation of these changes, "that looks suspiciously like a Roman road."[41]

THE FAILURE OF ATLANTIC UNITY

The military success of the Afghan campaign emboldened the Bush administration and sharpened the revisions to its initial foreign policy objectives prompted by September 11 attacks. In his 2002 State of the Union Address the president observed that "the American flag flies again over our embassy in Kabul" and in serving notice on the work yet to be done cited three rogue regimes, in Iran, Iraq, and North Korea, as an "axis of evil" arming terrorists and themselves with WMD.[42] Criticisms of Bush's remarks in the United States and Europe tended to object to Manichean rhetoric foremost, but there was accompanying awareness that something bigger was underway. This was confirmed in Bush's speech to the 2002 graduating class of West Point Military Academy, wherein he maintained that the Cold War principles of containment and deterrence had lost their utility to U.S. strategic doctrine, because terrorists with no territory to defend could not be deterred, just as rogue states prepared both to use WMD or supply terrorists could not be contained. While the administration's commitment to missile defenses was not downgraded—in part because it was itself the product of the obsolescence of deterrence—its place in the rank order of security priorities had obviously slipped. "The war on terror will not be won on the defensive," Bush warned, "we must take the battle to the enemy, disrupt his plans, and confront the worst threats before they emerge."[43]

Apprehension that Washington regarded Cold War institutions too as obsolete prompted NATO Secretary General Lord Robertson to claim the Alliance's continuing relevance. For the Eastern European applicants to NATO this was certainly true, as preparations were made for the Alliance's annual conference scheduled for November in Prague. The Alliance was about to undertake the largest single enlargement of its history—extending membership invitations to Bulgaria, Estonia, Latvia, Lithuania, Romania, Slovakia, and Slovenia—and yet experienced no debate akin to that which eventually brought in the Visegrad states in the mid-1990s.

Indeed, NATO enlargement hardly had Washington's attention. When, in response to the mounting violence between Israel and the Palestinians, President Bush called for the ouster of Yasser Arafat as leader of the Palestinian Authority, along with the demand that a democratically accountable alternative be found, he was anointed a "Wilsonian" in the conservative press and advised that the real test of the Bush Doctrine would be its application to Iraq.[44] That doctrine still awaited a more comprehensive articulation, but the administration seemed to draw a sense of vindication from its critics as much as from its supporters. In late August Secretary of Defense Rumsfeld indicated that the United States would not necessarily wait for international approval for military action in taking up the unfinished work of *Operation Desert Storm*.[45]

European government spokesmen were joined by the elite of European journalism in lamenting the confidence of "the Bushists" in Washington that they can put together a coalition-of-the-willing to confront Iraq rather than work through established institutions.[46] Another camp countered that American assertiveness was hardly surprising given that Turkey, China, India, and Japan were now more critical to U.S. geostrategic calculations than Western Europe; the European Union had since 1989 come to resemble less an emerging great power than an oversized shopping mall, on whose political maturation the United States could wait no longer.[47] From European governments, separately and in chorus, Washington meanwhile received expressions of concern over the treatment of Al Qaeda prisoners held at Guantanamo Bay; an insistence that the war on terrorism and the resolution of

Israeli-Palestinian conflict are necessarily linked; a call for a return of UN weapons inspectors to Iraq; and the demand that the Bush administration seek a UN resolution mandating the use of force against Iraq—above and beyond the series of Security Council resolutions dating to 1990–1991. Alone among European leaders, Prime Minister Blair defended the option of military action against the regime in Baghdad, in the of face strong opposition from within his own Labour Party and British public opinion. In a ninety-minute press conference, Blair reminded the assembled journalists of the nature of the Iraqi regime and its continuing efforts to develop WMD; "some of the talk about this in the past few weeks I have to say has astonished me," he chided, "you would think that we were dealing with some benign little democracy out in Iraq."[48] At the time, the published expert verdict on Iraq's weapons program, widely available to any interested public, tended to support Blair's position.[49]

But it counted for little in the fever of the German 2002 general election campaign in which the chancellor essentially reversed the position of his government at the time of the confidence vote in November 2001. In an unusually close contest in which his Social Democratic/Green coalition was vulnerable on domestic issues, Schröder's critical stance on the Bush administration's Iraq policy elicited sufficient positive response from opinion polls to tempt the chancellor into positions he might otherwise never have taken. In a televised debate against the Christian Democrat challenger, Edmund Stoiber, Schröder declared that under his leadership Germany would not take part in military action against Iraq even if Washington were to secure a UN mandate—an extraordinarily preemptive statement from the leader of a country where multilateralism is the prerequisite of all legitimate foreign policy. Yet Schröder took another step by warning that in the event of a U.S. attack on Iraq his government would withdraw Germany's small nuclear, chemical, and biological warfare unit stationed in Kuwait in support of operations in Afghanistan. In a stroke, the chancellor portrayed war against Iraq as nearly inevitable, stoked the fires of popular anti-Americanism in Germany, and in effect declared the United Nations irrelevant to Berlin's policy.[50] Admittedly, German support for the military effort in Afghanistan could not be assumed to prefigure approval for a war against Iraq. Schröder's explicit rejection of military action in advance of any Security Council debate on the issue, however, precluded any unified European backing for a UN-mandated threat of force against Baghdad. The parliamentary opposition pointed to press reports in which UN weapons inspectors are said to have judged the chancellor's categorical rejection of the use of force as "crazy" because it reduced diplomatic pressure on Baghdad.[51] Even balanced assessments that judged the Bush administration arrogant also accused the Schröder government of cheap and tasteless anti-Americanism. Others, not so concerned with balance, were much less charitable. The editor of the business weekly *Wirtschaftswoche* judged the prospect of an American war on Iraq a "service to all of humanity" and the attempt to hinder it "another chapter from the madhouse of German history."[52]

At a meeting of European foreign ministers in Elsinore, Denmark, British foreign secretary Jack Straw cultivated support from Spain and the Netherlands for military measures contingent on a serious effort by Washington to explore all possibilities at the United Nations. At the same meeting France's foreign minister, Dominique de Villepin, agreed that the threat of force was necessary in order to motivate Baghdad to admit weapons inspectors. A week later French defense minister, Michèle Alliot-Marie, conceded that France might join a UN-mandated attack on Iraq in spite of public opposition, thereby prompting one security analyst to observe that the three most important countries in the European Union now had three distinct positions on Iraq and that Europe was effectively absent from the international stage.[53]

It was into this atmosphere that the Bush administration officially released its national security doctrine, certainly among the most coherent articulations of foreign policy goals since the advent of containment in 1947 and potentially as significant.[54] A furor arose over the document's declaration that the United States was henceforth prepared to act preemptively to thwart the use of WMD against itself or its allies,[55] a somewhat false controversy in that preemptive military action was not entirely novel in the history of American foreign relations. Of greater importance was the cautioning assurance that "while the United States will constantly strive to enlist the support of the international community, we will not hesitate to act alone" combined with the statement in the document's overview that "the unprecedented and unequaled" strength of the United States "*must* be used to promote a balance of power that favors freedom" and indeed "look outward for possibilities to expand liberty."[56] The sense of an obligation to the spread of liberty emanating from the very fact of American power—in Bush's West Point speech, his insistence on a democratically accountable Palestinian leadership, and now in the *National Security Strategy*—was greeted simultaneously as imperial and Wilsonian.[57] But if one of Wilson's principles, the international vitality of democracy, was now at the core of U.S. national security policy, another, the organization of world opinion, was on trial. This became apparent in Bush's September 12 address to the UN General Assembly in which he reviewed the hope initially placed in the United Nations as a fundamental improvement on the League and proceeded to outline the case for UN action against Iraq, starting with its 1990 invasion of Kuwait and moving on to its failure to meet its obligations under successive UN resolutions over the next twelve years. Saddam Hussein's Iraq, Bush pointed out, was "exactly the kind of aggressive threat the United Nations was born to confront." He added that unless Baghdad fulfilled the UN resolutions, "a regime that has lost its legitimacy will also lose its power." The United Nations had before it the authority and opportunity to make a stand, but the assembled delegates were put on notice that "by heritage and by choice, the United States of America will make that stand."[58]

With *Resolution 1441*, adopted on November 8 by a 15–0 vote in the Security Council, the United Nations was officially on track in holding Hussein's regime accountable for its noncompliance with previous resolutions, particularly its failure to provide weapons inspectors unimpeded, unconditional, and unrestricted access to any and all of its facilities capable of producing or storing WMD. The resolution reiterated the warning that Iraq "will face serious consequences as a result of its continued violations of its obligations" and demanded that Baghdad provide the United Nations

Monitoring, Verification and Inspection Commission (UNMOVIC) and the International Atomic Energy Agency (IAEA) with immediate access. Thus, the first major project of enforced disarmament since the destruction of the axis forces in 1945 was to pick up where it had sputtered to a stop in 1998.[59] Despite Iraqi delays and obstructions from the outset, the inspection effort had achieved many of the UN objectives by the end of 1993. The strength of the UN position was somewhat undermined by its imposition of punitive economic sanctions and the extraordinary suffering caused to ordinary Iraqis over the course of the decade. While ultimate moral responsibility for this suffering remained with Saddam Hussein, the notion that sanctions represented a "soft option" alternative to compelling military force was valid only for the states imposing them; although by 1990 advanced weaponry facilitated impressive precision and discrimination in the application of violence, sanctions remained a blunt instrument usually much more effective in bringing misery to innocents than in wringing compliance from tyrants.[60] It was nevertheless the potential of Iraq's biological, chemical, and nuclear weapons, plus the record of Saddam Hussein's serial territorial aggressions, that set the Security Council's agenda in late 2002 and early 2003. As long as he remained in power, it was only prudent to assume the worst as to his intentions.[61]

The evidence in support of such an assumption had mounted steadily through the 1990s. Two years after the defeat of 1991, Iraqi newspapers reiterated Baghdad's claim to Kuwait. When Britain, France, and the United States belatedly banned Iraqi aircraft from attacking Shiite rebels in the south, Baghdad's response was to deploy SAM missiles to the no-fly zone to threaten allied aircraft enforcing it. Confrontations between allied aircraft and Iraqi air defenses over the southern and northern no-fly zones became routine. Early in 1993 British and American bombers and warships attacked Iraqi targets after Baghdad stopped flights of UN aircraft supporting the inspections regime. The inspections regime broke down entirely in December 1998, when Anglo-American aircraft launched *Operation Desert Fox* after another round of Iraqi obstruction. France, Russia, and China withdrew their support for the enforcement of Security Council resolutions for which they, as permanent members, bore a special responsibility.[62]

In the fall of 2002 there was no doubt that the Bush administration meant to deal decisively with Iraq. Bush himself pressed this point at the Prague NATO Summit, which made official the second post–Cold War enlargement, noting additionally that unless the Alliance developed capabilities permitting it to operate outside Europe its relevance to emerging security challenges would be marginal.[63] The critical question was whether the *Resolution 1441* gave the green light to military action in the event of a continuation of the tactics Baghdad had applied to the inspections from 1991 to 1998. The administration believed that with 1441 the Security Council had rededicated itself to the demands placed on Baghdad in 1991 along with consequences stipulated.

But when France repeated its previous position that an additional resolution would be needed in order to define the exact consequences of non-compliance with 1441 — in effect gravitating toward Germany's position — and the Blair government

urged European sympathy for Washington's position, the stage was set for the destruction of UN and NATO unity. Because Britain's efforts had been critical to the
passage of 1441, the Bush administration was willing to accommodate Blair's insistence on Security Council approval but would brook no obstruction or delay
that undermined the intimidatory value of what Bush saw as a UN ultimatum directed at Baghdad. Blair reciprocated by fixing his signature to an open letter of eight
European leaders backing Washington's position. This action was received in Paris
as a challenge to Franco-German leadership of Europe, coming as it did a week after
Bush's Secretary of Defense, Donald Rumsfeld, had argued that in an expanding
Atlantic Alliance, Paris and Berlin represented only the "old Europe."

At this point the Chirac government lost its equilibrium, reacting to the spirit
of Rumsfeld's remarks rather than the substance of Secretary of State Colin Powell's
arguments to the Security Council. The result was that, at the point where the Bush
administration had reluctantly returned Washington's Iraq diplomacy to United Nations, Powell's soft-spoken multilateralism in the Security Council was rewarded
with less rather than more sympathy for the administration's goals from its French
ally. Evidence of Washington's growing impatience with the inspection process occasioned a French proposal to triple the number of inspectors; this was backed by
Germany and Russia and then fleshed out into a proposal that all Iraq be turned into
a UN protectorate, presumably with Baghdad's cooperation. A threshold of an altogether different order was crossed, however, when France, Germany and Belgium
blocked NATO from activating plans for the defense of Turkey against attack from
Iraq in the event of war. Turkey invoked Article IV of the North Atlantic Treaty—
according to which member-states are to consult whenever any of their number ex-
presses concern for its territorial integrity, political independence, or security—but
was again refused.[64] French Foreign Minister Dominique de Villepin implied furthermore that France in effect spoke for Europe at the United Nations—"like the
continent to which it belonged"—while President Chirac used the occasion of the
EU summit in Brussels in mid-February to chide aspiring member-states for their
"childish and irresponsible" joint statements in support of Washington.[65] Both Powell and British Foreign Secretary Jack Straw accused France of going wobbly, the latter rather pointedly with the remark that "a peaceful solution could only be achieved
if the Council held its nerve, gave meaning to its word and ensured that Iraq would
face the consequences of its actions."[66] When, in the last week of February 2003, the
United States, Britain, and Spain tabled a resolution laying the legal groundwork for
military action while France and Germany had tabled an alternative calling for a
strengthened weapons inspection regime, the division not only of NATO but also
of the EU was almost complete. The circle was squared with Turkey's refusal to
allow U.S. troops to invade Northern Iraq from Turkish territory.

Under pressure from within his own parliamentary majority and faced with
antiwar demonstrations on the streets of London, Prime Minister Blair defended
the use of military force against Iraq by arguing that France—a NATO ally, EU
member, and permanent seat on the UN Security Council—had eliminated any
chance of compelling cooperation from Baghdad with its announcement that it

intended to veto a resolution containing an ultimatum.[67] France had abdicated on its responsibility as a great power to act in concert with other permanent members of the Security Council to bring a rogue regime to heel with the threat of force. While Blair's interpretation of Baghdad's behavior over the history of Saddam Hussein's regime amounted to a case for just war, his peroration predicted that a failure on Britain's part to do the right thing would simultaneously drive the United States to unilateralism and "turn the United Nations back into a talking shop."[68] No less a figure than Jacques Delors, whose vision and administrative drive had pushed the project of European integration from the Single European Act of 1985 to the Maastricht Summit of 1991, agreed with Blair in the essentials. In his judgment Chirac had led France into a diplomatic *cul de sac* through an obstructionist policy, not least of all because Europe was clearly not united behind France's position. The Iraq crisis had demonstrated further that a common European foreign policy would remain a vain hope for the next twenty years.[69] Possibly the most damning verdict, returned before France had promised to veto a second resolution, was that Chirac had violated Gaullist principles and had done so, absurdly, to celebrate the symbolism of Franco-German unity on the fortieth anniversary of the Elysée Treaty. It was observed that if Chirac thought himself closer to the European mainstream than Tony Blair, Silvio Berlusconi, or José Maria Aznar, then it was not the mainstream Washington wanted to hear from, and it was advised that "the way to influence a U.S. empire, if only at the margin, is through critical support, not abstention."[70]

   The withdrawal of the second resolution ended the weapons inspections and the Security Council's role in the crisis, setting the stage for an Anglo-American invasion of Iraq and a remarkably swift defeat of its armed forces. As the major fighting drew to a close, a review of the past six months of diplomacy tempted the conclusion that both the regime of Saddam Hussein and the Atlantic Alliance lay in the rubble of Baghdad and that a good part of the blame lay not with the swagger of the Bush administration.[71] There is no disputing that fact that the Bush administration's assertiveness — before and after September 11, 2001 — did a good deal to arouse the pique of its NATO allies. But it is a superficial judgment to place primary responsibility for the wreckage at the steps of the White House or to say in effect that "more Powell and less Rumsfeld" would have made a critical difference. What was made obvious by the Iraq crisis had been true before it began or indeed before Bush became president: that the radically changed conditions of the NATO allies had altered their respective strategic priorities. Admittedly, those priorities had changed more radically for the United States than any of the other member states. At Prague Bush had called for allies prepared to cooperate militarily with the United States beyond the frontiers of Europe and had found that only one old ally, Britain, and one new ally, Poland, were prepared to follow. At base, however, France and Germany had demonstrated that they resented Washington's assumptions concerning their obligations to an alliance in which the American pacifier was no longer of existential importance. For its part, the United States would not accept the constraint of multilateral institutions — in the new age of rogue regimes, proliferation, and asymmetric threats — which could not constrain Iraq. A multilateralist diplomacy that served primarily to thwart, restrain, or delay decisive action by the world's leading democracy against a threat to international order was fast becoming the errand boy of appeasement. European allies who deemed American unilateral action against Iraq a greater threat to the delicate construct of international law than Baghdad's repeated flouting of the same had chosen process over policy.

There had been no "rush to war" or "drive to preemption." During the UN debate both American and European academic circles scoffed at Bush's use of the word "evil" in reference to Iraq, but at least two years before the president dared to state the self-evident, former UN weapons inspector Richard Butler had pondered Saddam Hussein's continuing defiance of Security Council Resolutions as a "triumph of evil."[72] Integral to that defiance were repeated violations of the cease-fire provisions of the 1991 Security Council Resolution 687 by Iraqi air defense installations firing upon British and American aircraft enforcing the northern and southern no-fly zones. Viewed from this perspective, the decision to go to war had been taken in Baghdad in August 1990 and the terms of armistice in 1991 never truly accepted.[73] Tony Blair's March 18 arguments to the Commons devoted considerable attention to the "regime factor" in Iraq, noting that too many glib comparisons to the 1930s had been made, yet conceding that they were unavoidable. Indeed, Saddam's record of domestic repression, territorial aggression, and experimental genocide on his own people was more damning than Hitler's record up to the invasion of Poland in September 1939, and Blair's was in substance a strong argument that action against such a regime to deny it the destructive capacity it sought would not violate the defense-against-aggression principle of just war.[74] Given the deeper sources of disunity within the Alliance exposed by the UN debate on Iraq, just war arguments are for our purposes here nonetheless quaintly beside the point. It is to these sources and to the future prospects of the Atlanticism that the concluding chapter turns.

NOTES

1. Ira Straus, "Atlantic Federation and the Expanding Atlantic Nucleus," *Peace & Change* 24, no. 3 (1999): 299.
2. Quoted in John Lamberton Harper, *American Visions of Europe: Franklin Roosevelt, George F. Kennan, and Dean Acheson* (New York: Cambridge University Press, 1994), 79.
3. John Lewis Gaddis, *The Long Peace: Inquiries into the History of the Cold War* (New York: Oxford University Press, 1987), 245.
4. Edward Rhodes, "The Imperial Logic of Bush's Liberal Agenda," *Survival* 45, no. 1 (2003): 131–154; Raymond Aron, *The Imperial Republic: The United States and the World, 1945–1973*, trans. Frank Jellinek (Cambridge: Winthrop, 1973).
5. A superb review of the literature is that of Michael Cox, "September 11th and U.S. Hegemony—Or Will the 21st Century Be American Too?" *International Studies Perspectives* 3, no. 1 (2002): 53–70. A representative sampling includes H. Brandon, *The Retreat of American Power* (New York: Doubleday, 1973); D. Calleo, *Beyond American Hegemony: The Future of the Western Alliance* (New York: Basic Books, 1987); R. O.

Keohane, *After Hegemony: Cooperation and Discord in the World Political Economy* (Princeton, NJ: Princeton University Press, 1984); K. A. Oye, D. Rothchild, and R. J. Lieber, eds., *Eagle Entangled: U.S. Foreign Policy in a Complex World* (New York: Longman, 1979).

6. Paul Kennedy, *The Rise and Fall of the Great Powers: Economic Change and Military Conflict from 1500 to 2000* (London: Unwin Hyman, 1988), 689.

7. Henry Nau, *The Myth of America's Decline: Leading the World into the 1990s* (New York: Oxford University Press, 1990); J. S. Nye, Jr., *Bound to Lead: The Changing Nature of American Power* (New York: Basic Books, 1990).

8. Niall Ferguson, *The Cash Nexus: Money and Power in the Modern World, 1700–2000* (New York: Basic Books, 2001), 390–418.

9. E. H. Carr, *The Twenty Years's Crisis, 1919–1939* (London: Macmillan, 1939), 168. *Hegemony* here is used in the same classical sense as Cox, implying "overwhelming power but power employed and deployed to lead others," 55.

10. Michael Mandelbaum, *The Ideas That Conquered the World: Peace, Democracy and Free Markets in the Twenty-First Century* (New York: Public Affairs, 2002), 28.

11. Ferguson, *The Cash Nexus*, 418; Donald Kagan and Frederick W. Kagan, *While America Sleeps: Self-Delusion, Military Weakness, and the Threat to Peace Today* (New York: St. Martin's, 2000), 400–435.

12. George W. Bush, "A Distinctly American Internationalism," Ronald Reagan Presidential Library, Simi Valley, California, November 19, 1999, <http://www.mtholyoke.edu/acad/intrel/bush/wspeech.htm>.

13. Ibid.

14. Condoleezza Rice, "Promoting the National Interest," *Foreign Affairs* 79, no. 1 (2000): 45–62.

15. *New Statesman*, April 9, 2001, 4.

16. Remarks as delivered by Secretary of Defense Donald H. Rumsfeld, Munich, Germany, Saturday, February 3, 2001.

17. On Reagan's thinking, see George P. Schultz, *Turmoil and Triumph: My Years as Secretary of State* (New York: Charles Scribner's, 1993), 246–264.

18. Ivo H. Daalder, James Goldgeier, and James M. Lindsay, "Deploying NMD: Not Whether, But How," *Survival* 42, no. 1 (Spring 2000): 6–28; *CQ Weekly*, January 13, 2001, 125.

19. Philip Towle, "Missile Defenses: Implications for NATO," in Carl C. Hodge, ed., *NATO for a New Century: Atlanticism and European Security* (Westport, CT: Praeger, 2002), 123–134; David Goldfischer, *The Best Defense: Policy Alternatives for U.S. Nuclear Security from the 1950s to the 1990s* (Ithaca, NY: Cornell University Press, 1993); Roger Handberg, *Ballistic Missile Defense and the Future of American Security* (Westport, CT: Praeger, 2002). The term *Weapons of Mass Destruction* refers broadly to nuclear weapons as well as chemical, biological, and nerve agents capable of destroying whole populations. Because of the ease and cheapness with which such weapons can be developed they are the choice of weak and militarily challenged nations or terrorist organizations. Although unreliable, unpredictable, and frequently awkward and difficult to use, there is an international consensus that the killing capacity of biological, chemical, and nerve agents makes them the moral equivalent of nuclear weapons. Colin S. Gray, *Modern Strategy* (New York: Oxford University Press, 1999), 350–353.

20. Stefan Kornelius, "Bush auf dem Boden," *Süddeutsche Zeitung*, June 14, 2001, 4; *The Economist*, June, 16, 2001, 29–30; Karl-Heinz Kamp, "The Transatlantic NMD Debate: Skip Ridiculous Arguments," *RUSI Newsbrief* 20, no. 11 (November 2000): 3–5.

21. See Colin Gray's commentary in Ashton B. Carter and David N. Schwartz, eds., *Ballistic Missile Defense* (Washington, D.C.: Brookings, 1984), 400.

22. "Ballistic Missile Defense: 12 Years of Achievement," prepared statement of Lt. Gen. Malcolm R. O'Neill, USA, Director, Ballistic Missile Defense Organization, to the

House National Security Committee, April 4, 1995. *Defense Issues* 10, no. 37, available at <http://www.defenselink.mil/speeches/1995/19950404-oneill.html>; Keith B. Payne, "The Case for National Missile Defense," *Orbis* 44, no. 2 (2000): 187–196.

23. Camille Grand, "Missile Defense: The View from the Other Side of the Atlantic," *Arms Control Today* (September 2000): 13–14; Marc Lacey, "Powell Fails to Persuade NATO on Antimissile Plan," *New York Times*, May 30, 2001.

24. Compare Henry Nau, *At Home Abroad: Identity and Power in American Foreign Policy* (Ithaca, NY: Cornell University Press, 2002), 57, with Walter Russell Mead, *Special Providence: American Foreign Policy and How It Changed the World* (New York: Alfred A. Knopf, 2001), 266–267.

25. Daniel Nelson, "Transatlantic Transmutations," *Washington Quarterly* 25, no. 4 (2002): 51–66.

26. Cathal J. Nolan, "The OSCE: Nonmilitary Dimensions of Cooperative Security in Europe," in Carl C. Hodge, ed., *Redefining European Security* (New York: Garland, 1999), 314.

27. Philip Zelikow, "The Masque of Institutions," in Philip H. Gordon, ed., *NATO's Transformation: The Changing Shape of the Atlantic Alliance* (Lanham, MD: Rowman & Littlefield, 1997), 88.

28. Patrick M. Morgan, "Multilateralism and Security: Prospects in Europe," in John Gerard Ruggie, *Multilateralism Matters: The Theory and Praxis of an Institutional Form* (New York: Columbia University Press, 1993), 346.

29. Nelson, "Transatlantic Transmutations," 60.

30. Compare the Clinton administration's Policy on Reforming Multilateral Peace Operations (PDD-25) <http://www.fas.org/irp/offdocs/pdd25.htm> with Governor George W. Bush, "A Distinctly American Internationalism."

31. Lawrence Freedman and Efraim Karsh, *The Gulf Conflict, 1990–1991: Diplomacy and War in the New World Order* (Princeton, NJ: Princeton University Press, 1993), 228–295.

32. Ibid., 438–439.

33. Andrew J. Bacevich, "Different Drummers, Same Drum," *The National Interest*, no. 64 (2001): 67–77.

34. U.S. Department of State, Secretary, On-the-Record Briefing, Colin L. Powell Remarks to the Press, Washington, D.C., September 13, 2001, <http://www.state.gov/secretary/rm/2001/4910.htm>.

35. The nature of the normative dialogue of contemporary international affairs is brilliantly analyzed by Robert Jackson, *The Global Covenant: Human in a World of States* (New York: Oxford University Press, 2000), 1–25.

36. *Berliner Morgenpost*, November 7, 2001, 1

37. Deutscher Bundestag, *Stenographische Berichte*, 198 Sitzung, 8 November 2001.

38. Ibid.

39. Rede von Bundesaußenminister Fischer vor der 56. Generalversammlung der VN in New York an 12 November 2001, <http://www.auswaertiges-amt.de/www/de/aussenpolitik/ausgabe-archiv>; *Süddeutsche Zeitung*, November 16, 2001.

40. Paul Kennedy, "The Eagle has Landed," *Financial Times*, February 3, 2002; Robert S. Litwak, "The Imperial Republic after 9/11," *Wilson Quarterly* 26, no. 3 (2002): 76–83.

41. Thomas W. McShane, "Blame It on the Romans: Pax Americana and the Rule of Law," *Parameters* 32, no. 2 (2002), 71.

42. The President's State of the Union Address, The United States Capital, Washington, D.C., January 29, 2002, <http://www.whitehouse.gov/news/releases/2002/01>.

43. Remarks by the president at 2002 Graduation Exercise of the United States Military Academy, West Point, New York, June 1, 2002, <http://www.whitehouse.gov/news/releases/2002/06>.

44. Max Boot, "George W. Bush: The 'W' Stands for Woodrow," *Wall Street Journal*, July 1, 2002.

45. *Financial Times*, August 28, 2002.
46. Josef Joffe, "Neue Weltordnung," *Die Zeit*, Politik, 07/2002; also Bruce Stokes, "Our Allies New Slogan: Constrain America," *National Journal* 34/24 (June 15, 2002): 1803.
47. Egon Bahr, "Amerika schaut in die Zukunft, Europa in die Vergangenheit," *Die Welt*, May 15, 2002.
48. *Financial Times*, September 2, 2002; *Washington Post*, September 3, 2002.
49. See Richard Butler, *The Greatest Threat: Iraq's Weapons of Mass Destruction and the Crisis of Global Security* (New York: Public Affairs, 2001); Kenneth M. Pollack, *The Threatening Storm: The Case for Invading Iraq* (New York: Random House, 2002).
50. Nico Fried, "Die Bagdad-Wahl," *Süddeutsche Zeitung*, September 19, 2002; *Berliner Morgenpost*, September 9, 2002; *Financial Times*, September 5, 2002; Helmut Jung, "Analyse der Bundestagswahl 2002," *Politische Studien* 54, no. 387 (2003): 21–33.
51. Robert Gerald Livingston, "A Rare Opportunity for the German Opposition," *Financial Times*, February 24, 2003; Deutscher Bundestag, 37 Sitzung, April 3, 2003; Jochen Bittner and Reiner Luyken, "Die deutsche Schuld am Krieg," *Die Zeit* 14, 2003.
52. Stefan Baron, "The Real Meaning of the War in Iraq," *Wirtschaftswoche* 13, March 20, 2003, available at <http://www.aicgs.org/c/baron2.shtml>; Gert Krell, "Arroganz der Macht, Arroganz der Ohnmacht: Der Irak, die Weltordnungspolitik der USA und die transatlantischen Beziehungen," HSFK-Report 1/2003, Hessische Stiftung Friedens und Konfliktforschung.
53. François Heisbourg quoted in *Neue Zürcher Zeitung*, September 17, 2002. President Chirac stipulated that an attack on Iraq should be preceded by two resolutions, one demanding the return of UN weapons inspectors and a second to decide what to do should the inspectors be prevented from completing their work, *Financial Times*, September 10, 2002.
54. *The National Security Strategy of the United States of America*, September 2002.
55. Ibid., 15.
56. Ibid., 1, 3, 15.
57. Fareed Zakaria, "Our Way," *New Yorker*, October 14, 2002, 72–81; Rhodes, "The Imperial Logic of Bush's Liberal Agenda," 131–154.
58. Remarks by the president in Address to the United Nations General Assembly, New York, NY, September 12, 2002, <http://www.whitehouse/gov/news/releases/2002/09>.
59. United Nations Security Council, S/RES/1441 (2002), 3–5. Philip Towle, *Enforced Disarmament: From the Napoleonic Campaigns to the Gulf War* (Oxford: Clarendon Press, 1997), 183–201.
60. Towle, *Enforced Disarmament*, 196–198; Albert C. Pierce, "Just War Principles and Economic Sanctions," *Ethics & International Affairs* 10 (1996): 199–213; Joy Gordon, "A Peaceful, Silent, Deadly Remedy: The Ethics of Economic Sanctions," *Ethics & International Affairs* 13 (1999): 123–142.
61. Ibid., 200–201.
62. Ibid., 193–194. Richard Butler, *Saddam Defiant: The Threat of Weapons of Mass Destruction and the Crisis of Global Security* (London: Weidenfeld & Nicolson, 2000), 214–236.
63. Remarks by the president of the United States, George W. Bush, to the Atlantic Student Summit, Prague, 20 November 2002, <http://www.nato/int/docu/speech/2002/s021120f.htm>.
64. *Financial Times*, February 10, 2003.
65. United Nations, Press Release SC/7664, February 14, 2003, <http://www.un.org/news/press/docs/2003/sc7664.doc.htm>; *Financial Times*, February 18, 2003.
66. Ibid.
67. *Hansard*, March 18, 2003, Column 766.
68. Ibid., Columns 773–774.

69. Jo Johnson, George Parker, and Brian Groom, "Delors Warns against Outright Opposition to 'Messianic' U.S.," *Financial Times*, April 3, 2003.
70. Dominique Moïsi, "Chirac Should Follow the Spirit of de Gaulle," *Financial Times*, February 9, 2003.
71. See in particular Charles Kupchan, "The Atlantic Alliance Lies in the Rubble," *Financial Times*, April 10, 2003, and Stanley Hoffmann, "America Goes Backward," *New York Review of Books*, June 12, 2003.
72. Butler, *Saddam Defiant*, 257–258.
73. Tom M. Nichols, "Just War, Not Prevention," *Ethics & International Affairs* 17, no. 1 (2003): 25–29.
74. *Hansard*, March 18, 2003, Column 767; George Weigel, "Moral Clarity in a Time of War," *First Things*, no. 128 (December 2002).

A FUTURE FOR ATLANTICISM

On a European continent safer from the prospect of a major war than at any time since the late nineteenth century, the formal dissolution of NATO would be less than a tragedy but more than a mistake. After all, any alliance capable of remaining intact during four decades of confrontation and political competition with an opposing alliance and then of securing the peaceful surrender of its opponent on overwhelmingly advantageous terms has achieved every imaginable goal of a military coalition of states. And the Atlantic Alliance has gone beyond the diplomatic victories of 1989–1991 in helping to extend the habits of democratic self-government to most of the former Warsaw Pact.

Yet to say that NATO *as we have known it* is dead is a non-controversy. The Alliance has for more than a decade undergone relentless change in response to altered circumstance. This change has repeatedly demonstrated two interrelated features of the Atlantic relationship: the inability of even the major powers of Europe to improve their collective military capability so as to constitute a European partner for the United States, and Washington's declining willingness to heed the mixed message of its European allies regarding American rights and obligations in European and global security. A graduated American withdrawal from Europe has been underway since the early 1990s. It is conditioned less by a desire to leave Europe than the conviction that in the twenty-first century the Old Continent cannot hold the rank in the order of American global priorities it occupied during the twentieth.

In June 2003 the Pentagon announced its intention to reduce the size of the American garrison in Germany and Britain in order to redeploy forces to Africa, Eastern Europe, and the Caucasus. If the Alliance is to retain a measure of relevance despite its diminished military utility it will do so as an organization embodying the political ideals of the Atlantic heritage. That Wilsonian principles have become fully integral to that heritage has been a recurrent argument of this book. It is true that Wilsonianism secured its place in American diplomacy as an internationalist response to the twentieth century crisis of European civilization, 1914–1989, but it does not follow that the resolution of the crisis justifies dispensing with its principles.[1] Inasmuch as their resilience within the Atlantic Alliance during and after the Cold War is self-evident, the task of a concluding chapter is to speculate on their possible contribution to the Atlantic future.

THE INTERNATIONAL COMMUNITY

In a symposium on September 11, Paul A. Rahe, author of the magisterial *Republics Ancient and Modern,* observed that the time had come to admit to ourselves that the specter of war is not about to disappear from global affairs and that only lazy thinking would conclude otherwise. He then stated a heresy:

> There is no international community. The phrase is an empty rhetorical gesture that conceals the worst of all wishful thinking. We rely for our security, as we always have, on our capacity to defend ourselves. In apparently choosing to deny the gravity of the threat, our cousins on the other side of the Atlantic are allowing the provisions we have made on their behalf over the last decades to lull them into an almost childish self-indulgence. Should we retire from the scene, they would confront the harsh reality of their vulnerability and rediscover the capacity for self-defense. Otherwise they would not last long.[2]

Rahe's central point is all the more refreshing for being an overstatement about the relationship of the United States to the world around it. To the extent that an international community exists, the United Nations and NATO are rightly regarded as core institutions. Wishfulness about their institutional vitality and the inherent moral force of the multilateralism they embody is evidenced in the demonstrated inability of the wealthy states of the European Union to bring a semblance of order to the unruly Balkans without American leadership, and is set against the remarkable appetite of European states, singly and in combination, to hold forth on international security issues well beyond Europe. This ranges from public criticisms of the alleged strategic folly of missile defense to Brussels' pretensions as a peace broker in the Middle East where European governments have maintained ties with violently anti-American and anti-Israel regimes. A popular view in Washington foreign policy circles is that Europeans have for so long enjoyed low-cost security under the American umbrella, all the while committing proportionally greater resources to the social welfare programs so critical to "social cohesion" in the European Union, that they are convinced they have developed a more evolved and compassionate society. At its more extreme the idealist perspective on European integration is that the EU has developed a system for preserving peace, based on moral consciousness, rejection of force, and rule of law.[3] It is not surprising then that the contemporary

American skepticism regarding the inherent virtues of multilateralism is informed in large part by Washington's awkward post–Cold War relations with its European allies. Nations with whom the United States has deep historic, cultural, economic, and military bonds have thwarted the pursuit of unity—in the United Nations and in NATO—over confronting Iraq, a state in flagrant and repeated violation of every norm crafted to maintain peace since 1945.

The Security Council debate over Iraq accounted for only the most recent and spectacular breach of unity. In May 2001, the United States was ousted from its seat on the UN Human Rights Commission, in part the Cairo newspaper *Al-Ahram* pontificated, due to Washington's "blind support of Israel regardless of the atrocities committed against the defenseless Palestinian people,"[4] atrocities offensive to the sensibilities of UNHRC members such as Croatia, Sierra Leone, Sudan, Togo, and Uganda. The United States has occupied a seat since the Commission was created—at American insistence—in 1948. More serious was the chorus of international indignation over the Bush administration's refusal to assent to the jurisdiction claimed by the International Criminal Court (ICC) and veto of a UN Security Council Resolution renewing the Bosnian peace mission after the Council refused Washington's request that UN peacekeepers be placed beyond the ICC's reach. The administration was accused from several quarters of undermining the entire future of international peacekeeping by threatening to pull American forces out of Bosnia in response. The more serious peril to the mission was that several NATO states warned they would withdraw their own contribution if the United States were to leave. What kind of international community calls off a mission critical to the very viability of international peacekeeping when just one of its members folds its tent? What kind of European community would so much as contemplate abandoning its mission to peace in a region that was the cradle of the Great War?

Since 1989 the international community has too often amounted to an empty rhetorical gesture unless and until American diplomatic leadership and military power conjure it into meaningful existence. A look back on the last decade of the twentieth century from the first decade of the twenty-first tempts the conclusion not that the United States has been too assertive but rather that it has been reluctant to take up the role, to paraphrase George Kennan, that history plainly intended it to bear. For want of a better word, that role is best described as *imperial*. Three times in the twentieth century a realignment of the international balance-of-power favoring the United States challenged Washington's political leadership to reorder national foreign policy goals. To the contrasting performance of American diplomacy after 1918 and 1945, a verdict on the post-1989 period has yet to be added.[5] The Atlantic project begun aboard the *Augusta* by Churchill and Roosevelt in 1941 ultimately provided the basis for a stability in Western Europe imposed by the United States; a stability that went missing in Europe during the interwar decades. The Atlantic formula was a synthesis of historical experience, combining Wilson's imperative that the United States make a world "safe for democracy" with the balance-of-power requisites of strategic equilibrium and military security for Western

Europe. In the United States it involved an ideological commitment to defeat communism, powerfully articulated in order to convince and commit a people separated by thousands of miles from the theater of conflict to stay the course of containment.[6] The European settlement of 1989–1991 rewarded this commitment with one of the greatest diplomatic triumphs of modern history. Yet because no formula for the consolidation and extension of American hegemony was developed by either the senior Bush or the Clinton administration—and because American power was not supplemented by European power—the new world order frayed quickly on the European periphery and beyond. By the turn of the millennium the wayward course of Washington's foreign policy was being compared to that of Britain's between the wars; if its 1930s were not yet upon it, its 1920s were clearly over.[7] Insofar as the United States faced looming security challenges in Asia and an unresolved crisis with Iraq, its continuing commitment to Europe through NATO weakened its capacity to meet the challenges. Even NATO enlargement could be seen as a form of defeat, because the Alliance's capabilities were not enhanced in proportion to its longer frontier; "just as Britain signed the Treaty of Locarno in 1925 knowing that it could not support it militarily, so the United States and its allies have expanded the NATO alliance without any plans to meet the military commitments thereby involved."[8]

The 1990s meanwhile witnessed a world where the number of sovereign states had increased manifoldly since 1945; more of them were democratic than ever before; and the sovereign state remained the fundamental guarantor of its people's security and freedom. Yet in the decade of "globalization" there was precious little recognition that a viable state is a *moral* achievement. British Foreign Secretary Jack Straw speculated in the wake of September 11 that, "if the main challenge before the collapse of the Soviet empire and throughout much of the 20th century consisted of states with too much power, the problems of the 21st century may be states with too little power."[9] The apparent decay in the effectiveness and legitimacy of the sovereign state was accompanied and conditioned by the aggressive promotion of international human rights standards by governments, international organizations, and nongovernmental organizations. This, in turn, nurtured a growing contempt for the very principle of national sovereignty and a tendency to regard any ethnonationalist secessionist cause as the expression of a legitimate right to self-determination; by the mid-1990s rampant secessionism had indeed helped to bring democracy to post-Soviet Europe but had caused pandemonium elsewhere, not least of all in Yugoslavia.[10] The general trajectory of international affairs favored Hedley Bull's notion of a "new medievalism" more visibly than an international community and global governance.[11] This world of rogue nations, failed states, and asymmetric threats challenges the intellectual capacity, political ingenuity, and moral courage of the Atlantic democracies that have prospered under American leadership.

The United States is bound to the world around it by a thousand diplomatic, institutional, and organizational ligatures. Multilateral diplomacy is a tradition that should not, indeed cannot, be jettisoned by a single administration in Washington, regardless of its definition of national interest. But the best evidence of the past decade is that the United States must be prepared to exert its power and influence unapologetically in order to secure the essential modicum of world order in which the "Wilsonian triad" of peace, free markets, and democracy can flourish. The United States could almost certainly survive and prosper from a position of consolidated withdrawal to the North American continent, but it is doubtful in the present circumstances that the rest of the world can prosper in the absence of an imperial America.[12] The Bush administration's "American internationalism" means that Washington cannot be bound by the lowest common denominator of resolve available from established multilateral institutions. As the more prescient studies acknowledge, the crude dichotomy of multilateralism/unilateralism offers neither descriptive value to scholars nor prescriptive utility to policymakers.[13] The past success and present enlargement of the Atlantic and European communities suggests that the project of international democratic peace is a Western project and that this institutional "double nucleus" of Western democracy represents the real hope for extending the ambit of peace internationally.[14]

THREE VERSIONS OF EUROPE

In the near-term it is hard to imagine Europe contributing to this project in proportion to its collective wealth and political experience. Germany's preemptive unilateralism over Iraq in 2002 recalls its precipitative unilateralism in recognition of Croatian and Slovenian sovereignty in 1991. In 1991 Bonn sought to avoid direct European responsibility for the Yugoslav crisis and to internationalize any response through the United Nations as quickly as possible; in 2002 Berlin in effect announced well in advance of France's Security Council maneuvers that there would be no unified European support for a UN mandated application of force against Iraq. What the two episodes have in common is a determination to avoid the assumption of major international obligations. The key to Germany's foreign policy is thus at root a determined parochialism, for which a multilateral diplomacy articulated "in Europe's name" is the calling card.[15] It is possible that a center-right coalition might have adopted a position altogether different from that of Schröder's center-left in the autumn of 2002, but it is by no means a certainty. Cutting against the introspective pacifism evident in broad swaths of German public opinion would require moral courage from any government.

In the 1950s and 1980s the Christian Democratic-led governments of Adenauer and Kohl demonstrated the requisite backbone. The Socialist/Liberal coalition of Helmut Schmidt actually fell in 1983 over the chancellor's commitment to the INF deployments. But without the Soviet menace the temptation is ever present to earn easy political capital by opposing international security initiatives that do not have direct implications for Germany. On the German left in particular NATO is regarded as an artifact of the Cold War, and the idea of Europe is meaningless unless Europeans are prepared to draw a line between themselves and the

Anglo-Americans.[16] During the 1991 Persian Gulf War German preoccupation with the immediate burdens of reunification provided a legitimate reason for a nation with Germany's past to limit its participation to the checkbook diplomacy of helping to finance a war to which it would send no troops. But the political potential of pacifism was visible in the demonstrations staged in Germany's large cities and university towns as *Desert Storm* got underway. That Iraq was the aggressor, that the United Nations Security Council had endorsed the use of force against Saddam Hussein, that Scud missiles from Iraq had slammed into Israel could not divert the peace demonstrators from the idea that Germany had a duty to oppose a war led by American imperialists. Critics of the demonstrators noted that they obviously drew no connection between the recovery of national sovereignty and the assumption of greater responsibility to global security, and that the slogan "no German soldiers to the Gulf" could be interpreted abroad as just another variation of nationalist narcissism.[17]

France has sought with considerable success to enhance its own position internationally *through* Europe. What was true in 1968—that Gaullism was "indifferent" to the Atlantic dimension of Europe and stressed the bolstering of European power, not only to contain the Soviet Union, but also to challenge American supremacy[18]— remains true today. That goal is perhaps now more urgent because the thesis of relative American decline popular in the 1970s has been refuted. The Gaullist conception of the nation-state, meanwhile, still influences French society profoundly. Unlike Germany, France does not have a history that makes it apologetic either for the pursuit of military power or for a high-profile international role; unlike Britain it does not benefit from a cultural connection to the United States that would permit it to exercise collaborative influence on American policy.[19] There is something to the statement that in rejecting the Kyoto Protocol and the Comprehensive Test Ban Treaty the United States "seemed also to reject most of a European sense of how states ought to behave," but it is over-determined by a German and integrationist vision of Europe; the argument of German Foreign Minister Joschka Fischer that Europe has moved beyond power politics is indulged, but not genuinely shared, by France.[20]

De Gaulle's founding of the Fifth Republic and conduct of its foreign policy were in large part acts of defiance against decay and decline; to the extent that defiance was balanced with unsentimental pragmatism, France has since nonetheless achieved a very real recovery of economic vitality, military capacity, and influence in European and international affairs.[21] To say that in 2002–2003 President Chirac led France to diplomatic dead-end over Iraq is not to deny that his country has a *mission civilisatrice* in the world. But in openly obstructing American efforts to topple a brutal and revisionist Middle Eastern dictatorship with a string of United Nations resolutions against it, Chirac's government abandoned pragmatism to a degree that can only set back such a mission—by imperiling French influence in the Middle East while dividing NATO and the EU.[22] None of these outcomes was the necessary price of staking out an independent and skeptical French position on the Bush administration's Iraq policy.

The Iraq crisis also witnessed the emergence of a French/German/Russian troika in opposition to the UN initiatives of Britain and the United States—a manifestation of the "Tripolar Pan-Europe" recently envisaged by David Calleo.[23] Since the mid-1990s, both the Yeltsin and Putin presidencies regarded a vigorous Russian diplomacy in Western Europe as a way to foster a "Concert of European Powers" in international affairs against a "unipolar" order dominated by the United States. Germany's view of Russia is colored predominantly by economic interests. This motivates Berlin to set a comparatively high bar for Russian internal reforms, since an anarchic Russia represents a problem for Germany's growing economic sphere of influence in Central Europe and the Baltic. Because France sees a strong Russia as a useful partner in a "multipolar" world order, it stresses strategic vision over economic interest and sets a lower bar for Russian internal reforms. Just as the United States prefers a strong Ukraine as an essential part of European geopolitical pluralism, France sees a strong Russia as essential to global pluralism.[24] Yet to listen to French and Russian UN delegations congratulating themselves during the Iraq war on changing the wording of a Security Council resolution was to be reminded of a university international relations seminar in which it is possible to imagine that the wording of a resolution could actually make the world multipolar.

Beyond the realm of global trade, there is little sense in the United States that Europe constitutes a pole in contemporary international affairs. The impulses governing British, French, and German diplomacy alone exhibit divergence; when they are considered together with other EU states the prospects of a European strategic culture seem remote.[25] The French investment in partnership with Germany in building "deep Europe" has since the Elysée Treaty of 1963 established an array of privileged links, yet constitutes a far from secure edifice for the broader elaboration of European security and defense capabilities. Reconciliation with Germany was intended to offset the Anglo-American special relationship at the core of NATO, De Gaulle's initial veto of Britain's application to the European Community representing a determination to secure a dominant position for France in the integrative project before admitting Britain.[26] In the post–Cold War context, Chirac's 1998 Saint-Malô summit with Tony Blair was by contrast an acknowledgement that Germany could not substitute for Britain as a partner in building European capabilities in expeditionary warfare. Because Chirac sought greater European decision-making independence from a NATO mortgaged to continued borrowing of American capabilities, Saint-Malô was an attempt to extract an unequivocal choice for Europe from the only other nation that could bring meaningful military heft to European security. The Iraq crisis demonstrated that, for Blair, the European project could not trump loyalty to the Atlantic Alliance, and it laid bare for Chirac the real limitations in venturing a European Defense and Security Policy with partners from across the Rhine or across the Channel.

But the evidence was there long before Washington turned its attention to Iraq. To press this point, President Bush issued a joint statement with Blair endorsing Britain's interpretation of the Helsinki Headline Goals in which the European Rapid

Reaction Force was regarded as an adjunct to NATO, to be used when the Alliance chose not to be involved. A similar joint statement issued with Chancellor Schröder then turned Chirac's other flank. Even as the European Union's economic power increased and its member states marched toward a quasi-federal union, the role of the United States as Europe's preeminent military power was thus consolidated.[27] Beyond the naked facts of the "capabilities gap" the maintenance of the Anglo-American connection helped to ensure this. Among prime ministers willing to bring strong leadership to foreign policy, what distinguished Tony Blair from Margaret Thatcher was a refusal to look upon the Atlantic and European options as mutually exclusive. From the outset Blair was eager to engage Britain in the European project, yet refreshingly free of the garden variety assumptions of what building Europe necessarily entailed. His government plowed through domestic reforms such as the abolition of hereditary peerage and the devolution of certain self-governing powers to Scotland and Wales, which in theory prepared Britain for a federal Europe, but Blair's European diplomacy has shunned long-term alliances in favor of fluid issue-based coalitions of convenience.[28] Blair has simultaneously applied a "new bilateralism" to Britain's relations with other EU states such as Italy, Spain, and the former Warsaw Pact states queued for admission to the EU; in combination with his embrace of the Thatcher legacy of neoliberal economic policy stressing free markets over the deep integration championed in Paris and Berlin, Blair's advocacy of a wider more heterogeneous Europe serves the traditional British aim of thwarting the formation of any coalition of continental power "that could threaten the isles' freedom and independence."[29] Moreover, in his attention to the Anglo-American relationship, Blair has been anything but a poodle to U.S. foreign policy. He was a forthright advocate of NATO's Kosovo intervention at the point where the Clinton administration hesitated. Among major international leaders he has a record of the strongest statements on behalf of NATO's specific obligations to champion Western democratic values, with force if necessary, on Europe's periphery. His statements on international security more generally connect international peace to respect for basic standards of human rights in terms of just-war doctrine. If no international community currently exists, in other words, Blair's policy has been to bring it into existence as much by example as by persuasion.[30] More than any other European leader Blair appreciated that, from Washington's perspective, both European governments and the EU had been less than indispensable in the resolution of European crises and very nearly irrelevant in the wider world.

ATLANTIC COMMONWEALTH AND WORLD ORDER

Neither the achievements nor the potential of the European Union should be sold short. When the Treaty of Rome was signed in 1957, few expected the collaboration of the original six to accomplish half as much as it has; since victory in the Cold War—a victory in which the economic, social, and political achievements of European integration were as critical in their own way as NATO military deter-rence—the anticipation of membership in the European Union has served to fos-ter economic and political reforms all over Central and Eastern Europe. Whether the short-term benefits of the EU's most sweeping expansion announced in the fall of 2002 will meet the expectations of the populations who have faced the rigors of those reforms is an issue of speculation beyond the scope of this study. It has to be said, however, that priority given to deeper over wider Europe for most of the post–Cold War decade has made the EU a much less flexible and adaptive club than NATO. An expanded EU will no doubt be called upon to develop a strategic cul-ture of sorts, as its frontiers abut on "zones of intractable conflict" in Yugoslavia, Northern Africa, and the Middle East, and the gap between the Brussels' custom-ary way of doing things and the Hobbesian reality of the wider world stands out in high relief.[31] While the EU member states are now "irreversibly committed" to the creation of a 60,000-strong rapid reaction force, it is in concrete terms more sig-nificant that European states provide the great majority of troops in the former Yu-goslavia; in March 2003, NATO formally relinquished its mission in the Former Yugoslav Republic of Macedonia to an EU force consisting of British, French, and Czech troops under the command of German Navy Admiral Rainer Feist. When Washington's relations with Berlin and Paris were at their worst in the wake of the UN debates over Iraq, congressmen visiting U.S. troops in Afghanistan found them in close collaboration with French and German troops represented in the twenty-nine-nation International Security Assistance Force (ISAF). The Atlantic Alliance's responsibility for the twenty-nine-nation force marks NATO's first deployment out-side Europe and will, claims Secretary General Lord Robertson, debunk the myth that America and Europe are drifting apart.[32] The ISAF deployment is significant, but the secretary general is putting a brave face on present circumstances. Fol-lowing quickly upon the Afghan war, the Anglo-American invasion of Iraq demon-strated that only one NATO member could muster both the expeditionary capacity and the political will to fight alongside the United States. Thus, what has been ob-vious to the European Union since the Balkan experience of the mid-1990s, is now painfully true for the great majority of the European NATO states as well as for Canada, namely, that for the foreseeable future they will have to "backfill the Amer-ican military and logistical presence" in order to make the Atlantic Alliance some-thing more than an artifact of the Cold War.[33]

As NATO takes over command of ISAF, the relationship between the United States and the Europeans in Afghanistan confirms that both sides were essentially right in their respective arguments over multilateral approaches to international crises: the problems *are* too many and too complex for the United States to tackle alone and effective multilateral action in the future *will* consist more frequently of ad hoc coalitions-of-the-willing led by the United States. But the notion of strate-gic partnership and equilibrium between the United States and Europe is illuso-ry. The multilateral institutions erected after 1945, above all the United Nations, are ill-suited to any role approximating responsible leadership in the endeavor to deal with contemporary threats to international peace and security. World order requires robust American leadership, the more so because neither the European Union nor a looser coalition of European allies carries the requisite military heft or the moral authority to do more than supplement American power—even in Europe. The idea that Europe is abandoning the nation-state in favor of a postnational federation is also illusory. The European Union is in fact home to some of the strongest states in the history of the institution, and for Europeans the nation-state remains the real arena of democratic politics. The integrative project of a half century has indeed domesticated relations between them, but integration has done as much to supplement the sovereign legitimacy and governing effectiveness of European states as to replace them, which is prominent among the reasons for Jack Straw's appropriate remarks about the connection between durable statehood and international civil society.[34] The evidence of recent experience, as well as that extending back to the demise of the EDC and Germany's admission to NATO, is that a common European foreign policy will not emerge even from the wreckage of NATO's internal quarrel over Iraq. Time and again, the attempt to incorporate a defense dimension into European integration has revealed "a profound ambivalence, even of the Europeanists, to actually create a European security entity possessing the genuine ability to act in the interests of Europe."[35]

This being the case, the Atlantic Alliance will be the primary vehicle for Europe's security needs into the foreseeable future. Because NATO never developed supranational structures like those of the EU, the comparative specificity of its mission permitted it to adapt more quickly and radically to the changes of the 1990s, most especially in extending *Ostpolitik* to a post-Soviet Europe. Yet because the Alliance is not an exclusively military organization and has an attendant political mission dating to the Atlantic Charter, it has since the end of the Cold War become in many respects *primarily* a political coalition. Its eastern enlargement and the success of the CFE Treaty mean that extending the parameters of the Atlantic realm has been and remains a balm to democratization—as indeed it was even during the Cold War—rather than a bulwark against a recidivist Russia.[36] As NATO has expanded, in fact, Russia's role in NATO and participation in the Atlantic Council has itself expanded. The Alliance's new members sought admission not solely—perhaps not even primarily—in pursuit of a security guarantee but rather in terms of a "Western vocation," and signed up for the political, economic, and ideological affiliations entailed therein.[37]

The United States is "leaving Europe" in the sense that the uncertainties and ambiguities involved in consolidating the Cold War victory in Europe are now giving way to new missions with vast implications for American global leadership. This change was posted both in candidate Bush's November 1999 speech at Simi Valley and in National Security Advisor Condoleezza Rice's 2001 *Foreign Affairs* article, but it has acquired an understandable sense of urgency since the events of September 11, 2001. Woodrow Wilson was not the first American president to recognize that the growth of American power had made a policy of isolation impossible; the administrations of McKinley and Theodore Roosevelt before him had already begun to conceive American interests in global terms, in deed more than word. Rather, Wilson was first to *declare* in progressive liberal terms, during and after WWI, that isolation was unviable because American strength would henceforth be decisive in the outcome of major wars.[38] The dilemma of all foreign policy leadership in Washington has since been that American overseas commitments reflect the growth of power rather than a decline of security, "yet the full and effective deployment of that power has required from the American people disciplines and sacrifices that they are prepared to sustain only if they are persuaded that the nation's safety is directly at stake."[39] Because during the presidency of George W. Bush, American vulnerability was suddenly revealed with brutal clarity, this dilemma has given way to the new one of explaining to the American people the reality of new and unanticipated burdens. Because, as Colin Gray has rightly observed, "the civilized world is trapped somewhat in a time warp of arguably obsolescent political, ethical, and strategic assumptions and practices,"[40] the president of the United States will have to be forgiven for the time being if his message has departed from the received etiquette of multilateralism.

Those principles vindicated by the twentieth-century experience of Europe above all the others, democracy and free markets, are ingrained features of the political culture of Atlanticism. Europe has a responsibility to leaven the application of American power but will first have to catch up to the logic and acknowledge the legitimacy of its use. It should begin, advises Pierre Hassner, by facing "the tragic reality that, in order to preserve and promote good, it is necessary to resist evil and inflict harm."[41] If NATO is to survive and mature as a provider of security to regions of instability, its members will have to at last make a break with its Cold War orientation with a broader vision of the Atlantic realm in which the defense of democratic self-government and the promotion of free markets take priority. The Alliance in principle supported this regional agenda since the launch of its Mediterranean Initiative in 1995. The Initiative was intended to promote stability in the Mediterranean as a whole, and it involved NATO in a dialogue with Egypt, Israel, Mauritania, Morocco, and later Jordan on matters ranging from the Palestinian issue and proliferation of WMD to drug-trafficking, organized crime, and terrorism.[42] The potential importance of a dialogue incorporating both traditional, "hard" security concerns and non-military "soft" security to the export-dependent economies of Western Europe—and to the wider trade horizons of new NATO and EU members in Eastern Europe—can hardly be overemphasized. The experience of the EU, as well as of such Helsinki institutions as the Organization for Security and Cooperation in Europe (OSCE), can be of enormous benefit in extending the ambit of the civil society upon which Western Europe has prospered since the 1950s.[43]

Nonetheless, the challenge is now also enormous, and the Alliance's member states cannot bank on a peace separate from the one the United States has taken upon itself to build in the Middle East. The extraordinary speed of the Anglo-American victory over Iraqi forces has inevitably been followed by a difficult occupation; UN *Resolution 1483* legitimates the invasion to a degree after the fact by giving the United States and Britain the authority to rebuild the country, but a large and lengthy Anglo-American presence in Iraq is likely to complicate the task by cultivating resentment among its people. Lowering the profile of American forces in Iraq in particular, by introducing a large multilateral coalition-of-the-willing, could well be critical to minimizing this danger.[44] "Backfilling" the American military and logistical presence will be in its own way as daunting a task as the invasion, so contributions from European NATO states is one way in which the Alliance can recover a measure of its relevance and unity through a pragmatic division of labor. This is already underway. As the non-American contingent in Iraq increases, with pledged contributions from the new and old NATO states of Poland, Spain, Bulgaria, Romania, Hungary, Lithuania, Denmark, Turkey, the Netherlands, and the Czech Republic, the importance of backfill will become ever more apparent. Meanwhile, the best candidate as an institutional "partner" for the United States is the European Union, not with a rapid deployment force deployed with more acronyms than arms but as an institution experienced in promoting good governance, free market reform, institution building, rule of law and democracy.[45] An Iraqi democracy is likely too much to hope for, but the Bush administration should not be derided for trying—especially if ultimately the result is a responsible government in Baghdad constrained by law.[46]

In the meantime, political leadership of North America and Europe should tie economic interest to democratic principles more explicitly by addressing multilateral trade on a scale greater than at any time since Europe initiated the Single European Act and Canada, Mexico, and the United States fashioned the North American Free Trade Agreement. Institutionalized multilateralism is most developed in trade but is in need of rejuvenation and extension. In its understandable determination to meet the challenge of September 11, Washington's leadership too often forgets that the world is moving in its direction as it clearly was not between 1914 and 1989. A closer union among NATO's members by way of a Trans-Atlantic Free Trade Agreement (TAFTA), broached unsuccessfully by transatlantic business leaders in the mid-1990s, and a new international trade round with emerging nations would offset the Cromwellian grimness of Washington's war against terrorism and jolt the European Union out of its self-absorption and regulatory sclerosis. Such an initiative would engage with Hamiltonian optimism the enthusiasm of the new NATO and EU members of Eastern and Central Europe, post-communist societies where "Euro-Atlanticism is a living choice, not a bureaucratic habit."[47] A Euro-Atlantic Community or Commonwealth of Nations of the mature democracies promoting peace and responsible governance along its periphery, even in the face of open transatlantic disputes over the appropriate response to global crises, is not a utopian vision but a down payment on an international community worthy of the name.[48] Answers to the question as to whether Wilsonian ideas have triumphed since the end of the Cold War get us nowhere.[49] To the extent that they are still with us, they clearly have triumphed.

But the question is wrong. It is not Woodrow Wilson who is being put to the test. The Atlantic Alliance has the advantage over Wilson of some eighty years of collective experience in testing his principles against the realities of peace and war. It is Atlanticism that is being put to the test, the idea that North America and Europe have a common political heritage and destiny—and can continue to carry the Western vocation beyond the West.[50]

NOTES

1. Frank Ninkovich, *The Wilsonian Century: U.S. Foreign Policy since 1900* (Chicago, IL: University of Chicago Press, 1999), 288–289.
2. Paul A. Rahe, "Averting Our Gaze," *The Journal of the Historical Society* 2, no. 2 (2002): 148–149.
3. Robert Kagan, *Of Paradise and Power: America and Europe in the New World Order* (New York: Alfred A. Knopf, 2003), 54–73.
4. *Al-Ahram Weekly Online*, 10–16 May 2001, <http://www.ahram.org.eg/weekly/2001/533/in5.htm>.
5. Charles Maier, "Empires or Nations? 1918, 1945, 1989 . . .," in Carl Levy and Mark Roseman, eds., *Three Postwar Eras in Comparison: Western Europe 1918–1945–1989* (Basingstoke: Palgrave, 2002), 41–66; Donald Kagan and Frederick W. Kagan, *While America Sleeps: Self-Delusion, Military Weakness, and the Threat to Peace Today* (New York: St. Martin's, 2000).
6. Raymond Aron, *The Imperial Republic: The United States and the World, 1945–1973* (Cambridge: Winthrop, 1974), 313–314.
7. Kagan and Kagan, *While America Sleeps*, 424–435.
8. Ibid., 7.
9. "Order out of Chaos: The Future of Afghanistan," speech by the Foreign Secretary, Jack Straw, to the International Institute for Strategic Studies, London, Monday, 22 October 2001.
10. Daniel Patrick Moynihan, *Pandaemonium: Ethnicity in International Politics* (New York: Oxford University Press, 1993).
11. Hedley Bull, *The Anarchical Society: A Study of Order in World Politics* (New York: Columbia University Press, 1995), 254–266.
12. Michael Mandelbaum, *The Ideas That Conquered the World: Peace, Democracy, and Free Markets in the Twenty-First Century* (New York: Public Affairs), 17–44; Niall Ferguson, *The Cash Nexus: Money and Power in the Modern World, 1700–2000* (New York: Basic Books, 2001), 390–418.
13. See Henry R. Nau, *At Home Abroad: Identity and Power in American Foreign Policy* (New York: Century Foundation, 2002), 57–59; Joseph S. Nye, *The Paradox of American Power: Why the World's Only Superpower Can't Go It Alone* (New York: Oxford University Press, 2002), 137–171.
14. Robert H. Jackson, *The Global Covenant: Human Conduct in a World of States* (New York: Oxford University Press, 2000), 350–368; Ira Straus, "Atlantic Federalism and the Expanding Atlantic Nucleus," *Peace & Change* 24, no. 3 (1999): 295.
15. Timothy Garton Ash has minted the term *attritional multilateralism* to capture the spirit of German foreign policy. The Federal Republic has prospered diplomatically by pursuing national goals exclusively through multilateral institutions such as the EU, NATO, and the Helsinki process. Additionally, German foreign policy features a "habitual conflation of German and European interests." See "Germany's Choice," *Foreign Affairs* 73, no. 4 (1994): 71. See also Garton Ash's *In Europe's Name: Germany and the Divided Continent* (London: Jonathan Cape, 1993), 359.
16. Heinrich August Winkler, *Der lange Weg nach Westen*, 2 vols. (Munich: C. H. Beck, 2000), II, 624.

17. Ibid., 623–624.
18. Stanley Hoffmann, *Gulliver's Troubles, or the Setting of American Foreign Policy* (New York: McGraw-Hill, 1968), 417.
19. Philip H. Gordon, *A Certain Idea of France: French Security Policy and the Gaullist Legacy* (Princeton, NJ: Princeton University Press, 1993), 185; also Gilles Martinet, *Le Reveil des nationalismes français* (Paris: Le Seuil, 1994).
20. Daniel Nelson, "Transatlantic Transmutations," *Washington Quarterly* 25, no. 4 (2002): 61; Fischer's remarks are noted by Kagan in *Of Paradise and Power*, 56–57.
21. Andrew Knapp, *Gaullism since de Gaulle* (Aldershot: Dartmouth, 1994), 401.
22. *The Economist*, March 29, 2003.
23. David Calleo, *Rethinking Europe's Future* (Princeton, NJ: Princeton University Press, 2001), 348–350; Jean-Pierre Froehly, "Frankreich-Deutschland-Russland im neuen Dialog: eine Troika für Europa," *Politische Studien* 52, no. 376 (March/April 2001): 24–30.
24. Froehly, "Frankreich-Deutschland-Russland im neuen Dialog."
25. Paul Cornish and Geoffrey Edwards, "Beyond the EU/NATO Dichotomy: The Beginnings of a European Strategic Culture," *International Affairs* 77, no 3 (2001): 598–599. The authors define *strategic culture* as "the institutional confidence and processes to manage and deploy military force as part of the accepted range of legitimate and effective policy instruments," 587.
26. Charles G. Cogan, *Forced to Choose: France, the Atlantic Alliance, and NATO—Then and Now* (Westport, CT: Praeger, 1997), 138–139.
27. John Gillingham, *European Integration, 1950–2003: Superstate or New Market Economy?* (New York: Cambridge University Press, 2003), 402–403; Robert Wilkie, "Fortress Europa: European Defense and the Future of the Atlantic Alliance," *Parameters* 32, no. 4 (2002–2003): 41–42.
28. Ibid., 401–402; Hugo Young, *This Blessed Plot: Britain and Europe from Churchill to Blair* (New York: Overlook, 1998), 483–508.
29. Ibid., 402–403.
30. See Jackson's discussion of Blair and the "doctrine of international community" in *The Global Covenant*, 355–360.
31. Cornish and Edwards, "Beyond the EU/NATO Dichotomy," 598–599.
32. *Wall Street Journal*, June 17, 2003.
33. Compare Peter Ludlow, "Wanted: A Global Partner," *Washington Quarterly* 24, no. 3 (2001): 163–171, with Wilkie, "Fortress Europa," 46–47.
34. Gillingham, *European Integration*, 446–479.
35. Simon Duke, *The Elusive Quest for European Security, from EDC to CFSP* (New York: St. Martin's, 2000), 298.
36. Nau, *At Home Abroad*, 135; Mark Smith, *NATO Enlargement during the Cold War: Strategy and System in the Western Alliance* (Basingstoke: Palgrave, 2000), 174–175.
37. Smith, *NATO Enlargement*, 176.
38. John A. Thompson, "The Exaggeration of American Vulnerability: The Anatomy of a Tradition," *Diplomatic History* 16, no. 1 (1992): 23–43; also Frank Ninkovich, *The Wilsonian Century: U.S. Foreign Policy since 1900* (Chicago, IL: University of Chicago Press, 1999), 17–101; Walter A. McDougall, *Promised Land, Crusader State: The American Encounter with the World since 1776* (Boston, MA: Houghton Mifflin, 1997), 101–146.
39. Ibid., 43.
40. Colin Gray, "Thinking Asymmetrically in Times of Terror, *Parameters* 32, no. 1 (2002): 10.
41. Pierre Hassner, "The United States: The Empire of Force or the Force of Empire?" *Chaillot Papers*, no. 54 (September 2002): 49.
42. Gareth Winrow, *Dialogue with the Mediterranean: The Role of NATO's Mediterranean Initiative* (New York: Garland, 2000); Raymond A. Millen, "Pax NATO: The Opportunities of Enlargement," Strategic Studies Institute, U.S. Army War College (2002), 28.

43. See Emanuel Adler, "Seeds of Peaceful Change: The OSCE's Security Community-Building Model," in Emanuel Adler and Michael Barnett, eds., *Security Communities* (Cambridge: Cambridge University Press, 1998), 119–160.
44. Andrew Rathmell, Theodore Karasik, and David Gompert, "A New Persian Gulf Security System," *RAND Issue Paper* IP-248-CMEPP (2003).
45. Ibid., 9.
46. Fareed Zakaria, *The Future of Freedom: Illiberal Democracy at Home and Abroad* (New York: W. W. Norton, 2003), 239–256.
47. Nau, *At Home Abroad*, 104–105; Straus, "Atlantic Federalism and the Expanding Atlantic Nucleus," 304.
48. James Kurth, "The Next NATO: Building an American Commonwealth of Nations," *The National Interest*, no. 65 (2001): 5–16.
49. Robert W. Tucker, "The Triumph of Wilsonism?" *World Policy Journal* 10, no. 4 (1993–1994): 83–99.
50. Mandelbaum, *Ideas That Conquered the World*, 67.

ACRONYMS

ABC Atomic, Biological, and Chemical Weapons

ABM Anti-Ballistic Missile Treaty

ASRAAM Advanced Short Range Air-to-Air Missile

AFSOUTH Allied Forces Southern Europe

AWACS Airborne Warning and Control System

BMD Ballistic Missile Defense

BTWC Biological and Toxin Weapons Convention

BW Biological Weapons

C³I Command, Control, Communications, and Intelligence

CAP Combat Air Patrol

CDM Council of Defense Ministers

CESDP Common European Security and Defense Policy

CFE Conventional Forces in Europe

CFSP Common Foreign and Security Policy

CIA Central Intelligence Agency

CJTF Combined Joint Task Forces

CSBM Confidence and Security Building Mechanism

CW Chemical Weapons

DCI Defense Capabilities Initiative

DoD Department of Defense

DPPI Disaster Prevention and Preparedness Initiative

EADC European Aeronautics and Defense Company

EADRCC   Euro-Atlantic Disaster Response Coordination Centre

EADS   European Aeronautics, Defense, and Space Company

EAPC   Euro-Atlantic Partnership Council

EC   European Community

ECR   Electronic Combat Role

EDC   European Defence Community

EEA   European Armaments Agency

ESDI   European Security and Defense Identity

ESDP   European Security and Defense Policy

EU   European Union

EUMC   European Union Military Committee

EW   Electronic Warfare

FLIR   Forward-Looking Infrared

FRY   Former Republic of Yugoslavia

FYROM   Former Yugoslav Republic of Macedonia

HHG   Helsinki Headline Goal

ICBM   Inter-continental Ballistic Missile

ICC   International Criminal Court

ICTY   International Criminal Tribunal for the Former Yugoslavia

IFOR   Implementation Force

INF   Intermediate-range Nuclear Forces

IPTF   International Police Task Force

ISAF   International Security Assistance Force

ISR   Intelligence, Surveillance and Reconnaissance

JCS   Joint Chiefs of Staff

JDAM   Joint Direct Attack Munition

JSOW   Joint Stand-off Weapon

JSTARS   Joint Surveillance and Target Attack Radar System

KFOR   Kosovo Force

KPC   Kosovo Protection Corps

MAP   Membership Action Plan

MBFR   Mutual Balanced Force Reductions

MC   Military Committee

MoD   Ministry of Defence

NAC   North Atlantic Council

NACC   North Atlantic Cooperation Council

NAFTA   North American Free Trade Agreement

NATO   North Atlantic Treaty Organization

NMD   National Missile Defense

OSCE   Organization for Security and Cooperation in Europe

PfP   Partnership for Peace

PHARE   Poland and Hungary Assistance for Economic Restructuring

PIC   Peace Implementation Council

PSC   Policy and Security Committee

RMA   Revolution in Military Affairs

RRF   Rapid Reaction Force

SACEUR   Supreme Allied Commander in Europe

SACLANT   Supreme Allied Commander Atlantic

SALT   Strategic Arms Limitation Talks

SDI   Strategic Defense Initiative

SEA   Single European Act

SEAD   Suppression of Enemy Air Defenses

SEEGROUP   Southeast Europe Security Cooperation Steering Group

SEEI   Southeast Europe Initiative

SFOR   Security Force

SLBM   Submarine-launched Ballistic Missile

START   Strategic Arms Reduction Talks

TAFTA   Trans-Atlantic Free Trade Agreement

THAAD   Theater High Altitude Air Defense

TMD   Theater Missile Defense

UN   United Nations

UNHCR   United Nations High Commissioner for Refugees

UNHRC   United Nations Human Rights Commission

UNMIBH   United Nations Mission in Bosnia and Herzogovina

UNMIK   United Nations Interim Administration Mission in Kosovo

UNPROFOR   United Nations Protection Force

UNSCR   United Nations Security Council Resolution

WEAG   West European Armaments Group

WEU   West European Union

WMD   Weapons of Mass Destruction

WTO   World Trade Organization

BIBLIOGRAPHY

BOOKS

Adler, Emanuel, and Michael Barnett, eds. *Security Communities.* Cambridge: Cambridge University Press, 1998.

Ahmann, R., A. M. Birke, and M. Howard, eds. *The Quest for Stability: Problems of West European Security, 1918–1955.* London: Oxford University Press, 1993.

Allard, Kenneth. *Somalia Operations: Lessons Learned.* Washington, D.C.: National Defense University Press, 1995.

Ambrose, Stephen. *Rise to Globalism: American Foreign Policy since 1938.* New York: Penguin, 1991.

Aron, Raymond. *The Imperial Republic: The United States and the World, 1945–1973.* Trans. Frank Jellinek. Cambridge: Winthrop, 1973.

———. *On War.* Trans. Terence Kilmartin. New York: Doubleday, 1959.

Asmus, Ronald D. *Germany's Geopolitical Maturation: Public Opinion and Security Policy in 1994.* Santa Monica, CA: RAND, 1995.

———. *German Strategy and Opinion after the Wall, 1990–1993.* Santa Monica, CA: RAND, 1994.

Baker, James A. III. *The Politics of Diplomacy: Revolution, War, and Peace, 1989–1992.* New York: G. P. Putnam's, 1995.

Baring, Arnulf. *Unser neuer Größenwahn: Deutschland zwishen Ost und West.* Stuttgart: Deutsche Verlags-Anstalt, 1988.

Barry, Charles, ed. *Reforging the Trans-Atlantic Relationship.* Washington, D.C.: National Defense University Press, 1996.

Bebler, Anton, ed. *The Challenge of NATO Enlargement.* Westport, CT: Praeger, 1999.

Bellany, Ian, and Coit D. Blacker. *The Verification of Arms Control Agreements.* London: Frank Cass, 1983.

Berman, Larry. *Planning a Tragedy: The Americanization of the War in Vietnam.* New York: W. W. Norton, 1982.

Betts, Richard K. *NATO Deterrence Doctrine: No Way Out.* Los Angeles, CA: University of California Press, 1996.

Bildt, Carl. *Peace Journey: The Struggle for Peace in Bosnia.* London: Weidenfeld & Nicolson, 1998.

———, et al., eds. *What Global Role for the EU?* Brussels: The Philip Morris Institute for Public Policy Research, 1997.

Bilinsky, Yaroslav. *Endgame in NATO's Enlargement.* Westport, CT: Praeger, 1999.

Bonvicini, Gianni, Tapani Vaahtoranta, and Wolfgang Wessels, eds. *The Northern EU: National Views on the Emerging Security Dimension.* Helsinki: Finnish Institute of International Affairs, 2000.

Boutwell, Jeffrey. *The German Nuclear Dilemma.* Ithaca, NY: Cornell University Press, 1990.

Bozo, Frédéric. *La France et l'OTAN.* Paris: Masson, 1991.

Brandon, H. *The Retreat of American Power.* New York: Doubleday, 1973.

Brogan, Denis. *The Development of Modern France, 1870–1939.* London: Hamish Hamilton, 1967.

Brzezinski, Zbigniew. *The Grand Chessboard: American Primacy and Its Geostrategic Imperatives.* New York: Basic Books, 1997.

———. *The Game Plan: The Geostrategic Framework for the Conduct of the U.S.-Soviet Contest.* New York: Atlantic Monthly Press, 1986.

———. *Power and Principle: Memoirs of the National Security Advisor, 1977–1981.* New York: Farrar, Strauss, Giroux, 1983.

Bulkeley, Rip, and Hans Gunter Brauch. *The Anti-Ballistic Missile Treaty and World Security.* New York: AFES Press, Report Number 14, 1988.

Bull, Hedley. *The Anarchical Society: A Study of Order in World Politics.* New York: Columbia University Press, 1995.

Calleo, David. *Rethinking Europe's Future.* Princeton, NJ: Princeton University Press, 2001.

———. *Beyond American Hegemony: The Future of the Western Alliance.* New York: Basic Books, 1987.

———. *The Atlantic Fantasy: The U.S., NATO and Europe.* Baltimore, MD: Johns Hopkins University Press, 1970.

Carnovale, Marco. *The Control of NATO Nuclear Forces in Europe.* Boulder, CO: Westview, 1993.

Carpenter, Ted Galen. *NATO Enlargement: Illusions and Reality.* Washington, D.C.: Cato Institute, 1998.

Carr, E. H. *The Twenty Years Crisis, 1919–1939.* London: Macmillan, 1939.

Carter, Ashton B., and David N. Schwartz, eds. *Ballistic Missile Defense.* Washington, D.C.: Brookings, 1984.

Carter, Jimmy. *Keeping Faith: Memoirs of a President.* Fayetteville, AR: University of Arkansas Press, 1995.

Chauvistré, Eric. *The Implications of IAEA Inspections under Security Council Resolution 687.* New York: UNIDIR, UN, 1992.

Clark, I. *The Hierarchy of States: Reform and Resistance in the International Order.* Cambridge: Cambridge University Press, 1989.

Clark, Wesley. *Waging Modern War: Bosnia, Kosovo, and the Future of Combat.* New York: Public Affairs, 2001.

Claude, Inis L., Jr. *Swords Into Plowshares: The Problems and Progress of International Organization.* New York: Random House, 1964.

Clausewitz, Carl von. *On War*, ed. Michael Howard and Peter Paret. Princeton, NJ: Princeton University Press, 1976.

Cogan, Charles G. *The Third Option: The Emancipation of European Defense, 1989–2000.* Westport, CT: Praeger, 2001.

———. *Forced to Choose: France, the Atlantic Alliance, and NATO—Then and Now.* Westport, CT: Praeger, 1997.

Cohen, Lenard J. *Broken Bonds: Yugoslavia's Disintegration and Balkan Politics in Transition.* Boulder, CO: Westview, 1994.

Craig, Campbell. *Destroying the Village: Eisenhower and Thermonuclear War.* New York: Columbia University Press, 1998.

Daalder, Ivo H. *Getting to Dayton: The Making of America's Bosnia Policy.* Washington, D.C.: Brookings, 2000.

———, and Michael O'Hanlon. *Winning Ugly: NATO's War to Save Kosovo.* Washington, D.C.: Brookings, 2000.

Dallek, Robert. *Franklin Roosevelt and American Foreign Policy, 1932–1945.* New York: Oxford University Press, 1979.

Danopoulos, Constantine P., and Kostas G. Messas, eds. *Crisis in the Balkans: Views from the Participants.* Boulder, CO: Westview, 1997.

Dean, Jonathan. *Ending Europe's Wars: The Continuing Search for Peace and Security.* Washington, D.C.: Brookings, 1994.

Decret, François. *Carthage ou l'empire de la mer.* Paris: Editions du Seuil, 1977.

Deporte, A. W. *Europe between the Superpowers: The Enduring Balance.* New Haven, CT: Yale University Press, 1986.

Deutsch, Karl, et al. *Political Community in the North Atlantic Area.* Princeton, NJ: Princeton University Press, 1957.

Dobosiewicz, Zbigniew. *Foreign Investment in Eastern Europe.* London: Routledge, 1992.

Dockrill, Saki. *Britain's Policy for West German Rearmament, 1950–1955.* New York: Cambridge University Press, 1988.

Duffield, John S. *World Power Forsaken: Political Culture, International Institutions, and German Security Policy after Unification.* Stanford, CA: Stanford University Press, 1998.

———. *Power Rules: The Evolution of NATO's Conventional Force Posture.* Stanford, CA: Stanford University Press, 1995.

Duke, Simon. *The Elusive Quest for European Security: From EDC to CFSP.* New York: St. Martin's, 2000.

Durrell-Young, Thomas. *The Normalization of the Federal Republic of Germany's Defense Structures.* Carlisle, PA: U.S. Army War College, 1992.

Eliassen, Kjell A., ed. *Foreign and Security Policy in the European Union.* London: Sage, 1998.

Falkenrath, Richard A. *Shaping Europe's Military Order: The Origins of the CFE Treaty.* Cambridge, MA: MIT Press, 1995.

Ferguson, Niall. *The Cash Nexus: Money and Power in the Modern World, 1700–2000.* New York: Basic Books, 2001.

Flynn, Gregory, ed. *Remaking the Hexagone: The New France in the New Europe.* Boulder, CO: Westview, 1995.

Foschepoth, Joseph, ed. *Adenauer und die deutsche Frage.* Göttingen: Vandenhoeck und Ruprecht, 1988.

Freedman, Lawrence, and Efraim Karsh. *The Gulf Conflict 1990–1991.* Princeton, NJ: Princeton University Press, 1993.

Fromkin, David. *Kosovo Crossing: American Ideas Meet Reality on the Balkan Battlefields.* New York: Free Press, 1999.

Gacek, Christopher M. *The Logic of Force: The Dilemma of Limited War in American Foreign Policy.* New York: Columbia University Press, 1994.

Gaddis, John Lewis. *The United States and the Cold War: Implications, Reconsiderations, Provocations.* New York: Oxford University Press, 1992.

——. *The Long Peace: Inquiries into the History of the Cold War.* New York: Oxford University Press, 1987.

——. *Strategies of Containment: A Critical Appraisal of Postwar American National Security Policy.* New York: Oxford University Press, 1982.

Gammer, Nicholas. *From Peacekeeping to Peacemaking: Canada's Response to the Yugoslav Crisis.* Montréal: McGill-Queen's University Press, 2001.

Garnett, Sherman. *The CFE Flank Agreement.* Washington, D.C.: Carnegie Endowment for International Peace, 1997.

Garthoff, Raymond L. *The Great Transition: American-Soviet Relations and the End of the Cold War.* Washington, D.C.: Brookings, 1994.

——. *Détente and Confrontation: American-Soviet Relations from Nixon to Reagan.* Washington, D.C.: Brookings, 1985.

Garton Ash, Timothy. *In Europe's Name: Germany and the Divided Continent.* London: Jonathan Cape, 1993.

Gelman, Harry. *The Brezhnev Politburo and the Decline of Détente.* Ithaca, NY: Cornell University Press, 1984.

Genscher, Hans-Dietrich. *Erinnerungen.* Berlin: Siedler, 1995.

Gillingham, John. *European Integration, 1950–2003: Superstate or New Market Economy?* New York: Cambridge University Press, 2003.

Goldblat, Jozef. *Arms Control: A Guide to Negotiations and Agreements.* London: PRIO/Sage, 1996.

Goldgeier, James M. *Not Whether but When: The U.S. Decision to Enlarge NATO.* Washington, D.C.: Brookings, 1999.

Goldstein, Joshua S. *Long Cycles: Prosperity and War in the Modern Age.* New Haven, CT: Yale University Press, 1988.

Gompert, David C., et al. *Mind the Gap: Promoting a Transatlantic Revolution in Military Affairs.* Washington, D.C.: National Defense University Press, 1999.

——, and Stephen L. Larrabee, eds. *America and Europe: A Partnership for a New Era.* New York: Cambridge University Press, 1997.

Gordon, Philip H., ed. *NATO's Transformation: The Changing Shape of the Atlantic Alliance.* Lanham, MD: Rowman and Littlefield, 1997.

——. *France, Germany and the Western Alliance.* Boulder, CO: Westview, 1995.

——. *A Certain Idea of France: French Security Policy and the Gaullist Legacy.* Princeton, NJ: Princeton University Press, 1993.

Gottlieb, Gidon. *Nation against State: A New Approach to Ethnic Conflict and the Decline of Sovereignty.* New York: Council on Foreign Relations Press, 1993.

Gow, James, and James D. D. Smith. *Peace-making, Peace-keeping: European Security and the Yugoslav Wars.* London: Brassey's, 1992.

Gray, Colin S. *Modern Strategy.* Oxford: Clarendon, 1999.

——. *House of Cards: Why Arms Control Must Fail.* Ithaca, NY: Cornell University Press, 1992.

Haass, Richard N. *Intervention: The Use of American Military Force in the Post–Cold War World*. New York: Carnegie Endowment for International Peace, 1999.

——, ed. *Transatlantic Tensions: The United States, Europe, and Problem Countries*. Washington, D.C.: Brookings, 1999.

——, ed. *Economic Sanctions and American Diplomacy*. New York: Council on Foreign Relations Press, 1998.

——. *The Reluctant Sheriff: The United States after the Cold War*. New York: Council on Foreign Relations Press, 1997.

Haglund, David G. *Alliance within the Alliance? Franco-German Military Cooperation and the European Pillar of Defense*. Boulder, CO: Westview, 1991.

Hanrieder, Wolfram F. *Germany, America, Europe: Forty Years of German Foreign Policy*. New Haven, CT: Yale University Press, 1989.

Harper, John Lamberton. *American Visions of Europe: Franklin Roosevelt, George Kennan, and Dean Acheson*. New York: Cambridge University Press, 1994.

Harrison, Michael M. *The Reluctant Ally: France and Atlantic Security*. Baltimore, MD: Johns Hopkins University Press, 1981.

Hashmi, Sohail H., ed. *State Sovereignty: Change and Persistence in International Relations*. University Park, PA: Pennsylvania State University Press, 1997.

Heraclides, A. *Helsinki II and Its Aftermath: The Making of the CSCE into an International Organization*. London: Pinter, 1993.

Heuser, Beatrice. *Nuclear Mentalities? Strategies and Beliefs in Britain, France and the FRG*. New York: St. Martin's, 1998.

——. *NATO, Britain, France and the FRG: Nuclear Strategies and Forces for Europe, 1949–2000*. New York: St. Martin's, 1997.

Hodge, Carl C., ed. *Redefining European Security*. New York: Garland, 1999.

Hoffmann, Stanley. *Gulliver's Troubles, or the Setting of American Foreign Policy*. New York: McGraw-Hill, 1968.

Hogan, Michael. *The Marshall Plan: America, Britain, and the Reconstruction of Europe*. New York: Cambridge University Press, 1987.

Horsman, Matthew, and Andrew Marshall. *After the Nation State: Citizens, Tribalism, and the New World Disorder*. New York: Harper-Collins, 1994.

Howard, Michael. *The Invention of Peace: Reflection on War and International Order*. New Haven, CT: Yale University Press, 2000.

——. *The Lessons of History*. New York: Oxford University Press, 1991.

Huntington, Samuel. *The Clash of Civilizations*. New York: Simon & Schuster, 1996.

Hyde-Price, Adrian. *European Security beyond the Cold War. Four Scenarios for the Year 2010*. London: RIIA/Sage, 1991.

Ignatieff, Michael. *The Warrior's Honor: Ethnic War and the Modern Conscience*. London: Chatto & Windus, 1998.

——. *Virtual War: Kosovo and Beyond*. New York: Henry Holt, 1998.

Ikenberry, John G. *American Foreign Policy: Theoretical Essays*. New York: Addison-Wesley, 1996.

Jackson, Robert H. *The Global Covenant: Human Conduct in World Affairs*. New York: Oxford University Press, 2000.

Joffe, Josef. *The Limited Partnership: Europe, the United States, and the Burdens of Alliance*. Cambridge: Ballinger Publishing, 1987.

Jordan, Nicole. *The Popular Front & Central Europe: The Dilemmas of French Impotence*. New York: Cambridge University Press, 1992.

Judah, Tim. *Kosovo: War and Revenge*. New Haven, CT: Yale University Press, 2000.

Kagan, Donald, and Frederick W. Kagan. *While America Sleeps: Self-Delusion, Military Weakness, and the Threat to Peace Today*. New York: St. Martin's, 2000.

———. *Of Paradise and Power: America and Europe in the New World Order*. New York: Alfred A. Knopf, 2003.

Kaiser, Karl, and Pierre Lellouche, eds. *Deutsch-französische Sicherheitspolitik: Auf dem Weg zur Gemeinsamkeit?* Bonn: Europa Union Verlag, 1986.

Kaplan, Lawrence S. *The Long Entanglement: NATO's First Fifty Years*. Westport, CT: Praeger, 1999.

Kay, Sean. *NATO and the Future of European Security*. Lanham, MD: Rowman & Littlefield, 1998.

Keaney, Thomas A., and Eliot A. Cohen. *Gulf War Air Power Survey*, 6 vols. Washington, D.C.: USGPO, 1993.

Keegan, John. *The First World War*. London: Random House, 1998.

———. *War and Our World: The Reith Lectures, 1998*. London: Hutchinson, 1998.

Kegley, Charles W., and Kenneth L. Schwab, eds. *After the Cold War: Questioning the Morality of Nuclear Deterrence*. Boulder, CO: Westview, 1991.

———, ed. *The Long Postwar Peace*. New York: HarperCollins, 1991.

Kennedy, David M. *Freedom from Fear: The American People in Depression and War, 1929–1945*. New York: Oxford University Press, 1999.

Kennedy, Paul. *The Rise and Fall of the Great Powers: Economic Change and Military Conflict from 1500 to 2000*. London: Unwin Hyman, 1988.

Keohane, R. O. *After Hegemony: Cooperation and Discord in the World Political Economy*. Princeton, NJ: Princeton University Press, 1984.

Kissinger, Henry. *Years of Renewal*. New York: Simon & Schuster, 1999.

———. *Diplomacy*. New York: Simon & Schuster, 1994.

———. *White House Years*. Boston, MA: Little, Brown & Company, 1979.

Knapp, Andrew. *Gaullism since de Gaulle*. Aldershot: Dartmouth, 1994.

Kocs, Stephen A. *Autonomy or Power? The Franco-German Relationship and Europe's Strategic Choices, 1955–1995*. Westport, CT: Praeger, 1995.

Korey, William. *The Promises We Keep: Human Rights, the Helsinki Process, and American Foreign Policy*. New York: St. Martin's, 1993.

Kozhemiakin, Alexander V. *Expanding the Zone of Peace? Democratization and International Security*. New York: St. Martin's, 1998.

Krasner, Stephen D. *Sovereignty: Organized Hypocrisy*. Princeton, NJ: Princeton University Press, 1999.

Kunz, Dianne B., ed. *The Diplomacy of the Crucial Decade: American Foreign Relations in the 1960s*. New York: Columbia, 1994.

Lacouture, Jean. *De Gaulle, The Ruler, 1945–1970*. Trans. Alan Sheridan. London: Harvill, 1991.

Laird, Robbin F. *The Revolution in Military Affairs: Allied Perspectives*. Washington, D.C.: Institute for National Strategic Studies, 1999.

Lambeth, Benjamin S. *NATO's Air War for Kosovo: A Strategic and Operational Assessment*. Santa Monica, CA: RAND, 2001.

Larkin, Maurice. *France since the Popular Front: Government and People, 1936–1986*. Oxford: Clarendon Press, 1988.

Leffler, Melvyn. *A Preponderance of Power*. Stanford, CA: Stanford University Press, 1992.

Lesser, Ian O. *NATO Looks South: New Challenges and New Strategies in the Mediterranean*. Santa Monica, CA: RAND, 2000.

Levin, N. Gordon, Jr. *Woodrow Wilson and World Politics: America's Response to War and Revolution.* New York: Oxford University Press, 1968.

Levy, Carl, and Mark Roseman, eds. *Three Postwar Eras in Comparison: Western Europe 1918–1945–1989.* Basingstoke: Palgrave, 2002.

Libal, Michael. *The Limits of Persuasion: Germany and the Yugoslav Crisis, 1991–1992.* Westport, CT: Praeger, 1997.

Lindsay, James M., and Michael E. O'Hanlon. *Defending America: The Case for Limited National Missile Defense.* Washington, D.C.: Brookings, 2001.

Link, Arthur S. *Wilson: Campaigns for Progressivism and Peace, 1916–1917.* Princeton, NJ: Princeton University Press, 1965.

Litwak, Robert S. *Détente and the Nixon Doctrine: American Foreign Policy and the Pursuit of Stability, 1969–1976.* New York: Cambridge University Press, 1984.

Lukacs, John. *The End of the Twentieth Century and the End of the Modern Age.* New York: Ticknor & Fields, 1993.

Lyons, Gene, and Michael Mastanduno, eds. *Beyond Westphalia? State Sovereignty and International Intervention.* Baltimore, MD: Johns Hopkins University Press, 1995.

Mandelbaum, Michael. *The Ideas That Conquered the World: Peace, Democracy and Free Markets in the Twenty-First Century.* New York: Public Affairs, 2002.

——. *NATO Expansion: A Bridge to the Nineteenth Century.* Chevy Chase, MD: Center for Political and Strategic Studies, 1997.

——. *The Dawn of Peace in Europe.* New York: Twentieth Century Fund Press, 1996.

Martinet, Gilles. *Le Reveil des nationalismes français.* Paris: Le Seuil, 1994.

Mastny Vojtech, ed. *Helsinki: Human Rights and European Security.* Durham, NC: Duke University Press, 1986.

Mayers, David. *George Kennan and the Dilemmas of U.S. Foreign Policy.* New York: Oxford University Press, 1988.

Mazarr, Michael J. *The Revolution in Military Affairs: A Framework for Defense Planning.* Carlisle, PA: Institute of Strategic Studies, 1994.

——. *Missile Defenses and Asia-Pacific Security.* New York: St. Martin's, 1989.

McCullough, David. *Truman.* New York: Simon & Schuster, 1992.

McDougall, Walter A. *Promised Land, Crusader State: The American Encounter with the World since 1776.* New York: Houghton Mifflin, 1997.

McFaul, Michael. *Russia's Unfinished Revolution: Political Change from Gorbachev to Putin.* Ithaca, NY: Cornell University Press, 2001.

McNamara, Robert S., and James G. Blight. *Wilson's Ghost: Reducing the Risk of Conflict in the Twentieth Century.* New York: Public Affairs, 2001.

Mead, Walter Russell. *Special Providence: American Foreign Policy and How It Changed the World.* New York: Alfred A. Knopf, 2001.

Menon, Anand. *France, NATO and the Limits of Independence, 1981–1997: The Politics of Ambivalence.* New York: St. Martin's, 2000.

Middlemas, Keith. *Orchestrating Europe: The Informal Politics of European Union, 1973–1995.* London: Fontana, 1995.

Mileham, Patrick, and Lee Willett, eds. *Military Ethics for the Expeditionary Era.* London: Royal Institute for International Affairs, 2001.

Miller, Steven E., and Stephen Van Evera. *The Star Wars Controversy.* Princeton, NJ: Princeton University Press, 1986.

Miscamble, Wilson D. *George F. Kennan and the Making of American Foreign Policy.* Princeton, NJ: Princeton University Press, 1992.

Mitrany, David. *A Working Peace System.* New York and London: Royal Institute of International Affairs, 1946.

Morgan, Kenneth O. *The People's Peace, 1945–1989.* New York: Oxford University Press, 1990.

Morgenthau, Hans J. *Politics among Nations.* New York: Knopf, 1948.

Mowat, Charles Loch. *Britain between the Wars, 1918–1940.* London: Methuen, 1955.

Moynihan, Daniel Patrick. *Pandaemonium: Ethnicity in International Politics.* New York: Oxford University Press, 1993.

Muir, William Ker, Jr. *The Bully Pulpit: The Presidential Leadership of Ronald Reagan.* San Francisco, CA: Institute for Contemporary Studies, 1992.

Muravchik, Joshua. *The Uncertain Crusade: Jimmy Carter and the Dilemmas of Human Rights Policy.* Lanham, MD: Hamilton Press, 1986.

Nau, Henry. *At Home Abroad: Identity and Power in American Foreign Policy.* Ithaca, NY: Cornell University Press, 2002.

———. *The Myth of America's Decline: Leading the World into the 1990s.* New York: Oxford University Press, 1990.

Newhouse, John. *De Gaulle and the Anglo-Saxons.* New York: Viking Press, 1970.

Nicolson, Harold. *Peacemaking 1919.* New York: Grosset & Dunlap, 1965.

Ninkovich, Frank. *The Wilsonian Century: U.S. Foreign Policy since 1900.* Chicago, IL: University of Chicago Press, 1999.

Nolan, Cathal J., ed. *Ethics and Statecraft: The Moral Dimension of International Affairs.* Westport, CT: Praeger Publishers, 1995.

———. *Principled Diplomacy: Security and Rights in U.S. Foreign Policy.* Westport, CT: Greenwood Press, 1993.

Nordlinger, Eric. *Isolationism Reconfigured: American Foreign Policy for a New Century.* Princeton, NJ: Princeton University Press, 1995.

Nye, Joseph S. *The Paradox of American Power: Why the World's Only Superpower Can't Go It Alone.* New York: Oxford University Press, 2002.

———. *Bound to Lead: The Changing Nature of American Power.* New York: Basic Books, 1990.

O'Hanlon, Michael. *Technological Change and the Future of Warfare.* Washington, D.C.: Brookings, 2000.

———. *Saving Lives with Force: Military Criteria for Humanitarian Intervention.* Washington, D.C.: Brookings, 1997.

O'Rourke, Kevin, and Jeffrey Williamson. *Globalization and History: The Evolution of a Nineteenth Century Atlantic Economy.* Cambridge, MA: MIT Press, 2000.

Owen, David. *Balkan Odyssey.* London: Victor Gollancz, 1995.

Oye, K. A., D. Rothchild, and R. J. Lieber, eds. *Eagle Entangled: U.S. Foreign Policy in a Complex World.* New York: Longman, 1979.

Paterson, Thomas G., ed. *Kennedy's Quest for Victory: American Foreign Policy, 1961–1963.* New York: Oxford University Press, 1989.

———. *Meeting the Communist Threat, Truman to Reagan.* New York: Oxford University Press, 1988.

Payne, Keith. *Missile Defense in the 21st Century: Protection against Limited Threats, Including Lessons from the Gulf War.* Boulder, CO: Westview, 1992.

Peters, John E., Stuart Johnson, Nora Bensahel, Timothy Liston, and Traci Williams. *European Contributions to Operation Allied Force: Implications for Transatlantic Cooperation.* Santa Monica, CA: RAND, 2001.

Philpott, Daniel. *Revolutions in Sovereignty: How Ideas Shaped Modern International Relations.* Princeton, NJ: Princeton University Press, 2001.

Pipes, Richard. *U.S.-Soviet Relations in the Era of Detente.* Boulder, CO: Westview Press, 1981.

Ramet, Sabrina Petra, and Ivo Banac. *Balkan Babel: The Disintegration of Yugoslavia from the Death of Tito to Ethnic War.* Boulder, CO: Westview, 1996.

Reddaway, Peter, and Dmitri Glinski. *The Tragedy of Russia's Reforms: Market Bolshevism against Democracy.* Washington, D.C.: United States Institute of Peace, 2001.

Rieff, David. *Slaughterhouse: Bosnia and the Failure of the West.* New York: Touchstone, 1995.

Rivkin, David B., Lee A. Casey, and Darin R. Bartram. *The Collapse of the Soviet Union and the End of the 1972 Anti-Ballistic Missile Treaty.* Washington, D.C.: Hunton and Williams, 1998.

Rodley, Nigel S., ed. *To Loose the Bands of Wickedness: International Intervention in Defence of Human Rights.* London: Brassey's, 1992.

Rosenthal, Joel, ed. *Ethics and International Affairs: A Reader.* Washington, D.C.: Georgetown University Press, 1999.

Ruane, Kevin. *The Rise and Fall of the European Defence Community: Anglo-American Relations and the Crisis in European Defence, 1950–55.* London: Macmillan, 2000.

Ruggie, John Gerard. *Multilateralism Matters: The Theory and Praxis of an Institutional Form.* New York: Columbia University Press, 1993.

Rumer, Eugene. *Russian National Security and Foreign Policy in Transition.* Santa Monica, CA: RAND, 1995.

Rummel, Reinhardt, ed. *Toward Political Union: Planning a Common Foreign and Security Policy in the European Community.* Boulder, CO: Westview Press, 1992.

Rynning, Sten. *Changing Military Doctrine: Presidents and Military Power in Fifth Republic France, 1958–2000.* Westport, CT: Praeger, 2002.

Sauder, Axel. *Souveränität und Integration. Französische und deutsche Konzeptionen europäischer Sicherheit nach dem Ende des Kalten Krieges, 1990–1993.* Baden-Baden: Nomos, 1995.

Schmidt, Helmut. *Die Deutschen und Ihre Nachbarn.* Berlin: Siedler, 1990.

——. *Menschen und Mächte.* Berlin: Goldmann, 1987.

Schmidt, Peter. *Neuorientierung in der Europäischen Sicherheitspolitik? Britische und Britisch-Französische Initiativen.* Ebenhausen: Stiftung Wissenschaft und Politik, 1999.

——. *Frankreichs neues Verhältnis zur NATO: Preisgabe oder Verwirklichung gaullistischer Prinzipien?* Ebenhausen: Stiftung Wissenschaft und Politik, May 1996.

Schultz, George B. *Turmoil and Triumph: My Years as Secretary of State.* New York: Charles Scribner's Sons, 1993.

Schwarz, Hans-Peter. *Die gezähmten Deutschen: Von der Machtbessenheit zur Machtvergessenheit.* Stuttgart: Deutsche Verlags-Anstalt, 1985.

Sharp, Paul. *Thatcher's Diplomacy: The Revival of British Foreign Policy.* New York: St. Martin's, 1997.

Simonian, Haig. *The Privileged Partnership: Franco-German Relations on the European Community.* Oxford: Clarendon, 1985.

Smith, Mark. *NATO Enlargement during the Cold War: Strategy and System in the Western Alliance.* London: Palgrave, 2000.

Smith, Tony. *America's Mission: The United States and the World-Wide Struggle for Democracy in the Twentieth Century.* Princeton, NJ: Princeton University Press, 1994.

Sodaro, Michael J. *Moscow, Germany, and the West from Khrushchev to Gorbachev.* Ithaca, NY: Cornell University Press, 1990.

Steinbruner, John D. *Principles of Global Security.* Washington, D.C.: Brookings, 2000.

Stent, Angela E. *Russia and Germany Reborn: Unification, The Soviet Collapse, and the New Europe.* Princeton, NJ: Princeton University Press, 1999.

———. *From Embargo to Ostpolitik: The Political Economy of West German-Soviet Relations, 1955–1980.* New York: Cambridge University Press, 1981.

Szabo, Stephen, ed. *The Bundeswehr and Western Security.* London: Macmillan, 1990.

Szayna, Thomas S. *NATO Enlargement 2000–2015: Determinants and Implications for Defense Planning and Shaping.* Santa Monica, CA: RAND, 2001.

Teller, Edward. *Better a Shield than a Sword.* New York: The Free Press, 1987.

Thatcher, Margaret. *The Downing Street Years.* New York: HarperCollins, 1993.

Thomas, Daniel C. *The Helsinki Effect:International Norms, Human Rights, and the Demise of Communism.* Princeton, NJ: Princeton University Press, 2001.

Thomas, Raju G. C., and H. Richard Friman, eds. *The South Slav Conflict: History, Religion, Ethnicity and Nationalism.* New York: Garland Publishing, 1996.

Tilford, Earl. H. *The Revolution in Military Affairs: Prospects and Cautions.* Carlisle, PA: Strategic Studies Institute, 1995.

Towle, Philip. *Enforced Disarmament from the Napoleonic Campaigns to the Gulf War.* Oxford: Clarendon 1997.

Trachtenberg, Marc. *A Constructed Peace: The Making of the European Settlement, 1945–1963.* Princeton, NJ: Princeton University Press, 1999.

———. *History and Strategy.* Princeton, NJ: Princeton University Press, 1991.

Treverton, Gregory F. *America, Germany, and the Future of Europe.* Princeton, NJ: Princeton University Press, 1992.

Troebst, Stefan. *Conflict in Kosovo: An Analytical Documentation, 1992–1998.* Flensburg: European Center for Minority Issues, 1998.

Ullman, Richard H., ed. *The World and Yugoslavia's Wars.* New York: Council on Foreign Relations Press, 1996.

———. *Securing Europe.* Princeton, NJ: Princeton University Press, 1991.

Vance, Cyrus. *Hard Choices: Critical Years in America's Foreign Policy.* New York: Simon & Schuster, 1983.

Vogelgesang, Sandy. *American Dream, Global Nightmare: The Dilemma of U.S. Rights Policy.* New York: W. W. Norton, 1980.

Vulliamy, Ed. *Seasons in Hell: Understanding Bosnia's War.* New York: St. Martin's 1994.

Wallace, Helen, and William Wallace, eds. *Policy-Making in the European Union.* Oxford: Oxford University Press, 1996.

Wallander, Celeste A. *Mortal Friends, Best Enemies: German-Russian Cooperation after the Cold War.* Ithaca, NY: Cornell University Press, 1999.

———, ed. *The Sources of Russian Foreign Policy after the Cold War.* Boulder, CO: Westview, 1996.

Walt, Stephen M. *Revolution and War.* Ithaca, NY: Cornell University Press, 1996.

———. *The Origins of Alliances.* Ithaca, NY: Cornell University Press, 1987.

Waltz, Kenneth N. *Theory of International Politics.* Reading, MA: Addison Wesley, 1979.

———. *Man, the State, and War: A Theoretical Analysis.* New York: Columbia University Press, 1959.

Walzer, Michael. *Just and Unjust Wars: A Moral Argument with Historical Illustrations.* New York: Basic Books, 1977.

Weinberg, Gerhard L. *A World at Arms: A Global History of World War II.* New York: Cambridge University Press, 1994.

Wheeler, Nicholas. *Saving Strangers: Humanitarian Intervention in International Society.* New York: Oxford University Press, 2000.

Wilkening, Dean A. *Ballistic Missile Defence and Strategic Stability.* London: IISS and Oxford University Press, 2000.

Willis, F. Roy. *France, Germany, and the New Europe, 1945–1963.* Stanford, CA: Stanford University Press, 1965.

Winkler, Heinrich August. *Der lange Weg nach Westen: Deutsche Geschichte vom Ende des Alten Reiches bis zum Untergang der Weimarer Republik,* 2 vols. Munich: C. H. Beck, 2001.

Winrow, Gareth. *Dialogue with the Mediterranean: The Role of NATO's Mediterranean Initiative.* New York: Garland, 2000.

Woodward, Susan L. *Balkan Tragedy: Chaos and Dissolution after the Cold War.* Washington, D.C.: Brookings, 1995.

Wyatt-Walter, Holly. *The European Community and the Security Dilemma, 1979–1992.* London: Macmillan and St. Martin's Press, 1997.

Yost, David S. *NATO Transformed: The Alliance's New Roles in International Security.* Washington, D.C.: United States Institute of Peace, 1998.

Young, Hugo. *This Blessed Plot: Britain and Europe from Churchill to Blair.* Woodstock: Overlook Press, 1998.

Zakaria, Fareed. *The Future of Freedom: Illiberal Democracy at Home and Abroad.* New York: W. W. Norton, 2003.

Zelikow, Philip, and Condoleezza Rice. *Germany Unified and Europe Transformed: A Study in Statecraft.* Cambridge, MA: Harvard University Press, 1995.

Zielonka, Jan. *Explaining Euro-Paralysis: Why Europe Is Unable to Act in International Politics.* New York: St. Martin's, 1998.

Zitelmann, Rainer, and Karlheinz Weissmann, eds. *Westbindung.* Frankfurt: Propylaen, 1993.

ARTICLES AND ESSAYS

Abrams, Elliot. "To Fight the Good Fight." *The National Interest* 59 (2000): 70–78.

Adler, Les K., and Thomas G. Paterson. "Red Fascism: The Merger of Nazi Germany and Soviet Russia in the American Image of Totalitarianism, 1930s–1950s." *American Historical Review* 75, no. 4 (1970): 1046–1064.

Adomeit, Hannes. "Russia and Germany: A Normal Relationship." *RUSI Journal* (December 2000): 55–61.

Alexander, Michael, and Timothy Garden. "The Arithmetic of Defence Policy." *International Affairs* 77, no. 3 (2001): 509–529.

Anderson, Stephanie. "EU, NATO and CSCE Responses to the Yugoslav Crisis: Testing Europe's New Security Architecture." *European Security* 4, no. 2 (1995): 328–353.

Arbatov, Georgi. "Eurasia Letter: A New Cold War?" *Foreign Policy* 95 (1994): 90–103.

Archer, Clive. "Nordic Involvement in the Baltic States: Needs, Response, Success." *European Security* 7, no. 3 (1998): 43–62.

Asmus, Ronald D., Richard L. Kugler, and F. Stephen Larrabee. "Building a New NATO." *Foreign Affairs* 72, no. 4 (1993): 32–34.

Avant, Deborah D. "Are Reluctant Warriors Out of Control? Why the U.S. Military is Averse to Responding to Post–Cold War Low-level Threats." *Security Studies* 6, no. 2 (Winter 1996–1997): 51–90.

Bacevich, Andrew J. "Different Drummers, Same Drum." *The National Interest* 64 (2001): 67–77.

Bailes, Alyson. "Europe's Defense Challenge." *Foreign Affairs* 76, no. 1 (1997): 14–18.

Baldwin, K. J. "Can Europe Project Air Power without the Support of the United States?" *Royal Air Force Air Power Review* 4, no. 3 (2001): 61–62.

Baylis, Thomas. "Presidents versus Prime Ministers: Shaping Executive Authority in Eastern Europe." *World Politics* 48, no. 2 (1996): 297–323.

Becker, Jeffrey. "The Future of Atlantic Defense Procurement." *Defense Analysis* 16, no. 1 (2000): 9–32.

Bell, Coral. "Why an Expanded NATO Must Include Russia." *Journal of Strategic Studies* 17, no. 4 (1994): 27–41.

Betts, Richard. "The Lesser Evil: The Best Way out of the Balkans." *The National Interest* 64 (2001): 53–65.

——. "Compromised Command: Inside NATO's First War." *Foreign Affairs* 80, no. 4 (2001): 126–132.

Blank, Stephen J. "Russia and the Baltics in the Age of NATO Enlargement." *Parameters* 28, no. 3 (1998): 50–68.

——. "Russia, NATO Enlargement, and the Baltic States." *World Affairs* 60, no. 3 (1998): 115–125.

Borwaski, John. "Partnership for Peace and Beyond." *International Affairs* 71, no. 2 (1995): 233–246.

Bozo, Frédéric. "La France at l'Alliance: les limites du rapprochment." *Politique Etrangère* (1995–1996): 865–877.

Brown, Michael E. "The Flawed Logic of NATO Expansion." *Survival* 37, no. 1 (1995): 34–51.

Brzezinski, Zbigniew. "The Premature Partnership." *Foreign Affairs* 73, no. 2 (1994): 67–82.

Bugajski, Janusz. "Balkan in Dependence?" *Washington Quarterly* 23, no. 4 (2000): 177–192.

Buszynski, Leszek. "Russia and the West: Towards Renewed Geopolitical Rivalry?" *Survival* 37, no. 3 (1995): 104–114.

Chan, Steve. "The Impact of Defense Spending on Economic Performance: A Survey of Evidence and Problems." *Orbis* 29, no. 3 (1985): 403–434.

Clark, Mark T. "The Trouble with Collective Security." *Orbis* 39, no. 2 (1995): 237–259.

Cohen, Lenard J., and Alexander Moens. "Learning the Lessons of UNPROFOR: Canadian Peacekeeping in the Former Yugoslavia." *Canadian Foreign Policy* 6, no. 2 (1999): 85–101.

Coll, Alberto R. "Introduction: American Power and Responsibility in a New Century." *Ethics & International Affairs* 14 (2000): 3–10.

Cook, Martin. "Immaculate War: Constraints on Humanitarian Intervention." *Ethics & International Affairs* 14 (2000): 55–65.

Cornish, Paul, and Geoffrey Edwards. "Beyond the EU/NATO Dichotomy: The Beginnings of a European Strategic Culture." *International Affairs* 77, no. 3 (2001): 598–599.

——. "European Security: The End of Architecture and the New NATO." *International Affairs* 72, no. 4 (1996): 751–770.

Cox, Michael. "September 11th and U.S. Hegemony—Or Will the 21st Century Be American Too?" *International Studies Perspectives* 3, no. 1 (2002): 53–70.

Crawford, Beverley. "Explaining Defection from International Cooperation: Germany's Unilateral Recognition of Croatia." *World Politics* 48, no. 4 (1996): 482–523.

Daalder, Ivo H., James M. Goldgeier, and James M. Lindsay. "Deploying NMD: Not Whether, but How." *Survival* 42, no. 1 (2000): 6–28.

——, and Michael E. O'Hanlon. "Unlearning the Lessons of Kosovo." *Foreign Policy* 116 (1999): 128–141.

Dalsjö, Robert. "Are the Baltics Defensible?" *RUSI Journal* 143, no. 4 (1998).

Davis, Mark W. "Reagan's Real Reason for SDI." *Policy Review* (October–November 2000): 47–57.

Delors, Jacques. "European Unification and European Security." *Adelphi Paper* 284 (1994): 3–14.

——. "European Integration and Security." *Survival* 33, no. 2 (1991): 99–101.

Dorff, Robert H. "Germany and the Future of European Security." *World Affairs* 161, no. 2 (1998): 59–69.

Falkenrath, Richard A. "The CFE Flank Dispute, Waiting in the Wings." *International Security* 19, no. 4 (1995): 118–144.

——. "Theatre Missile Defence and the ABM Treaty." *Survival* 36, no. 4 (1994): 140–160.

Finlay, Brian, and Michael O'Hanlon. "NATO's Underachieving Middle Powers: From Burdenshedding to Burdensharing." *International Peacekeeping* 7, no. 4 (2000): 145–160.

Fleckenstein, Bernhard. "Bedingt einsatzfähig: Der lange Weg zur Neugestaltung der Bundeswehr." *Aus Politik und Zeitgeschichte* 43 (2000): 13–23.

Franck, Thomas L. "The Emerging Right to Democratic Governance." *American Journal of International Law* 86, no. 46 (1992): 46–91.

Froehly, Jean-Pierre. "Frankreich-Deutschland-Russland im neuen Dialog: eine Troika für Europa." *Politische Studien* 52, no. 376 (2001): 24–30.

Fukuyama, Francis. "The End of History?" *The National Interest* 16 (1989): 3–18.

Gagnon, V. P., Jr. "Ethnic Nationalism and International Conflict." *International Security* 19, no. 3 (1994–1995): 130–166.

——. "Yugoslavia: Prospects for Stability." *Foreign Affairs* 70, no. 3 (1991): 17–35.

Garton Ash, Timothy. "Germany's Choice." *Foreign Affairs* 73, no. 4 (1994): 65–72.

Gentry, John A. "The Cancer of Human Rights." *Washington Quarterly* 22, no. 4 (1999): 95–112.

Goldgeier, James M. "NATO Expansion: The Anatomy of a Decision." *Washington Quarterly* 21, no. 1 (1998): 85–102.

Gompert, David C., and Richard L. Kugler. "Rebuilding the Team: How to Get Allies to Do More in Defense of Common Interests." *Issue Paper, Rand National Defense Research Institute*, September 1996.

Gordon, Philip H. "Die Deutsch-Französische Partnerschaft und die Atlantische Allianz." *Arbeitspapiere zur Internationalen Politik* 82. Forschungsinstitut der Deutschen Gesellschaft für Auswärtige Politik (1994): 43–66.

Gow, James. "The Use of Coercion in the Yugoslav Crisis." *World Today* 48, no. 11 (1992): 198–202.

——. "Deconstructing Yugoslavia." *Survival* 33, no. 4 (1991): 291–311.

Grabbe, Heather. "The Sharp Edges of Europe: Extending Schengen Eastwards." *International Affairs* 76, no. 3 (2000): 519–536.

Graham, Thomas. "Strengthening Arms Control." *Washington Quarterly* 23, no. 2 (2000): 183–196.

Grand, Camille. "Missile Defense: The View from the Other Side of the Atlantic." *Arms Control Today* (September 2000): 13–14.

Grant, Robert P. "France's New Relationship with NATO." *Survival* 38, no. 1 (1996): 58–80.

Gray, Colin S. "Thinking Asymmetrically in Times of Terror." *Parameters* 32, no. 1 (2002): 5–14.

———. "The American Revolution in Military Affairs: An Interim Assessment." *The Strategic and Combat Studies Institute, Occasional Paper No. 28*, 1997.

———. "Arms Control Does Not Control Arms." *Orbis* 37, no. 3 (1993): 333–348.

Hammersen, Frederick P. A. "The Disquieting Voice of Russian Resentment." *Parameters* 28, no. 2 (1998): 39–55.

Hammond, Grant. "Myths of the Air War Over Serbia." *Aerospace Power Journal* 14, no. 4 (2000): 78–87.

Harries, Owen. "The Collapse of the West." *Foreign Affairs* 72, no. 4 (1993): 41–53.

Hassner, Pierre. "The United States: The Empire of Force or the Force of Empire?" *Chaillot Papers* 54 (2002).

Hawkins, William R. "Imposing Peace: Total versus Limited Wars and the Need to Put Boots on the Ground." *Parameters* 30, no. 2 (2000): 72–82.

Heisbourg, François. "L'Europe de la défense dans l'Alliance atlantique." *Politique etrangère* 2 (1999): 219–232.

———. "L'OTAN et le piler européen." *Politique internationale* 71 (1996): 55–64.

Hendrickson, David C. "The Ethics of Collective Security." *Ethics & International Affairs* 7 (1993): 1–15.

Herd, Graeme, and Joan Löfgren. "Societal Security, the Baltic States and EU Integration." *Cooperation and Conflict* 3, no. 3 (2001): 273–296.

Hodge, Carl Cavanagh. "Casual War: NATO's Intervention in Kosovo." *Ethics & International Affairs* 14 (2000): 39–54.

———. "Europe as a Great Power: A Work in Progress?" *International Journal* 53, no. 3 (1998): 487–504.

———. "Botching the Balkans: Germany's Recognition of Slovenia and Croatia." *Ethics & International Affairs* 12 (1998): 1–18.

Horsley, William. "United Germany's Seven Cardinal Sins: A Critique of German Foreign Policy." *Millennium* 21, no. 2 (1992): 225–241.

Howard, Michael. "1945–1995: Reflections on Half a Century of British Security Policy." *International Affairs* 71, no. 4 (1995): 705–715.

Howarth, Jolyon. "Britain, France and the European Defence Initiative." *Survival* 42, no. 2 (2000): 33–55.

Hulsman, John C. "The Guns of Brussels: Burden Sharing and Power Sharing with Europe." *Policy Review* 101 (2000): 35–50.

Hunter, Robert E. "Enlargement: Part of a Strategy for Projecting Stability into Eastern Europe." *NATO Review* 43, no. 3 (1995): 3–8.

Ignatieff, Michael. "The Virtual Commander." *New Yorker*, August 2, 1999.

Job, Cvijeto. "Yugoslavia's Ethnic Furies." *Foreign Policy* 92 (1993): 52–74.

Joffe, George. "European Security and the New Arc of Crisis." *Adelphi Papers* 265 (1991–1992): 53–67.

Joffe, Josef. "Bismarck or Britain? Toward an American Grand Strategy after Bipolarity." *International Security* 19, no. 4 (1995): 94–117.

———. "The New Europe: Yesterday's Ghosts." *Foreign Affairs* 72, no. 1 (1993): 17–44.

———. "Europe and America: The Politics of Resentment." *Foreign Affairs* 62, no. 3 (1984): 569–590.

Kaltefleiter, Werner. "Rakentenabwehr für Europa." *Zeitschrift für Politik* 43, no. 3 (1996): 235–261.

Katzenstein, Peter. "United Germany in an Integrating Europe." *Current History* 96, no. 608 (1997): 116–124.

Kegley, Charles W. "International Peacemaking and Peacekeeping: The Morality of Multi-national Measures." *Ethics & International Affairs* 10 (1996): 25–45.

Kennan, George. "The Sources of Soviet Conduct." *Foreign Affairs* 25, no. 4 (1947): 169–182.

Kennedy, Paul M. "The Tradition of Appeasement in British Foreign Policy, 1865–1939." *British Journal of International Studies* 2 (1976): 195–215.

Kerr, David. "The New Eurasianism: The Rise of Geopolitics in Russia's Foreign Policy." *Europe-Asia Studies* 6 (1995): 977–988.

Kirkpatrick, Jeane. "Dictatorships and Double Standards." *Commentary* 68, no. 5 (1979): 34–45.

Kissinger, Henry. "America at the Apex: Empire or Leader?" *The National Interest* 64 (2001): 9–17.

Kolankiewicz, George. "Consensus and Competition in the Eastern Enlargement of the European Union." *International Affairs* 70, no. 3 (1994): 477–495.

Kozyrev, Andrei. "The Lagging Partnership." *Foreign Affairs* 73, no. 3 (1994): 59–72.

Krauthammer, Charles. "The Short, Unhappy Life of Humanitarian Warfare." *The National Interest* 57 (1999): 5–9.

Krepinovich, Andrew. "Cavalry to Computer: The Pattern of Military Revolutions." *The National Interest* 37 (1994): 30–42.

Kupchan, Charles A. "In Defence of European Defence: An American Perspective." *Survival* 42, no. 2 (2000): 16–33.

———. "Defence Spending and Economic Performance." *Survival* 31, no. 6 (1989): 447–461.

Kurth, James. "The Next NATO: Building an American Commonwealth of Nations." *The National Interest* 65 (2001): 5–16.

Lambeth, Benjamin S. "Russia's Wounded Military." *Foreign Affairs* 74, no. 2 (1995): 86–98.

Lange, Peer. "Das Baltikum als eine Aufgabe für die integrative Gestaltung Europas." *Aus Politik und Zeitgeschichte* 37 (1998): 3–13.

Larres, Klaus. "Mutual Incomprehension: U.S. German Value Gaps Beyond Iraq." *Washington Quarterly* 26, no. 2 (2003): 23–42.

Layne, Christopher. "U.S. Hegemony and the Perpetuation of NATO." *Journal of Strategic Studies* 23, no. 3 (2000): 59–91.

Leffler, Melvyn. "The American Conception of National Security and the Beginnings of the Cold War, 1945–48." *American Historical Review* 89, no. 2 (1984): 346–400.

Lellouche, Pierre. "La France et l'OTAN." *Relations internationales et stratégiques* 7 (1992): 90–98.

Lieven, Anatol. "Russia's Military Nadir." *The National Interest* 44 (1996): 24–33.

———. "Russian Opposition to NATO Expansion." *World Today* 51, no. 10 (1995): 196–199.

Lukacs, John. "The End of the Twentieth Century." *Harper's* 286, no. 1712 (1993): 39–55.

Ludlow, Peter. "Wanted: A Global Partner." *Washington Quarterly* 24, no. 3 (2001): 163–171.

Luttwak, Edward N. "Give War a Chance." *Foreign Affairs* 78, no. 4 (1999): 36–44.

———. "A Post-Heroic Military Policy." *Foreign Affairs* 75, no. 4 (1996): 33–44.

———. "Towards Post-Heroic Warfare." *Foreign Affairs* 74, no. 3 (1995): 109–122.

MacFarlane, S. Neil. "Russian Conceptions of Europe." *Post-Soviet Affairs* 10, no. 3 (1994): 234–269.

———. "Russia, the West and European Security." *Survival* 35, no. 3 (1993): 3–25.

Mahant, Edelgard. "Foreign Policy and European Identity." *History of European Ideas* 21, no. 4 (1995): 485–497.

Mallaby, Sebastian. "The Reluctant Imperialist: Terrorism, Failed States, and the Case for American Empire." *Foreign Affairs* 81, no. 2 (2002): 2–7.

Mandelbaum, Michael. "Bad Statesman, Good Prophet: Woodrow Wilson and the Post–Cold War Order." *The National Interest* 64 (2001): 31–41.

——. "A Perfect Failure: NATO's War against Yugoslavia." *Foreign Affairs* 78, no. 5 (1999): 2–8.

Martel, William C. "The End of Non-Proliferation." *Strategic Review* 28, no. 4 (2000): 16–21.

Mathiopoulos, Margarita, and István Gyarmati. "Saint Malo and Beyond: Toward European Defense." *Washington Quarterly* 22, no. 4 (1999): 65–76.

Maull, Hanns W. "Germany and the Use of Force: Still a Civilian Power?" *Trierer Arbeitspapiere zur internationalen Politik*, no. 2 (1999).

——. "Zivilmacht Bundesrepublik Deutschland: Vierzehn Thesen für eine neue deutsche Aussenpolitik." *Europa Archiv* 47, no. 10 (1992): 269–278.

Mayall, James. "Democracy and International Society." *International Affairs* 76, no. 1 (2000): 61–75.

Mayer, Hartmut. "Early at the Beach and Claiming the Territory? The Evolution of German Ideas on a New European Order." *International Affairs* 73, no. 3 (1997): 721–737.

McGwire, Michael. "Why Did We Bomb Belgrade?" *International Affairs* 76, no. 1 (2000): 1–23.

Mearsheimer, John. "The False Promise of International Institutions." *International Security* 19, no. 3 (1995): 5–49.

Meiers, Franz-Josef. "The Reform of the Bundeswehr: Adaptation or Fundamental Renewal?" *European Security* 10, no. 2 (2001): 1–22.

Meimeth, Michael. "Frankreichs militärische Engagement in Afrika: Aufgaben und Perspektiven." *Stiftung Wissenschaft und Politik*, Working Paper 2960, June 1996.

Melinikas, Borisas. "Probleme der Intergration der baltischen Staaten in westliche Strukturen." *Berichte des Bundesinstituts für ostwissenschaftliche und internationale Studien* 40 (1999).

Millen, Raymond A. "Pax NATO: The Opportunities of Enlargement." Strategic Studies Institute, U.S. Army War College, August 2002.

Moltke, Gebhardt von. "Building a Partnership for Peace." *NATO Review* 42, no. 3 (1994): 3–7.

Nance, Bill. "An Update on National Missile Defense." *Comparative Strategy* 18, no. 3 (1999): 239–244.

Nelson, Daniel. "Transatlantic Transmutations." *Washington Quarterly* 25, no. 4 (2002): 51–66.

Newhouse, John. "The Diplomatic Round: Dodging the Problem." *New Yorker* 68, no. 27 (August 24, 1992): 60–72.

Nichols, Tom M. "Just War, Not Prevention." *Ethics & International Affairs* 17, no. 1 (2003): 25–29.

O'Connell, Mary Ellen. "The UN, NATO, and International Law after Kosovo." *Human Rights Quarterly* 22 (2000): 70–71.

Park, Bill. "Turkey, Europe, and ESDI: Inclusion or Exclusion?" *Defense Analysis* 16, no. 3 (2000): 315–328.

Parmentier, Guillaume. "Redressing NATO's Imbalances." *Survival* 42, no. 2 (2000): 96–112.

Pasic, Amir, and Thomas G. Weiss. "The Politics of Rescue: Yugoslavia's Wars and the Humanitarian Impulse." *Ethics & International Affairs* 11 (1997): 105–131.

Payne, Keith B. "The Case for National Missile Defense." *Orbis* 44, no. 2 (2000): 187–196.

——. "The Case against Abolition and for Nuclear Deterrence." *Comparative Strategy* 17, no. 1 (1998): 3–44.

Pierre, Andrew J., and Dmitri Trenin. "Developing NATO-Russian Relations." *Survival* 39, no. 1 (1997): 5–19.

Porter, Bruce D., and Carol R. Saivetz. "The Once and Future Empire: Russia and the 'Near Abroad.'" *Washington Quarterly* 17, no. 3 (1994): 75–90.

Rahe Paul A. "Averting Our Gaze." *The Journal of the Historical Society* 2, no. 2 (2002): 145–151.

Ramet, Sabrina Petra. "War in the Balkans." *Foreign Affairs* 71, no. 4 (1992): 79–98.

Reiter, Dan. "Why NATO Enlargement Does Not Spread Democracy." *International Security* 25, no. 4 (2001): 41–67.

Rhodes, Edward. "The Imperial Logic of Bush's Liberal Agenda." *Survival* 45, no. 1 (2003): 131–154.

Rice, Condoleezza. "Promoting the National Interest." *Foreign Affairs* 79, no. 1 (2000): 45–62.

Rieff, David. "The Humanitarian Trap." *World Policy Journal* 12 (1994–1995): 1–11.

Roberts, Adam. "NATO's 'Humanitarian War' over Kosovo." *Survival* 41, no. 3 (1999): 102–126.

———. "The Crisis in UN Peacekeeping." *Survival* 36, no. 3 (1994): 93–120.

Roberts, Guy B. "An Elegant Irrelevance: The Anti-Ballistic Missile Treaty in the New World Disorder." *Strategic Review* 23, no. 2 (1995): 15–25.

Roberts, Priscilla. "The Anglo-American Theme: American Versions of an Atlantic Alliance, 1914–1933." *Diplomatic History* 21, no. 3 (1997): 333–365.

Salmon, Patrick. "Reluctant Engagement: Britain and Continental Europe, 1890–1939." *Diplomacy & Statecraft* 8, no. 3 (1997): 141–163.

Schake, Kori, Amaya Bloch-Lainé, and Charles Grant. "Building a European Defence Capability." *Survival* 41, no. 1 (1999): 20–40.

Schake, Kori. "NATO after the Cold War, 1991–1996: Institutional Competition and the Failure of the French Alternative." *Contemporary European History* 7, no. 3 (1998): 379–407.

Schild, Georg. "The USA and Civil War in Bosnia." *Aussenpolitik* 47, no. 1 (1996): 22–32.

Schmidt, Hans-Joachim. "Auf dem Weg zum NATO-Beitritt: Die konventionellen Rüstungskontrolle als Stabilitätselement für den baltischen Raum." *HSFK-Report* 1 (2001): 25–44.

Schmidt, Peter. "German Security Policy in the Framework of the EU, WEU and NATO." *Aussenpolitik* 47, no. 3 (1996): 211–222.

———. "French Security Policy Ambitions." *Aussenpolitik* 44, no. 4 (1993): 335–343.

Sedivy, Jiri, Pál Dunay, and Jacek Saryusz-Wolski. "Enlargement and European Defence after 11 September." *Chaillot Papers* 53 (2002): 1–77.

Simonsen, Sven Gunnar. "Compatriot Games: Explaining the 'Diaspora Linkage' in Russia's Military Withdrawal from the Baltic States." *Europe-Asia Studies* 53, no. 5 (2001): 771–791.

Sloan, Stanley. "Transatlantic Relations: Stormy Weather on the Way to Enlargement." *NATO Review* 45, no. 5 (1997): 12–16.

Smith, Tony. "Morality and the Use of Force in a Unipolar World: The 'Wilsonian Moment'"? *Ethics & International Affairs* 14 (2000): 11–22.

———. "A Wilsonian World." *World Policy Journal* (Summer 1995): 62–66.

Sokolsky, Richard D. "European Missile Defense—Issues and Options." *Joint Force Quarterly* 29 (2001–2002): 46–51.

Sopko, John F. "The Changing Proliferation Threat." *Foreign Policy* 105 (1996–1997): 3–20.

Strachan, Hew. "Essay and Reflection: On Total War and Modern War." *International History Review* 22, no. 2 (2000): 340–370.

Straus, Ira. "Atlantic Federalism and the Expanding Atlantic Nucleus." *Peace & Change* 24, no. 3 (1999): 277–328.

Taylor, Trevor. "West European Security and Defence Cooperation: Maastricht and Beyond." *International Affairs* 70, no. 1 (1994): 1–16.

———. "Redefining Security." *International Security* 8, no. 1 (1983): 129–153.

Thompson, John A. "The Exaggeration of American Vulnerability: The Anatomy of a Tradition." *Diplomatic History* 16, no. 1 (1992): 23–43.

Trenin, Dmitri. "Silence of the Bear." *NATO Review* 50, no. 1 (Spring 2002): 7–9.

Tucker, Robert W. "A Benediction on the Past: Woodrow Wilson's War Address." *World Policy Journal* 17, no. 2 (2000): 77–93.

——. "The Triumph of Wilsonianism?" *World Policy Journal* 10, no. 4 (1993–1994): 83–99.

Ullmann, Richard. "The Covert French Connection." *Foreign Policy* 75 (1989): 3–33.

Van Eekelen, Willem. "WEU Prepares the Way for New Missions." *NATO Review* 41, no. 5 (1993): 19–23.

Vershbow, Alexander. "European Security and Defense Identity: Berlin, St. Malo, and Beyond." *Joint Forces Quarterly* 21 (1999): 52–55.

Vulliamy, Ed. "The Crime of Appeasement." *International Affairs* 74, no. 1 (1998): 73–91.

Wall, Robert. "Missile Defense's New Look to Emerge This Summer." *Aviation and Space Weekly* 156, no. 12 (2002): 28–29.

Wallin, Lars, and Bengt Andersson. "A Defence Model for the Baltic States." *European Security* 10, no. 1 (2001): 94–106.

Walzer, Michael. "The Politics of Rescue." *Social Research* 62 (1995): 53–66.

Webber, Steven. "Origins of the European Bank for Reconstruction and Development." *International Organization* 48, no. 1(1994): 1–38.

Weigel, George. "Moral Clarity in a Time of War." *First Things* 128 (2002): 20–27.

Weller, Marc. "The Rambouillet Conference on Kosovo." *International Affairs* 75, no. 2 (1999): 211–251.

Wheeler, Nicholas J. "Reflections on the Legality of NATO's Intervention in Kosovo." *International Journal of Human Rights* 4, no. 4 (2000): 145–163.

Wiener, Myron. "Security, Stability, and International Migration." *International Security* 17, no. 3 (1992–1993): 91–126.

Wilkie, Robert. "Fortress Europa: European Defense and the Future of the Atlantic Alliance." *Parameters* 32, no. 4 (2002–2003): 34–47.

Woodward, Susan L. "Bosnia after Dayton: Year Two." *Current History* 96, no. 608 (1997): 97–103.

Yost, David. "The NATO Capabilities Gap and the European Union." *Survival* 42, no. 4 (2000–2001): 97–128.

Zackheim, Dov S. "Old Rivalries, New Arsenals: Should the United States Worry?" *IEEE Spectrum* 36 (1999): 30–31.

Zakaria, Fareed. "The Rise of Illiberal Democracy." *Foreign Affairs* 76, no. 6 (1997): 22–43.

Zimmermann, Warren. "The Last Ambassador: A Memoir of the Collapse of Yugoslavia." *Foreign Affairs* 74, no. 2 (1995): 2–20.

INDEX